DISCARDED

13.6

A Connecticut Yankee In Criminal Court

A Mark Twain Mystery

Peter J. Heck

BERKLEY PRIME CRIME, NEW YORK

Historical Note and Acknowledgments

Mark Twain never, to my knowledge, solved a murder mystery. As with *Death on the Mississippi*, the previous volume of this series, this novel assumes that Mark Twain went on a lecture tour in the mid-1890s, hoping to recoup his lost fortune, and ended up solving a murder case. Although my novel is based on historical research into Mark Twain's character and times, and it makes an honest attempt to portray them as accurately as possible, it is of course a work of fiction. None of the events portrayed here actually happened.

A few characters other than Mark Twain are modeled on historical figures. George Washington Cable remains one of the most important writers to have come out of New Orleans. Buddy Bolden was the legendary founder of jazz, whose career was cut short by mental illness before the music became popular outside the Crescent City. Eulalie Echo was one of the many "hoodoo women" who followed in the footsteps of Marie Laveau, and she was the godmother of Jelly Roll Morton. Tom Anderson was the "Mayor of Storyville," although the New Orleans vice district had not acquired that name at the time this story takes place. Charley Galloway was a band leader and guitarist who gave Bolden some of his early jobs, and Judge J. J. Fogarty has been immortalized in one line of Morton's recording of "Buddy Bolden's Blues." I have treated all these characters, as well as the mysterious Widow Paris, as best suited my fictional needs, although I have done what

I could to make them plausible within the context of my story. Any historical or factual errors are strictly my own responsibility.

Anyone who has visited New Orleans will recognize many of the places mentioned. However, many of my settings, such as the old Parish Prison (located in today's Louis Armstrong Park), no longer exist. The Henry Clay monument has been moved from the center of Canal Street to Lafayette Square. A number of street names have been changed, especially in the upper Garden District where Buddy Bolden and Eulalie Echo lived. I hope that my portrayal of old New Orleans at one of the most colorful moments in its history does justice to this wonderful city, one of my favorite places to visit. Despite Mr. Clemens's baiting of George Cable, it really is almost impossible to eat a bad meal there.

My special thanks to my agent, Martha Millard; to my editor, Laura Anne Gilman; and to all the great New Orleans musicians whose music and spirit have filled my life with joy for many years.

1

My instructors at Yale always spoke confidently of preparing their students for life. I believe that, in general, they did their job well. Upon my graduation, I felt I had learned many things, both practical and theoretical, and had gone out to confront the world confident of my abilities and my training. But as I soon realized, nothing could have prepared me for the position of traveling secretary to Mr. Samuel L. Clemens—or, to use the name by which most of the world appeared to know him and his writings, Mark Twain.

What could have prepared me for a lecture tour that began with a murder in New York City and reached its climax (although not its conclusion) with the recovery of ten thousand dollars in buried gold? Along the way, I had survived a dunking in the Mississippi, tested my wits and skill against riverboat gamblers, and fought two strenuous battles with a backwoods bully. Somehow, through it all, I had also managed to perform my secretarial duties to Mr. Clemens's satisfaction, and after traveling nearly the whole length of the river, we came at last to New Orleans.

Mr. Clemens had known New Orleans well in his days as a steamboat pilot but, since then, the great national upheavals of the Civil War and Reconstruction had altered many things in the city. He himself was now a world-famous author, lecturer, and traveler who had seen the great cities of Europe as well as traveled extensively throughout

America, and his face was apparently as familiar to the man in the street as that of the President of the United States. But despite these far-reaching alterations in himself and in New Orleans, Mr. Clemens claimed that it remained the most singular city in the world.

It was our first morning in the city. We were waiting in the Café du Monde, an establishment that sits open to the sidewalk in the old section of the city, also known as the French Quarter. Our waiter had just brought us a plate of beignets (a sweet local pastry), and I was sipping one of the best cups of coffee I had ever tasted. George Washington Cable, a local writer with whom Mr. Clemens had shared a lecture tour some years before, was to join us for breakfast and an informal tour of the city.

Mr. Clemens puffed on a cigar and scanned the bustling crowds in nearby Jackson Square, beyond which I could see the impressive Roman Catholic cathedral. I sat there in silence, trying to absorb the sights, sounds, and smells of a city that might as well have been on some other continent. Even the light seemed to have a different quality from that of my hometown of New London, Connecticut. From down the way came the sounds of a thriving market, with vendors calling out their wares in French patois, Italian, and an English more melodious and liquid than any I had encountered in my travels thus far.

Finally Mr. Clemens said, "Here he comes." I looked up to see a diminutive fellow, with a full dark beard and a suit of somewhat old-fashioned cut, bustling across the street. "George, you old humbug, it's good to see you. I'd like to introduce my secretary, Wentworth Cabot. He went to Yale and played football, but it doesn't seem to have hurt him any."

The little man laughed and reached up to shake my hand, with a bright smile that was a marked contrast to his sober dress and demeanor, then sat down at the table. After ordering his own café au lait and another portion of beignets, Mr. Cable inquired about our trip downriver. With no further urging, Mr. Clemens embarked on a highly colored account of the voyage we had just undertaken. With considerable relish, he recounted how he had unraveled two murders, ending with our finding ten thousand dollars in hidden gold in an abandoned livery stable. "You should have been there, George," he said. "There's no feeling in the world like sticking your hand into a dark hole, not knowing what's waiting for you—maybe a snake, maybe nothing at all—and pulling it out, full of double eagles. Although standing up on a stage in front of a whole boatload of people and pointing my finger at a murderer was a pretty close second. That came close to trumping anything I've ever done on a stage."

"Having seen you in front of an audience, I call that a remarkable statement," said Mr. Cable. His voice was soft, with the distinctive accent of New Orleans. "But from what you've said, solving the murder couldn't have been very hard. There were only a few people on board who could have been guilty, and it must have been more or less obvious once you looked in the right place."

Mr. Clemens blew a ring of cigar smoke before replying to the other writer. "Obvious enough once it's explained, but I'm the only one who saw it, George, and there were plenty of other people looking for the answer. I was under considerable pressure because I had pretty good reason to think the killer was going to come after *me,* once we got to the place where the treasure was hidden. Some people say that personal danger helps focus a man's mind, but in my experience, it's a lot more likely to scare him out of his wits. So, all things taken into account, I think I did a pretty good job as a detective." He took a bite of his beignet, carefully brushed the powdered sugar off his mustache, and then continued.

"I've always scoffed at these Pinkertons and would-be Sherlocks, but that was before I tried my own hand at it. There's a knack to detection that not everybody has. I've always said that piloting taught me how to look at a set of

4 facts and see what's behind them, and of course, being a writer gives you a pretty good sense of people's character. If I were setting up in life again and had to pick a career, I could see myself trying out the detective business, with someone like Wentworth here to do the legwork for me.''

"Perhaps you could make a career of it," said our host. He sipped his coffee, a contemplative look on his face. "But you have to admit that the affair on the riverboat was very unusual. You had a limited number of suspects and a clear motive—child's play, compared to the usual run of unsolved murders. Besides, you were practically born on a riverboat. You'd have a much harder time of it in a city like New York or New Orleans, where you don't know the lay of the land so well."

"Harder still would be making a living at it," said Mr. Clemens. "I saw my share of murder investigations when I was writing for the newspapers. Nineteen times out of twenty, there's nothing mysterious about a murder: it's a couple of drunken bullies arguing over a woman or a domestic quarrel that gets out of hand. Everybody knows who did it. All the police have to do is arrest him. Half the time, the murderer confesses right on the spot. Not much work for a detective *there*."

Mr. Cable put down his coffee cup and leaned back in his chair. "That's true enough," he said, after a pause. "And the unsolved ones are usually where some poor fellow tried to resist an armed robber, or where a hardened criminal eliminated a business rival, as it were. Unless there's an eyewitness, the police have no place to start. Again, there's not much chance anyone will hire a detective to help solve it."

"That doesn't leave much room for the Sherlock to make a living, does it?" said Mr. Clemens, shaking his head. "Either the answer is obvious from the beginning, or there's no evidence and no incentive for the police to go digging for the answers. It's only when the victim has important friends that they do much more than go through the motions of investigating. If that's one case out of five hundred, I'd be surprised.''

"Curiously enough, there's just such a case right here in New Orleans,'' said Mr. Cable. "I've been following it in the local newspapers. John David Robinson, who was being talked about as a candidate for mayor next election, was found dead in his bed almost two weeks ago. Robinson was in the pink of health, so the family doctor asked the coroner to do an autopsy, and it turned out he'd been poisoned. If he'd been some no-account fellow off the street, they'd probably have written it off as stroke or maybe bad whisky and put him in Lafayette Cemetery without a second thought.''

"Have the police arrested anyone?'' Mr. Clemens leaned forward, his eyes lighting up.

"No,'' said Mr. Cable, shaking his head. "No arrests so far, although the police claim they're closing in on a suspect. But I think that's just the usual blarney, meant to make them look as if they're making progress on the case. Reading between the lines of the newspaper stories, I think they're baffled.''

"Poison's supposed to be a woman's weapon,'' I said, recalling something I'd read in a history book. "Wasn't it one of the Medicis who used it so much?''

"*All* of the Medicis, if you can believe the stories,'' said Mr. Clemens. "I doubt we can blame them for this one, though.''

Mr. Cable made a wry face. "Not that the police wouldn't jump at a chance to blame them, if there were any to be found. When the New Orleans police can't find anybody else to arrest, they're likely to claim the Mafia is involved and arrest some convenient Italian.''

"Failing that, they'll blame some mysterious outsider that nobody ever manages to locate,'' said Mr. Clemens. "Of course, there's a skeleton or two in everybody's closet, and they're likely to come tumbling out in a murder investigation.''

"Yes, and there's many a juicy story hidden behind those stately doors out in the Garden District," said Mr. Cable. "Now, here's your opportunity to play detective, Clemens. A genuine mystery, the police at an impasse, and a wealthy family to make it worth your while. It's exactly the kind of case where you could prove you have the knack." The little man's eyes twinkled over the rim of his coffee cup as he took another sip.

"Well, so it appears," said Mr. Clemens, "but I suspect the answer's easier to find than the newspapers make it out to be. You were a reporter, George. You know as well as I do that the point of the job is to sell newspapers, and the best way to do that is to create a sensation. And nothing's more sensational than murder in high places. I'd lay you odds that when the dust settles, this'll turn out to be a household accident—the poor fellow mistook rat poison for headache powder, or something of the sort. Next most likely is that his wife learned that he was seeing another woman and put arsenic in his soup."

"That would be quite a surprise," said Mr. Cable. "John David Robinson was the epitome of respectable New Orleans society, spoken of very highly by everyone who knew him. Which makes it even more an enigma why anyone would want to kill him. Doesn't that pique your interest, Sam? Here you were, telling me how you'd solved two murders and recovered a hidden treasure on your boat ride down here, and talking as if solving mysteries was the easiest thing in the world. Why don't you tackle this one, then? Are you worried that you'll fall short of your boasting?"

"Now, George, stop pulling my leg," said Mr. Clemens. "Even if I were in the detective business, which I'm not, I'd never get my foot in the door without the family's help. Unless someone in the family thinks the police aren't doing their job, why would they let some outsider paw through their dirty linen? And you can be sure the police will make this case a top priority. They know which side their bread is buttered on. I'll grant you the story is interesting enough, but I can't see any profit in poking my nose into it. Besides, I'm here on important business of my own. No time for me to go hunting for mysteries to solve.''

Mr. Cable smiled. ''I should have known you'd find some excuse to squirm out of it, Sam. Don't tell *me* about setting up as a detective anymore! Here I bring you a delicious murder case, full of dark secrets and whimsical characters, and you won't even rise to the bait.''

Mr. Clemens shook his head stubbornly, and Mr. Cable continued. ''But if you're not inclined to take the case, I suppose we'll have to read about it in the newspapers and speculate about the parts they can't print.''

''I'll content myself with that,'' said Mr. Clemens agreeably. ''I have a book to write and plenty of good stories to fill it with. The police can go about their business with no fear of competition from Mark Twain.''

''But we poor authors have to sit, quaking in our boots, knowing that our next book *will* be in competition with Mark Twain,'' said Mr. Cable with a chuckle. ''Perhaps I should persuade you to go unravel this murder and rush to get my next book to press while you're preoccupied!''

''Well, if you're writing a novel, you needn't worry,'' said Mr. Clemens. He waved his hand dismissively, although I could see that he was pleased by his fellow writer's compliment. ''I'm up to my ears just writing down the story of this latest trip down the river. The truth has always done better for me than anything I can dream up.''

''Do you expect anyone who knows you to believe that?'' said Mr. Cable, laughing. ''Your books may not always be strictly fiction, but that says nothing whatsoever about their relation to the truth. Why, there are more lies in your nonfiction than in all your novels put together.''

''That's the way it should be,'' said Mr. Clemens. ''Why should a man go to all the trouble of writing a novel if he was just going to fill it up with lies?''

2 ⌒

Mr. Clemens and I spent the rest of the morning walking about the French Quarter, with Mr. Cable acting as our native guide. He took a particular delight in pointing out details of the ornate wrought iron railings and colorful hanging plants that grace the second stories of so many otherwise ordinary buildings throughout the quarter. A common pattern in this district is for a building's street level to be given over to commerce, while the higher stories are apartments. An eastern visitor, used to looking straight ahead of him, has constantly to be reminded to look up, else he would miss much of the charm of the city. Also, in many of the houses, elegant courtyards invisible from the street offer a cool refuge from the noise and dust of the outside world. Among the houses Mr. Cable pointed out with special affection were two on Dumaine Street and another on Royal Street that figured in his own stories.

As the oldest section of New Orleans, the French Quarter was at one time populated almost entirely by Louisiana Creoles. It was then a fashionable and affluent area of the growing city. But the Vieux Carré has in recent years fallen on hard times: many buildings showed signs of disrepair, and we heard as much Italian as French spoken in the streets. Walking down Decatur Street, not far from the riverfront, Mr. Cable told us with a wry grin that the local newspapers had renamed that section Vendetta Alley on account of the frequent assassinations in the vicinity. Only a few years before our visit, the Italian Mafia was accused of murdering the New Orleans chief of police. That had set off a terrible outbreak of violence, culminating in the lynching of nineteen Italians, who may or may not have been involved in the murder of the chief.

Still, as Mr. Cable pointed out, the majority of the new immigrants are honest people making their way by hard work, and they can soon be expected to add their characteristic national flavor to the life of the city. To judge by the bustling commerce I saw on the streets of the French Quarter, it may be only a matter of time before it is again a prosperous area. Certainly, it would be a shame for such a picturesque district to remain in neglect.

We ate lunch in a little restaurant on Chartres Street that I would hardly have noticed if Mr. Cable had not led us to it. When I asked for the bill of fare, the waiter said, ''We don't need no menu, I know what we got.'' He proceeded to reel off a list of dishes, half of which I had never before heard of. Mr. Clemens noted my consternation and laughed. For his part, Mr. Cable said, ''Young man, I can see you're a newcomer to Creole cuisine. May I help you find something to your liking?''

I had been ready to order a plate of red beans and rice, that being the only item on the list of which I could guess the nature of the ingredients, but Mr. Cable's offer opened up other possibilities. ''Why, thank you,'' I said. ''What, pray tell, do all these odd names mean?''

''Well, a good bit of the local diet is based on seafood. We get excellent fresh fish from the Gulf, and the shellfish are mighty fine as well. For example, this place makes a very good seafood gumbo, which is a thick kind of soup.''

''Oh, it must be like chowder,'' I said. ''I think I'll have a bowl of that, thank you.'' And I settled back contentedly, thinking how long it had been since I'd tasted a good bowl of chowder. Mr. Cable and Mr. Clemens looked at each other with amused expressions, probably at my unadven-

10 turous choice. But I was more than satisfied, now that I had finally found one of my favorite dishes in a restaurant away from home. Of course, the local recipe would probably not be as good as the real thing from good old New England, but I was willing to take my chances. If the ingredients were as fresh as Mr. Cable said, it could hardly be that great a disappointment. The two older men placed their orders, and talk turned to other matters.

After an interval, the waiter returned with our food, placing a bowl of some outlandish concoction in front of me. "Excuse me, what is this?" I said.

The waiter gave me a puzzled look. "Why, sir, didn't you say you wanted gumbo?"

"Well, yes, but this is nothing like what I expected. Mr. Cable said it was like chowder."

"I don't know nothing 'bout no chowder, but if that ain't the best gumbo on Chartres Street, I'm quittin' my job this very day. Go on and try it," he said, and stood there waiting, with his arms folded across his chest. Mr. Cable and Mr. Clemens, for their parts, sat looking at me with unreadable expressions. Feeling as if I had suddenly been thrust out on a stage without a script, I picked up my spoon and dipped it in the bowl.

I could see good-sized bits of different kinds of seafood, as well as rice and chopped vegetables. And the aroma, while most unchowderlike, was not unpleasant. I took a tentative taste . . . and I think that only the three pairs of watching eyes kept me from spitting it out. Why, the cook must have spilled a whole pot of pepper into it!

Then the rich taste of crabmeat came through the spice. *That* was certainly good. Perhaps I could pick out the seafood from the rest of the soup, and not sear my palate beyond repair.

I was certainly hungry enough, after the morning's walking. I dipped my spoon into the bowl again, and the waiter said, "There! Didn't I tell you that's some mighty fine gumbo? Plenty tasty, plenty hot. You tell me when you're done, and I'll bring you 'nother bowl.'' And he turned and went back to the kitchen, satisfied that he had done his duty by me.

"Not much like chowder, is it?'' asked Mr. Clemens, a gleam in his eye.

I took another taste and found another flavor of seafood, this one not familiar, although quite good. "That's crawfish,'' said Mr. Cable, watching me eat. I had seen crawfish, looking somewhat like miniature lobsters, in streams back in Connecticut, but never thought of them as food. They seemed right at home in this gumbo, nonetheless. If I could only get used to the excess of pepper, it might be quite palatable. Luckily, I had ordered a glass of the local beer, and it served admirably to wash down the thick soup. And I *had* worked up quite an appetite. I took another spoonful, and another, and before I knew it, the bowl was empty, and I began to wonder if the waiter really would bring me another serving.

Seeing me devour the gumbo, Mr. Cable waxed eloquent about the cuisine of his native city. (He had ordered another dish with some barbarous name, a mixture of rice, vegetables, chicken, and sausage.) "Why, the worst New Orleans food makes anything you can get in a New York restaurant taste bland, never mind what passes for food in the rest of the North. You'd have a hard time finding a bad meal in this city if you tried for a month,'' he said in between forkfuls of his jambalaya.

His smug expression made me want to rise to the defense of my home region, although I knew little enough of the restaurants of New York. But just as I opened my mouth to reply, Mr. Clemens cut me off with a gesture. "Well, George,'' he said in the slow, drawling manner that was his characteristic way of speaking, "I'll have to call you on that. Back in my cub pilot days, I remember a New Orleans meal that nobody at the table could get past their noses. Once we realized it was unfit for human consumption, we tried to get the dog to eat it, and *he* wouldn't have any part of it. And when we threw it in the garbage, every single rat in that alley pulled up stakes and headed for Texas. The bugs ate it, though. I know that for a fact, because we found a passel of 'em dead up to a week afterward.'' He smiled and nodded, as if in confirmation of his own declaration.

Mr. Cable began to sputter at this slander on New Orleans cooking, but Mr. Clemens continued. ''Yes indeed, worst meal I ever had. Cooked it myself. I never made that mistake again.'' He took a sip of lager and patted his stomach. ''What's on the schedule this afternoon, George?''

Mr. Cable snorted and shook his head before succumbing to laughter. Finally, he said, ''I thought we'd ride out to Lake Pontchartrain and have dinner near West End. It's only a five-mile ride, but it'll be much cooler than here in the city, and I know a place where the chef is superb. Half the city migrates out there in the warm season.''

Mr. Clemens nodded. ''Fine. How do we get there?''

''The train's the easiest way, although a carriage ride out the Shell Road is more picturesque. Mr. Cabot might enjoy the view, since he's new to the city. And you can take the train back, if you're in a hurry then.''

Mr. Clemens agreed to this proposal, and we settled our bill and walked out to Jackson Square to find a carriage out to Lake Pontchartrain. We soon engaged a smart-looking rig, driven by a wiry little Irishman with bushy chin whiskers and a crooked smile. He took us along the famous Shell Road, a toll road running alongside a canal through swampy land. I saw my first live alligator swimming in this canal; Mr. Clemens, who had told me several stories about these animals during our steamboat trip, kindly offered to have the driver stop so I could inspect the reptile more closely. As the driver seemed to be in a hurry, I was unwilling to interfere with his schedule out of mere curiosity. I prevailed upon Mr. Clemens and Mr. Cable to postpone the opportunity to some indefinite future.

To the landward side, there was a thick forest full of

exotic foliage and dark shadows; an occasional path broke the wall of greenery, leading to some destination I could only guess at. Some of the plants could have been giant versions of the house plants I was used to seeing my mother grow, but here they grew—nay, flourished!—out of doors, all on their own. Mr. Cable told me that most of the inhabitants of this territory were poor Negroes who supported themselves by fishing and trapping. The canal itself seemed busy enough; twice we passed tugboats with barges of bricks or other building materials headed for the heart of the city. And the road itself was well-traveled, with a number of gentlemen driving their buggies past us at impressive speed.

Eventually, we broke out onto the lakeshore, a district much like the shore resorts I had seen in Rhode Island: large, lightly constructed hotels with broad verandas and expansive pavilions, close upon the blue waves of the broad lake. Gaily dressed vacationers seemed to be everywhere, enjoying themselves in the warm sunlight. From somewhere in the distance I heard music, a sprightly waltz tune. Small sailboats dotted the water, and a good number of people were taking advantage of the cool waters to escape the late afternoon heat. Mr. Cable told us that another, newer resort had been constructed a few miles away, at Spanish Fort, and that thousands of citizens would come out every evening to enjoy the view, the breeze, the food, the gambling houses, and the band concerts at the two resorts.

We stopped at a little café to wash the dust from our throats, Mr. Clemens and I with an excellent lager, and Mr. Cable (a teetotaler) with a glass of lemonade. Afterward, we strolled along the waterside a while, observing the sights and commenting idly on this or that. An occasional passerby would recognize Mr. Clemens and shout out a greeting, to which he would return some appropriate remark. Finally, at an intersection filled with happy vacationers, a newsboy's cry seized our attention.

"Read all about it, an arrest in the Robinson murder! Read all about it!"

"An arrest at last!" said Mr. Cable. He reached in his pocket for a nickel. "Here, boy, give me a copy!" The grinning urchin took the coin and gave him the paper and his change, then raised his cry again, hoping to attract more customers.

"It looks as if the New Orleans police know their business," said Mr. Clemens, as Mr. Cable scanned the front page. "The New York detective who came downriver with us took over a month to spot the man he was after and never did arrest him."

Mr. Cable's brow furrowed as his gaze moved down the column, and he finally slapped the paper against his leg. "Read that!" he said, abruptly throwing the paper in Mr. Clemens's general direction. It hit my surprised employer in the chest and landed on the sidewalk, and I bent to pick it up.

"A travesty if ever I heard of one," said Mr. Cable. He stamped away several paces, then whirled on his heel to face us again. "An absolute outrage!"

"What on earth is wrong, George?" said Mr. Clemens, looking at the little man with visible alarm.

"Read that story—that pack of lies," said Mr. Cable, gesturing at the paper I held.

Mr. Clemens took the paper from me, and I crowded in behind him to look over his shoulder. "Here, Wentworth, give me some room," he said after a moment. "Better yet, you take it and read it to me," and he handed me back the paper.

I found the story and read aloud: "Police in Orleans Parish today announced they had arrested Leonard Galloway, a Negro cook, on suspicion of poisoning the late John David Robinson. Mr. Robinson, widely recognized as one of the leading lights of Crescent City society, was found dead by his wife, Eugenia Holt Robinson, on Friday the 11th of this month. Dr. Alphonse Soupape, the family physician, recognized the cause of death as poisoning and alerted the authorities. Police had learned that the deceased reprimanded the Negro for drunkenness a few days before his untimely death. Following his arrest at his home on First Street between Howard and Liberty, Galloway was arraigned before J. J. Fogarty, of the First Recorder's Court, and remanded to Parish Prison to await trial.''

When I had finished, my employer looked at Mr. Cable expectantly. ''On the face of it, I don't see any reason to take issue. What do you know that makes you think otherwise?''

''I've known Leonard's family for twenty-five years,'' said Mr. Cable. ''His aunt Tillie was my cook when I lived in the Garden District, and Leonard used to come into my own kitchen, watching her work and learning the trade, when he was just a boy. It wasn't long before he was better than she was. I *know* that fellow, Clemens. He's about as likely to commit murder as you are.'' Cable's face was white, and the little man trembled as if he could barely hold back his emotions. One or two of the passersby looked at him strangely, though no one said anything.

''Don't say that, or they'll hang him for sure,'' said my employer, laughing. I could see that he was trying to cheer up his friend, who had obviously taken the news of the cook's arrest very much to heart. ''Now, if you'd compared him to Wentworth here''—he gestured in my direction—''I'd start raising funds for his defense this instant. But don't hang a millstone around the poor cook's neck by comparing him to an old reprobate like me.''

''It's no joking matter, Sam,'' said Mr. Cable earnestly. ''The police are obviously at wits' end, so they've arrested a defenseless black man and concocted a reason why he might have had some grudge against poor Robinson, may the Lord rest his soul. If the real killer doesn't somehow stumble into their hands, they *will* hang Leonard Galloway, without taking a single further step to find out who really killed Robinson and without even a semblance of a fair

16 trial.'' He looked thoroughly dejected as well as angry.

"Well, I wouldn't want to see the fellow hanged for a murder someone else committed,'' said Mr. Clemens, a bit chastened by Mr. Cable's indignant response. "If it came to that, I suppose I could scrape up some money—I'm not sure where, but I'm willing to try—to hire a good lawyer, if there's such a critter to be found in this city.''

"There are ways to help a man besides giving him money,'' said Mr. Cable thoughtfully. "Perhaps it would be easier for you to donate your time to the cause, instead. You said you thought you could be a detective; here's your chance. I was joking before, but now I think it would be a good way for you to help poor Leonard.''

"Oh, George, that was just daydreaming,'' said Mr. Clemens. "I don't have any intention of going into the detective business. Besides, I'm way behind schedule on the book I'm supposed to be writing.''

Mr. Cable shook his head. "I know as well as you how much time and effort writing requires, but some things take precedence over ordinary business. This newspaper story will convince the whole city that poor Leonard Galloway is a murderer. Getting him a good lawyer will help, if the case comes to trial, but I'd rather not put my faith in a Louisiana jury. Better to find some way to clear him entirely.''

"That may not be as easy as it sounds,'' said Mr. Clemens. "What makes you think he didn't do it?''

"I've eaten Leonard's cooking more than once. That man isn't a cook, he's an artist,'' said Mr. Cable. "For him to poison something he'd prepared would be close to sacrilege. But more than that, I *know* Leonard. He practically grew up in my house. He's no killer.''

"Maybe so,'' said Mr. Clemens. "But that won't get you very far in a court of law. And people do change, sometimes. Look here, George, you want me to jump into this thing head over heels just because you knew this fellow when he was a boy. But I've been bit a few too many times by taking on something when I didn't know all the facts. If it's that important to you, why don't you look into it yourself? You know this city far better than I do: the laws, the customs, the politics, where all the bodies are buried. You've done more newspaper work than I ever did. And you know the people. That's the single most important thing I had to draw on when I solved that riverboat murder. You know the people, and I don't. Why don't you do it, George?''

Mr. Cable lifted his head and returned Mr. Clemens's challenging stare for a moment, then sighed. ''I would do it myself, Sam. I'd love to make the pompous hypocrites who run this city quake in their boots. But it won't wash. I know them, but they know me, as well. Half of them wouldn't give me the time of day, let alone talk to me about a murder case. If I stuck my nose into what they consider their business, they'd be likely to hang poor Leonard just to teach me a lesson.''

He paced for a moment without saying a word, seemingly oblivious to the carefree vacationers around us. His serious expression was a strange contrast to those of the people walking and laughing as they passed by us. Down by the lake, I could see a group of children skipping stones, and the music of two bands came faintly from the distance. Then Mr. Cable turned and looked my employer in the eye again. ''You don't have enemies down here, Sam. You're the best-liked writer in America, bar none. Your name will open any door in this city. On top of that, you just solved a murder case that probably had the police chiefs up and down the Mississippi singing your praises. They'd listen to you, even if you were telling them things they didn't want to hear.''

Mr. Clemens's face seemed to harden, then a strange glint came into his eye. ''Well, I can see you might have a problem or two, George. Oh, hell, give me a chance to think about it a little bit and poke around to see what the facts are. If I'm convinced this fellow really needs help,

18 I'll do what I can for him. Is that good enough for you?''

"I suppose it'll have to be," said Mr. Cable, somewhat reluctantly, to my thinking. "I think you'll be eager to help once you've looked into the case. Can you promise me you won't shilly-shally around instead of making a decision?''

"First thing in the morning," said Mr. Clemens. "Meanwhile, there's important business to be looked into. It's been twelve years since I had a taste of pompano, and it was as delicious as sin. Find me a restaurant that makes it right, and we'll show Wentworth just how good New Orleans cooking can be.''

"You've come to the right place for that, and I'm just the man to show it to you," said Mr. Cable. He pointed down the street, and the three of us began walking toward the noise and lights of one of the waterfront resorts. "I'll tell you what. If we can get Leonard out of jail, I'll do better than that. I guarantee he'll cook up the best pompano you ever tasted, and you'll be my guest to share it with me.''

"You're trying to bribe me, George," said Mr. Clemens, grinning. "You know my weaknesses all too well. But are you sure you want to offer me a sample of the man's cooking before you've proven he's not a poisoner?''

Mr. Cable smiled back at Mr. Clemens. "Once you've tasted Leonard's cooking, poisoning will be the farthest thing from your mind. But come; I know just the place for a pompano, and until we have Leonard to cook for us, it'll be an acceptable substitute.''

He led us to a garden restaurant from which we could hear the music from a nearby bandstand. As if by tacit agreement to leave the question of the murder case until a better time, the two writers spoke of old times, old friends, and of books still to be written. And the pompano, a tropical fish from the Gulf of Mexico, was every bit as delicious as promised.

*　　*　　*

A Connecticut Yankee in Criminal Court

We parted company with Mr. Cable after dinner: he took a carriage back to the Garden District, and we caught a train to the corner of Canal and Bourbon Streets, a short walk from our pension on Royal Street, in the French Quarter. (I had followed the advice of my *Baedeker's Guide* and given the local hotels a miss in favor of a suite of furnished rooms.) We settled into a quiet corner of the smoking car and watched the lights of West End fade into the distance as Mr. Clemens puffed contemplatively on one of his corncob pipes.

After a brief silence, I asked, "Why is Mr. Cable so eager to involve you in exonerating this Negro cook? I am surprised at his vehemence on the issue."

"I'm not," said my employer. "There's a lot of courage in that little man, whether you agree with everything he believes or not. And when he makes up his mind about something, he doesn't give a damn what anybody else thinks. I found that out when we did our lecture tour together as the 'twins of genius.' If he'd been more willing to bend to the prevailing wind when he lived down here, he might have had an easier time of it."

"How do you mean?"

Mr. Clemens frowned. "George was a staunch advocate of a fair deal for the colored man long before I first met him. That has never been a popular position to take here in Louisiana, even a dozen years ago, and the tide has been running entirely against colored rights ever since."

I was surprised. "Is the situation really that bad? The Negroes I've seen on the streets seem happy and prosperous enough."

"You've still got a few things to learn, Wentworth," said Mr. Clemens. "There are laws on the books in Louisiana that deny a colored man the right to sit on a streetcar or in a train, if a white man wants his seat. It doesn't affect you, so of course you wouldn't notice it, but the colored man has to live with it every day. He can't eat in the same restaurant as you can, or shop in the same stores. Hell, it

20 doesn't matter if his skin's as light as yours and mine, if the law can prove he had one black great-grandparent. That's the way the *good* people of Louisiana want to run their state, and God help any man with the audacity to tell them they're wrong. George may have been a native, and a Confederate veteran, and the best writer Louisiana has ever produced. That didn't help his case at all. It just made him more a traitor in their eyes.'' His voice took on considerable heat as he spoke, and I looked apprehensively around the car to see if anyone had overheard him, but the nearby seats were vacant, and none of the other passengers seemed to be paying us any mind.

"The ironic part of it is," Mr. Clemens continued, "George fell out of favor with the Creoles, as well. He tried to portray them honestly and accurately in his writing, which is exactly what a writer is supposed to do."

"Who exactly are the Creoles?" I asked. "I thought they were the descendants of the original French settlers."

"They all speak the patois, but there's Spanish blood in the mix, as well as French, and sometimes a touch of the African or Indian, too. George probably has as much real affection for them and their way of life as any man alive. But when he published his books about the old times in New Orleans, some of the leading Creoles thought he was mocking them—the stiff-necked fools! And so, between them and the damned lily-white bigots, George found himself surrounded by enemies in his own hometown. Finally, a few years ago, his friends convinced him to move to Massachusetts, where his opinions were less likely to bring armed men to his door."

"Ah, I thought he still made his home in Louisiana. Why on Earth has he come back, then, if he has so many enemies here?"

"The same thing that brings me back: writing a book. A man can only trust his memory so far, Wentworth. There comes a time when you have to set foot on the ground you're writing about, even if it costs you a certain amount of pain. Despite all that's happened to him, George still loves this place. I can understand why. If you'd spent the first part of your life eating meals like that one tonight, could you live out your days in New England, knowing you were condemning yourself never to taste pompano again? For a plate of fish cooked like that, and an evening of talk like that, I'd make a dinner date with the devil himself, even if the table was set by the hottest furnace in Hell.''

I wasn't certain I'd go to quite that length, but I had to admit that, barring the local predilection for excessive spice, I could easily grow accustomed to the food in New Orleans. And, after Mr. Cable's extravagant praise of Leonard Galloway's prowess in the kitchen, I found myself almost wishing that Mr. Clemens would decide to help the poor fellow, if only so I could sample his cooking.

3 ⌇

Mr. Clemens spent the next morning catching up on his writing and correspondence, which despite our best efforts, he had fallen behind in during our journey down the Mississippi on the steamboat *Horace Greeley*. He dictated a number of business letters to me, and once again, I regretted that Yale had not offered courses in shorthand, although I had gotten the knack of quickly jotting down his intention, if not his exact words. Later, I would turn my notes into finished letters while he took care of matters that required his personal attention. As usual, he devoted much of his time to a long letter to his wife and daughters, whom he had sent to Europe, where they could live more cheaply than at home, while he worked to liquidate his debts.

Toward that end, he had boarded up his home in Hartford, Connecticut, and, with the backing of Mr. Henry H. Rogers, the oil millionaire, embarked on the steamboat cruise and lecture tour down the Mississippi on which I had served as his secretary. (While I was responsible only to Mr. Clemens, I had learned that Mr. Rogers was actually the one who paid my salary, as well as Mr. Clemens's traveling expenses.) At the same time, he had begun a book describing our journey, with plentiful observations on the customs, the history, and the life of the great American waterway. We were scheduled to give two final lectures here in New Orleans; meanwhile, Mr. Clemens worked on his newest book.

It was already after noon when a knock announced the arrival of Mr. Cable. Mr. Clemens greeted him enthusiastically, but his expression changed when Mr. Cable asked, "Have you looked into the Galloway case?"

"Damnation! I meant to, but I got involved in business, and it completely slipped out of my mind," said my employer, slumping back into his overstuffed chair. I was somewhat embarrassed, also having completely forgotten his promise to investigate the cook's arrest for poisoning his master.

"I wish you wouldn't swear, Sam," said Mr. Cable, a stern expression on his face. "I'm disappointed in you. You told me last night that you wanted to find out the facts before deciding whether to help poor Leonard Galloway, and the facts aren't going to walk up to your door and knock."

"I suppose you're right," Mr. Clemens admitted. "I'll work on it this afternoon, if I get the chance."

Mr. Cable gave my employer an indulgent look. "Sam Clemens, I know you better than that. You have the best intentions in the world, but you're lazy as an old dog on a hot summer day. Well, I'm here to see that you don't have any more excuse to put off fulfilling your promise."

"Promise? I don't remember promising to help the fellow."

"No," said Mr. Cable. "You promised to find out the facts—first thing this morning. Well, here it is after noon, and you don't know any more than you did last night. Luckily for you, I still have a few friends in New Orleans, and one of them has offered to meet us for lunch and talk about the Galloway case. The facts may not come knocking, but if you're willing to walk two or three blocks with me—and you'd *better* be, Sam!—I can promise you'll find out some things that didn't get into the newspapers."

"It doesn't look as if I have much choice," said Mr.

24   Clemens, standing up. "Come along, Wentworth, we might as well find out what George has up his sleeve. At worst, we'll get another good meal out of it."

We walked down to Saint Peter Street, where at a table in the courtyard of a little café, smoking a dark-colored cheroot, sat a rotund man of medium stature, meticulously dressed, and sporting a dark mustache waxed to sharp points. Mr. Cable introduced him as Richard LeJeune, a detective with the New Orleans Police Department, whom Cable had met when he was a writer for the New Orleans newspapers.

LeJeune stood and shook hands with Mr. Cable and Mr. Clemens. "I've heard about that business on the riverboat, where you caught that murderer, Mr. Clemens. A good piece of detective work," he said. "A lot of policemen don't like it when outsiders do their work for them. Me, I'm thankful for any kind of help we can get."

"Well, I appreciate the compliment, although I don't expect to make a habit of solving murders," said Mr. Clemens. "It's more work than I'm accustomed to, for one thing. But it was more or less in the line of self-preservation, and that's a pretty good antidote to indolence."

After the introductions, Mr. Clemens and Mr. Cable seated themselves on either side of the detective, and I took the fourth chair at the table. We ordered drinks, and when the waiter had gone to fetch them, Mr. Cable told my employer, "Richard is one of the few honest policemen still left in New Orleans. He's assigned to the Robinson murder, and he's agreed to tell us something about the case. So where would you like to begin?"

"Well, all I really know is what that newspaper said yesterday: that Robinson was poisoned and that the police have arrested his cook for it," said Mr. Clemens, looking at the detective. "That seems straightforward enough, but I was a reporter long enough to know that no newspaper ever gets the whole story. Why don't you start with the main facts. How did Robinson die, and how did the police decide it was a murder?''

The detective looked at Mr. Clemens intently for a moment, as if sizing him up. ''Well, Mr. Clemens, Robinson died of jimsonweed poisoning. Now, jimsonweed is powerful stuff. The whole plant is poison, and most people around here know it. There's not much chance Robinson would have took it by accident. For one thing, it has a pretty rank smell. The country folks call it stinkweed, and it's hard to mistake for much else. We found some of it growing in a vacant lot near where the cook lives, and the cook admits that he fixed Robinson's last meal.''

''How long was that before he died?''

''The coroner says four hours at least—maybe a lot longer. Sometimes the poison takes twelve, fifteen hours to kill a man. Split the difference and say eight or ten. We figure the poison was in his food at supper the evening before he died, disguised somehow so he wouldn't smell or taste it—most likely in some kind of spicy sauce. He was the only one who ate the meal, on account of his wife was out of town to visit family. Later that evening, Robinson saw his brother-in-law, and complained of a headache and blurry vision. The servants say he went to bed early. The next day—this was Friday, nearly two weeks ago—his wife arrived home late in the morning and got worried when she learned he hadn't come down for breakfast. She went into his room and found him. Old Doc Soupape was suspicious right away and asked for an autopsy.''

''And found evidence of the poison, I assume.'' Mr. Clemens took a puff on his cigar. ''Any reason to suspect the cook besides the plants growing near his home?''

''Yes. A couple of days before, Robinson found the cook drunk on the job. He dressed him down pretty fierce in front of the other servants, docked him the day's pay, and sent him home in shame. The cook didn't like it one bit. Would anybody? The way it looks is that he went home mad, stayed mad, noticed the weeds, and decided to put them in his master's soup or maybe his salad. Nobody else was home for the meal, so he didn't have to worry about killing the rest of the family.''

"Has he confessed any of this?''

"No,'' said the detective, "but that don't mean anything. Sometimes they confess, sometimes they deny everything. And sometimes they confess when they didn't do it.''

We were interrupted by the waiter arriving with our drinks: lemonade for me and Mr. Cable, a whisky and soda for Mr. Clemens, and a fresh coffee for the detective. We ordered our food, the waiter departed, and Mr. Clemens leaned both elbows on the table, a thoughtful look on his face. "So,'' he said at last, "the cook's guilt or innocence seems to ride on whether his motive is strong enough to make him poison his employer.''

"True enough,'' said LeJeune. "That's right where the case stands or falls, the way I see it. Nobody denies the cook had the chance to get the poison, though he claims he didn't know it was growing there, and he had a perfect opportunity to give it to the victim. The main question is whether being yelled at and docked his pay made him mad enough to kill the man who did it to him. George doesn't think so, and he claims to know this fellow pretty well. And the cook doesn't have any history of previous trouble with the law. So I think maybe there's some room for doubt.''

"Well, if everyone whose boss yelled at him turned into a killer, we'd be in a sad way,'' said Mr. Clemens. "From what you say, the cook had plenty of time after Robinson bawled him out to sober up and think things over. What makes the police think he stayed mad? Did any of the other servants hear him make threats, or anything like that?''

"No, but that's normal. These people always stick together—''

"As well they should, seeing how little help they can expect from anyone else!'' Mr. Cable interrupted angrily, but Mr. Clemens silenced him with a gesture.

"Now, George, let's stick to our business," said my employer. "Mr. LeJeune's come here to tell us what he knows about the case, not to argue about the racial question."

Mr. Cable glared at both Mr. Clemens and the detective for a moment. Then the detective looked at him with a wry smile and a shrug, and the little man's anger seemed to melt away. "That's all right, Mr. Clemens," said the detective. "George and I know where each other stand. We go back a long way. The fact is, one of the things that bothers me about this case is that the papers are talking as if the cook is some sort of black monster who killed his boss because he hated white men. Well, I was one of the men who questioned the cook when we arrested him, and if he hates anybody, I sure didn't see it. So when George asks me to take a closer look at the evidence, I think maybe I should listen to George. But the prosecutor wants to treat the Robinson murder as a closed case, now that we've made an arrest. And the captain has been making hints that maybe I should get on with the rest of my caseload, which is plenty big enough, no question about that. Trouble is, I don't think we've nailed the lid on it yet, and I guarantee you I don't like being told to stop looking when there's still something I'm not sure of."

"So you figure you'll let us do your looking for you," said Mr. Clemens.

"Couldn't have put it better myself," said the detective. He took a sip of his coffee, put his cup down precisely in the center of the saucer, and continued. "I'm going to give you enough information to let you start, and then you'll tell me anything you find out. I'm taking a bit of a chance, because most amateurs don't know the first thing about a murder investigation. But you did do a pretty good job in that riverboat murder, so maybe you will find something. If you can prove the cook is innocent or even raise enough of a doubt that he did it, maybe I can still arrest the right person instead of going into court with the wrong man in the dock and making myself have a guilty conscience. And if you find something to prove the cook really did kill Robinson, I will trust George to tell me. So I can't really lose, can I?''

"I suppose not, now that you put it that way," said Mr. Clemens. "George says you're an honest man, and coming from him, that means a good bit. I think we can all play straight with each other. If you promise you won't hold back anything we need to know about the case, I can promise to tell you anything we find out, one way or the other. Is it a deal?''

"I think we can work with one another," said LeJeune, and he reached out to shake Mr. Clemens's hand. Just then the waiter arrived with our food, and a lull fell over the conversation as we turned to eating, which I was beginning to realize took precedence over all other business in New Orleans. I had again taken Mr. Cable's advice on my selection, a spicy rice-and-meat concoction called jambalaya. Once again, it seemed to me that the cook had used too free a hand with the pepper pot, but with frequent sips of lemonade to quench the fire, I found it palatable enough. Strike that—I found myself asking for a second helping, much to Mr. Cable's satisfaction.

After the noise of forks and spoons had died down enough to permit conversation, Mr. Clemens wiped his mouth with a napkin and fixed the detective with his gaze. "Let's take a different angle on this murder business," he said. "Suppose there wasn't any reason to blame the cook for it, and you had to figure out the whole thing from scratch. What would you be looking at?''

"Well," said LeJeune, "we have a man killed in his own home, and by poison. That eliminates a lot of things you'd have to think about if he'd been shot, or stabbed. It's a good bet he didn't surprise a burglar in the act, for instance. On the other hand, we have to make sure it's not suicide, or an accident, which it might be, if the poison were something you'd expect to find around the house. But we can pretty much rule that out, if it's jimsonweed. Robinson wouldn't have been out picking greens for his own salad, and if he had, the cook would have known it wasn't fit to eat.''

''Never mind the cook,'' said Mr. Clemens. ''Pretend we don't know how Robinson was given the poison, just that we know it was poison. Who are your suspects? Are we sure it's not suicide?''

LeJeune rubbed his chin. ''I'd say suicide is even less likely than an accident. Odds are there are two or three faster and surer poisons he could have laid hands on: arsenic, maybe laudanum . . . besides, a man isn't as likely to take poison as to put a pistol to his head. There wasn't any note, or any kind of scandal he might have been trying to escape. And the autopsy would have found out if he'd had some incurable disease. I'd lay long odds against suicide.''

''Fine. We'll set it aside for now,'' said Mr. Clemens. ''That brings us back to murder. Assume for the sake of argument we've got a gilt-edged, government-bonded, iron-clad alibi for the cook. Let's say he was in Mexico. Who's the most logical suspect?''

''Usually, we'd be looking at the wife—except, this time, the wife's the one with the gilt-edged alibi. She was out of town, visiting family up near Baton Rouge, for nearly a week. She didn't get back until the morning Robinson was found dead. I checked her story myself, and it's solid as a rock.''

''Did you check her story just out of routine, or was there a reason to suspect her?'' asked Mr. Clemens.

''You always suspect the wife when a man's been poisoned in his own home,'' said LeJeune. ''Eugenia Holt had her choice of beaux twenty years ago, and she married John David Robinson. Now, I don't have any special reason to think Mrs. Robinson might have regretted her choice. These respectable people, they have a knack for keeping their scandals quiet. But she is still an uncommonly pretty woman, Mr. Clemens, and he was a very important man, and these very rich people don't live their lives the same way as you and I. Of course I checked. And she was where she claims to have been, when she claims to have been there. Unless she could poison him by long distance, she is no suspect.''

"How about other close family?'' Mr. Clemens had taken out one of his corncob pipes and was packing the bowl with tobacco. "Any domineering mother-in-law, or worthless brothers, or jealous sisters?''

"Mrs. Robinson has a brother and a sister, both living here in New Orleans. The brother, Reynold Holt, is a war veteran, a brooding fellow with a limp. He was wounded and captured by the Federals at Chancellorsville, and spent six months in a military prison. Her sister Maria has literary inclinations; if you wanted to talk to the family, she might be the one to start with. She's married to Percy Staunton, who's a bit of a reckless fellow, although he comes of good family. I don't know anything that would make any of them likely to kill Robinson. Of course, once we arrested the cook, we didn't really go prying for evidence against any of them.''

"What about other enemies?'' Mr. Cable asked. "Robinson was getting ready to run for mayor, or so say the papers. Who would have run against him? Whose share of the pie would have been smaller if he'd won?''

"Robinson was a Democrat, on the reform platform,'' said the detective. "There's been some noise about corruption in the city government in the last few months, and Robinson was one of the main agitators. So Mayor Fitzpatrick could be vulnerable, next election. That's two years off, though, and Fitzpatrick could turn things around. He might be stronger than ever by then. Or Joe Shakspeare might make another run, and a lot of the reform Democrats would stick with him. Or some other candidate might have knocked Robinson out of the lead—maybe dug up a scandal or found a hot issue to beat him on. So he wasn't guaranteed the nomination. I wouldn't be surprised at anything in New Orleans politics, but nobody's head is really on the block until '96.''

"No reason to suspect anybody of killing off the opposition, in other words," said Mr. Clemens. He'd gotten his pipe lit and was puffing away merrily. "But you probably didn't look far enough to eliminate anybody there, either, did you?"

LeJeune gave a nod and a wry smile. "Not really. Like I said, once we had the cook in custody, the investigation pretty much stopped. So, where do you think you want to start?"

"There doesn't seem to be any shortage of leads," said Mr. Clemens, "but there's no single area of suspicion strong enough to tell me I ought to concentrate on it alone."

He paused, puffing on his pipe and wrinkling his brow in thought. Finally, he said, "Let's go straight for the brass ring and see if we can prove or disprove the main argument all in one shot. The key to the whole case is Leonard Galloway. If I can satisfy myself once and for all whether he's innocent—or guilty, if that's how the cards fall—I know whether to stop right there or go looking for another killer. Can you get me a chance to talk to him?"

"I suspect so," said the detective, standing up. "Let me go make a telephone call. I know a place around the corner where I can use the phone. I'll have your answer before you've finished your pipe."

4 ⟿

"**D**o you really intend to embroil yourself in this murder case?" I asked Mr. Clemens. He was strolling at his usual leisurely pace (as I forced myself not to rush ahead) along Orleans Street, away from the river in the direction of the Parish Prison.

Detective LeJeune had arranged for my employer to visit the Parish Prison that afternoon, and to spend half an hour talking to a certain prisoner: Leonard Galloway, the cook accused of murdering John David Robinson. Somewhat to my surprise, Mr. Clemens had accepted the invitation without hesitation.

Mr. Cable, obviously pleased at how quickly events were moving, offered to accompany us to see the prison. At that, Mr. Clemens shook his head. "No, George, I have to do this one by myself—well, I'll want Wentworth to come along. But the point is for me to make up my own mind. It'll be hard enough to keep the cook from saying what he thinks *I* want to hear, without having somebody there he's known since he was a boy to complicate things. I promise I'll tell you everything when I get back." Mr. Cable reluctantly admitted that Mr. Clemens's objections were well-founded, and we left him and LeJeune sitting over their coffee.

"I still haven't decided what I'm going to do, Wentworth," said Mr. Clemens now. "George Cable believes that Galloway is an innocent man; it's damned near an article of faith with him. But George has been away from New Orleans for ten years, and a man can change a lot in that much time, especially if you figure that the cook couldn't have been much older than twenty then. And that's ten years of being told over and over again that he's less than a real man, and having his nose rubbed in it by every white man he meets.'' We paused a moment at the corner of Bourbon Street as a fully laden beer wagon rumbled past, the big horses straining at the traces, headed for some saloon.

We crossed the dusty street and Mr. Clemens continued. ''That's why I don't want to jump into the case just on Cable's say-so, Wentworth. Is Leonard Galloway a convenient victim chosen to appease the public, or is he a poisoner? If he really *is* a murderer, and I lend my name to the battle to defend him, who does it help? It doesn't help the blacks, it doesn't help Cable, it doesn't help the people of New Orleans, and it sure doesn't help me. So I want to be sure I know what kind of man Galloway is, and the best way I know to decide that is to talk to him. I can tell more about a man in five minutes of talking to him, face-to-face, than in a year of hearing what other people say about him. So here's a chance to talk to him and see what I can learn.

''Besides, this is as good a chance as I'll ever have to get a look around the old Parish Prison. It's a New Orleans landmark in a dismal sort of way, on the order of the Bastille. It dates from before I was born, and there are a lot of strange stories about it. They've finally decided to build a new prison up on Tulane Avenue, and tear the old one down. So this is probably my last chance to see the inside of the place. I imagine I'm unlikely to see it as an overnight guest, now that I'm supposedly an honest citizen.''

''I should hope not!'' I said, shocked at the notion of my employer spending a night in prison. Perhaps respected authors of mature years were still imprisoned in Russia, or other barbaric places with no constitution, but I could not imagine Mr. Clemens being jailed. Well, perhaps it might have happened in the bygone era of debtor's prisons—but hardly in these enlightened times.

We walked up Orleans Street to the corner of Tremé, where we found a grim-looking structure, three stories high and covering an entire city block. We presented ourselves at the entrance, where the policeman on duty instantly recognized "Mark Twain," and waved us through the doors where many wretches undoubtedly met a much less congenial welcome and entered with far less hope of a timely exit than we experienced.

Even at first glance it was clear that the building sadly needed repair—better yet, replacement. One of the senior keepers, Mr. DeBusschere, appointed himself our guide and led us into the heart of the ancient dungeon.

Mr. DeBusschere was a thick, muscular man with a full white mustache and a clean-shaven head. He wore a blue uniform with a holstered pistol at the waist, along with a large ring of keys. He was obviously impressed at the chance to escort a world-famous author, and so he took us on a roundabout route, giving us a full commentary on all the sights and history of the Parish Prison, smiling broadly all the time, although the smile stopped short of his eyes. Mr. Clemens looked at everything with lively interest, and so I refrained from expressing my annoyance that we were not taken directly to see the cook.

Mr. DeBusschere put great emphasis on the lynching of the Italians accused of shooting the police chief a few years earlier; his theme appeared to be the valiant but unsuccessful efforts of the guards (himself prominent among them) to protect the prisoners. "Here's Cell Number Two, where six of the Italians hid the night the lynch mob came," he said. "We left the dagos free to run inside the prison, hoping they'd have a chance to save themselves, but the citizens followed them down that way into the courtyard—we'll see that in a little while—and shot them down."

I peered into the gloomy cell, lit by a single gas flame from the hall where we stood. Several prisoners stared back, with no sign of recognizing their distinguished visitor. "What a terrible place! It must be a very hotbed of vermin and disease," I said.

"Well, we have the very answer for that," said Mr. DeBusschere, proudly. He pointed to the ceiling with a sweeping gesture. "We let the bats nest in the rafters undisturbed so they can kill off the flies and mosquitos. That's a sure preventative to yellow fever, you know." I peered into the dark, but could not make out anything. Still, the notion of bats swooping down over the poor souls in the cells sent a chill up my back.

"Yes, and Cable tells me they fumigated the place back in '82," said Mr. Clemens, conversationally. "They took out over a hundred barrels full of dead rats."

"Well, that's what the newspapers claimed, but it's an exaggeration," said the keeper. "I was here at the time, and I doubt there were more than ninety-five barrels. But good riddance to the filthy vermin, says I." He rattled his keys self-importantly and led us on to the next section of the prison. I resisted the temptation to ask whether the place had been given a proper cleaning since.

Mr. DeBusschere took us through several different sections of the prison, pointing out places he thought we might find interesting: a doghouse where two of the arrested Italians had hidden and escaped the mob; bullet holes in the wall where two others had been found and shot to death; and the infamous sweatbox that, until very recently, had been used to coerce recalcitrant prisoners to confess. At every turn, prisoners crowded forward, some of them pleading pathetically, asking for their lawyers, for food, for their wives or mothers. A few of them tried to beckon me over to the bars, but Mr. DeBusschere had warned me not to listen to such invitations. "I can't guarantee your safety," he said. Still, my indignation grew to see such inhumane and uncivilized treatment, even of murderers and thieves, let alone the unfortunates whose only crimes were mental deficiency or lunacy, but who were indiscriminately thrown in with the worst kind of hardened criminal.

I think our guide must have detected my revulsion at the barbaric conditions prevailing within the prison, for at last he took us up a stairway to a different section of the building. "Now, I don't want you to think we don't know how to treat decent folks who somehow fall afoul of the law," he said. Much to my surprise, we found ourselves surrounded by cells far cleaner and more roomy than those we had just seen.

We entered a large common room with comfortable chairs and writing tables and curtains concealing the bars on the windows. A couple of guards stood casually by the door, conversing with the prisoners as if they were the best of friends. The inmates here were far better fed and dressed than their fellows in the cells we had just left. Mr. DeBusschere told us that they were even allowed to order dinner sent in from restaurants in the neighboring community. One fellow was being measured for a suit of clothes, and another, a stout man with long stringy hair combed upward across his skull in a futile attempt to cover a large bald spot, recognized Mr. Clemens and had the audacity to walk over and offer him a cigar. "You'll find this as good a smoke as you'll get this side of Cuba," he told him. Mr. Clemens stared at the fellow, but took the cigar and put it in his breast pocket, politely thanking the prisoner.

After a short while in this comparatively comfortable section of the prison, we headed for the courtyard where we would meet Leonard Galloway, the cook arrested for Robinson's murder. "Who was that rascal who gave me the cigar?" asked Mr. Clemens, as we came down the stairs.

"Adolf Mueller," said Mr. DeBusschere. "He's a precinct worker in the Fourth Ward. He beat up a policeman who went to question him about extorting money from a house over on Customhouse Street, and the cop pressed charges. The madam and the girls were too scared to testify, but the cop wouldn't be scared off or bought off, and neither would the judge. Now Adolf's doing ninety days in the Orleans Hotel,'' the prison guard concluded, chuckling. Upon hearing this, Mr. Clemens took the cigar out of his pocket and sniffed the wrapper with an expression that combined evident relish and profound regret. Then, as we passed an open window, he flung it through the bars.

''Waste of a good cigar,'' said Mr. DeBusschere, with a surprised look on his face.

''Damned good cigar, unless my nose has failed me in my old age,'' said Mr. Clemens. ''But somebody else is bound to find it before it gets rained on, and I hope he'll enjoy it more than I ever could have, once I knew what kind of son of a bitch gave it to me.''

Mr. DeBusschere brought us down a rickety flight of stairs to a large courtyard, surrounded on all sides by the prison buildings and walls. Along one side, three tiers of rounded arches created a pleasant contrast to the stark purpose of the building. Prisoners of all races and nationalities filled the courtyard, although they tended to stay in groups with their own kind. Some chatted animatedly with their fellows, while others simply paced or sat dejectedly against a wall, out of the direct rays of the hot afternoon sun. Among the latter was a dark-skinned man who did not even look up at our approach, until Mr. DeBusschere prodded him and said, ''Leonard, there's a man here to see you.''

The man looked up, squinting into the sun, and rose quickly to his feet. ''Excuse me, mister, but aren't you Mr. Mark Twain?'' he said to my employer. His voice was a deep baritone with the soft inflections I'd come to associate with the New Orleans accent.

''That's who he is, and he wants to ask you some questions, so mind your manners,'' said the keeper, in a gruffer voice than he'd used speaking to Mr. Clemens or me.

''That's who I am, and this is my secretary, Wentworth Cabot,'' said Mr. Clemens, extending his hand. ''George

Cable heard about your case, and asked me to come see you. Is there any chance Leonard and I can speak some in private?'' he asked, turning to Mr. DeBusschere.

The keeper grumbled a bit about regulations, but the complaints were evidently strictly pro forma. Mr. Clemens took something out of his pocket and slipped it into DeBusschere's hand, and the smile returned to the keeper's face. He quickly ushered us into an unoccupied cell just off the courtyard. ''I can let you talk for twenty minutes. There'll be a keeper in earshot if the boy causes any trouble,'' he told Mr. Clemens. ''But I think Leonard knows that he'll get back any trouble he starts, with compound interest. Ain't that right, Leonard?''

''Yessir, Mr. DeBusschere,'' said the Negro with a frightened look. Evidently satisfied, the keeper nodded to Mr. Clemens and left, pulling the barred door shut behind him.

I looked around and saw that we were in a clean, sparsely furnished room, perhaps six by eight feet, with a small, high, barred window that let in the bright southern sun from the courtyard. There was a small bench bolted to the wall beneath the window. ''Sit down and relax, if you can,'' said Mr. Clemens, waving in the direction of the bench. The Negro took the seat, still looking warily toward the door through which the keeper had left. There was nobody within sight, but anyone could have stood around the nearest corner and overheard all we said.

I took the opportunity to observe Galloway more closely: he was a bit over average height, possibly five feet eleven inches, and solidly built, although not with the kind of bulky muscle that comes from heavy manual labor. His skin was a rich chocolate color, and his hair was cut short. His clothes were not expensive, but they were relatively new and clean, despite his overnight stay in prison. I guessed his age at about thirty, judging by his unlined face and trim waist. At present, he looked thoroughly miserable.

''I remember you, now that I can get a look at you,''

said Mr. Clemens. "I saw you in the kitchen a couple of times when I last visited George Cable in New Orleans. Ten, maybe twelve years ago, if I'm not mistaken."

"Yessir, that's right," said Galloway. "I 'member you, too. 'Course, I was just a boy, and you was a writer, a friend of Mr. George's."

"Well, there's the difference between us. I'm still a writer, but you're hardly a boy these days. Cable tells me you've become a mighty good cook."

Galloway gave a little smile. "Thank Mr. George for saying that about me. I learnt how to cook from my old Aunt Tillie, right in his kitchen. I sure do miss them days." And then, the memory of where he was seemed to strike home, and he slumped forward and his gaze dropped to the floor. I felt immediate sympathy for his plight. But was I looking at an innocent man or a cold-blooded killer? I couldn't tell, and I wondered how Mr. Clemens meant to spot the difference.

"We've all seen better days, Leonard. But I've come here on business, and that keeper will be back soon enough, so let's get down to it while we have the time. The police say you murdered Robinson, and Cable says you couldn't have. I know Cable, and I put a lot of faith in his word. So I'd like to believe you're innocent, and see you back in your own home. But I'm not the judge, and not about to become one. What can you tell me that might help me get you out of this place?" He leaned casually against the wall, his eyes fixed on the prisoner.

"I don't know," said Galloway, wringing his hands. "I told the police everything, 'cause I don't have nothing to hide. I told 'em all I didn't put poison in Mr. Robinson's food. I'd be crazy to try that. I'd be the first man they come looking for. If I done it, you know I'd have gone and lit out for Texas. I *sure* wouldn't be catching a nap on my front porch when they come looking for me. Not after it was in all the newspapers he was poisoned."

Mr. Clemens pointed his finger at the prisoner. "They

say he yelled at you because you were drunk on the job. Fined you a day's pay and sent you home.''

Galloway hung his head. "He did, and I deserved it. Me and a few other people on the block was at a funeral the day before, and stayed up late consoling the widow—and joining in the singing, and having a few drinks. The next day I had a bad headache, so I figured a little hair of the dog that bit me was the answer. And I 'spect I had a little too much of that hair, 'cause I fell asleep in the kitchen. Mr. Robinson found me and cussed me out and sent me home to sober up without my pay." He paused, as if gathering his thoughts, then shook his head and looked up with a rueful expression.

"Yeah, I was mad when I went home, even though I knew better. But Mr. Robinson came out to the kitchen looking for me the next day, and he acted as if *he* was the one that done something wrong. Said he shouldn't have yelled at me in front of the others, I was the best cook he ever had, and I had a job with him as long as I wanted. And he gave me the pay for the day before, even though he sent me home! I didn't want to take it, Mr. Twain. I didn't earn it, and I didn't want it. But he made me take it. What kind of fool would want to go and kill a man that treated him like that?'' I could see tears on his face.

Mr. Clemens sat down next to Galloway, putting his hand on his shoulder. "A bigger fool than anybody in this room," he said. "Or a worse monster. You've convinced me, Leonard. I'm going to do my best to get you out of here. But to do that, I'm afraid I'll have to prove that somebody else is the real killer." He stood and looked up at the window. "Do you have any idea who that could be?''

"None of the other servants, anyhow," said the cook. "The only one in the family they didn't like is Miz Eugenia. She's got a real temper. It wasn't like Mr. Robinson to yell at folks or order 'em around. That's why I was so flabbergasted when he cussed me out. I figured it was 'cause Miz Eugenia wasn't there, and he felt he had to do something. Maybe he was mad over something else and took it out on me, although that wasn't his way, either.'' There was the beginning of hope on Galloway's face.

"What about the family? Visitors to the house? Were there any that you know of that day?'' Mr. Clemens stopped and looked at him.

The Negro clasped his hands and lifted them to his chin, thinking deeply. At last he shrugged. "If there was, I didn't see them. But out in the kitchen, I wouldn't have known it, anyway, unless they called for some kind of refreshments. It was a weekday, so the mailman would have come by twice, and we got a delivery of ice just before lunchtime. But Mr. Robinson was out a good bit of the afternoon, doing business in town. After dinner, Miz Eugenia's brother, Mr. Reynold Holt, came by as I was packing up to leave. I don't know how late he stayed, though, or if anybody else came later on. Arthur, the butler, might could tell you.''

"Write down those names, Wentworth, the butler and the brother-in-law," said Mr. Clemens. He paced a few steps across the cell, and I took out my notebook. "I'll have to see if I can talk to the butler. But think, Leonard. Did you hear any talk among the servants that might suggest why someone would want Robinson dead? Did he have any enemies?'' Mr. Clemens's mind seemed to be moving at high speed, although as usual he spoke and walked as if there were all the time in the world.

Galloway shook his head. "If he had any enemies, they sure never came to dinner at the house. But he was always talking politics, always politics—who going to run for mayor, how to clean up the Quarter, what to do about the Mafia—this and that and the other thing. There was loud arguments sometimes, 'cause I could hear 'em from the kitchen, but they didn't sound like the kind of thing to kill a man for. They'd laugh as much as they argued.''

"Who's *they?*" said Mr. Clemens. "Was it family,

42   businesspeople, old friends? Think hard, Leonard, this could be important.''

"Mostly the same few folks. Mr. Reynold Holt, old Dr. Soupape, Mr. Dupree the lawyer, Mr. Percy Staunton, Professor Maddox, and their wives . . . some family, some friends from way back. Mr. Robinson was in the army with some of 'em, during the war. They weren't the only guests, but they were the regulars.'' Galloway moved forward on the bench, arching his back as if to stretch sore muscles.

But Mr. Clemens was not done yet. He leaned over him and continued with his questions. "Were there any family quarrels you heard about?''

"Sure, that's what family's like, ain't it? But nothing really hot or nasty, that I heard. Me and my brother Charley get into worse fights all the time. Some of the live-in servants might know more, though. You ought to talk to them. Go and see Arthur. Or that girl Theresa, Miz Eugenia's maid. Tell 'em I said to tell you what they know. They'll talk to you.''

"Get those names, too, Wentworth," said Mr. Clemens, but I was already scribbling them into my notebook. I finished the list and had my pencil poised for Mr. Clemens's next question, when a knock at the door announced the return of Mr. DeBusschere.

"Well," said the keeper, "looks like y'all had a nice little talk. Sorry to rush you, but Leonard's got to get back to his own cell." His hands were on his hips, and the keys dangled by his waist. Behind him, I could see the sunlit courtyard and the other prisoners.

The hope I'd seen on Leonard Galloway's face had disappeared again. The cook rose from the bench and, without being ordered, walked toward the door. But as he passed Mr. Clemens, he paused for a moment and said in a low voice, "I sure do 'preciate you coming to see me, Mr. Twain. It do mean a lot to me, even if nothing comes of it.''

"Come along, now," said Mr. DeBusschere. "You

know you shouldn't waste Mr. Twain's time.''

"Just one thing more, can I please, Mr. Keeper?" said Galloway. DeBusschere nodded, and the cook said, "Get word to my Aunt Tillie, over at my place on First Street. Tell her you saw me, and I'm all right. That you're gonna help me, if you can.''

"I will," said Mr. Clemens, and Galloway nodded, evidently satisfied. I put my notebook in my pocket and stepped out into the sun. Mr. Clemens and the cook were right behind me. My employer turned and shook hands with our guide. "Thank you for the tour, Mr. DeBusschere," he said. "You've given me a lot of good stories to put in my new book, and I'll make sure to give you credit for them.''

DeBusschere beamed, and it was clear he was already planning how he would tell his family and friends about escorting the famous author around the old prison house, and maybe even getting into a book. As he escorted us to the front door, Mr. Clemens turned and said, as if in an afterthought, "I'm glad you were able to let us talk to Galloway awhile. Take good care of him, now. I think he'll be going home sooner than you expect.''

"We try to take good care of all our guests," said the keeper with a chuckle that wasn't entirely pleasant to my ears. "Y'all come back sometime, and we'll do the same for you.''

Mr. Clemens laughed heartily at this sally, although I myself saw nothing humorous about it. "There are some who might think I belong here," he said, "but I reckon I'll just have to disappoint them. Good day, Mr. DeBusschere.'' Thus we took our leave of the Parish Prison. I can think of very few places I have been gladder to walk away from.

5

After a leisurely walk back from the Parish Prison along the seedy but undeniably picturesque steets of the French Quarter, we arrived at Mr. Clemens's rooming house on Royal Street, where we found Mr. Cable awaiting us in the courtyard, reading a book of French poems. "Aha, I was beginning to wonder when you'd be back," he said. "Did Leonard convince you of his innocence?"

"He convinced me there's more to the case than the police are letting on," said Mr. Clemens. "But come up to the room, so we can all sit down and talk freely. Besides, I need a drink." We went upstairs, and after I had made drinks for all of us—whisky and soda for Mr. Clemens and me, soda water for Mr. Cable—Mr. Clemens returned to the subject, summarizing our conversation with Galloway in the Parish Prison.

"Galloway told us that Robinson apologized for bawling him out after finding him drunk. Not only that, but he paid him for the day even though he'd sent him home," he concluded. "If that's the truth, then Galloway's reason for killing him has just disappeared—or so it seems to me. But we need more than his word for that if we're going to clear him. Maybe we can find somebody else that Robinson told what he was going to do, preferably someone the police will believe. Better yet, maybe we can figure out who the real murderer is. I'm not sure how we're going to do either one of those things, though.''

Cable drew himself up to his full height—something just over five feet—and said, ''Remember what Detective LeJeune told us about the Robinson case? In this kind of murder, a poisoning in the victim's own home, the killer is more likely than not one of the victim's close acquaintances. We should go talk to the Robinson family, ask a few unostentatious questions, and see what we can find out.''

''Now, hold on, Cable,'' said Mr. Clemens, holding up his hand in protest. ''I can't walk into a house where I've never shown my face before and start asking questions about a murder in the family. It's hard enough for the police to get straight answers in a case like this, let alone some outsider. You, of all people, ought to know how close-knit these Louisiana gentry are. What makes you think they'll give me any more than the time of day?''

''Because you're the most famous writer in America, and because you're going to tell them you're going to put them in a book,'' said Cable. ''If that won't start them talking, there's nothing on Earth that will.''

''Excuse me, gentlemen,'' I said. The two men turned to face me, and suddenly my mouth went dry at the thought of trying to give either of them advice. But for once, I happened to know something about the subject under discussion. I forged ahead. ''I can't claim to know the customs here in Louisiana, but I do have a good notion how an old established New England family would act, and there surely can't be very much difference. I'd think that offering to put Mr. Robinson's widow in a book, this soon after her husband has died of unnatural causes, is likely to make her slam the door in your face—even more so, if she has reason to fear it might bring more scandal to the family. Nor is she likely to be enthusiastic about your quizzing the servants.''

''Good points, Wentworth,'' said Mr. Clemens, nodding.

46   "I'm flattered that George thinks my name would open
their doors, but I'm afraid you've hit the nail on the head.
How would you suggest we go about getting in to talk to
them?"

"Try to talk to the servants away from the Robinson
house," I suggested. "Possibly you can catch them at their
own homes, or out running errands, or even after church. I
think they'll be more forthcoming if we can interview them
away from their employer's eyes."

"The butler and the maid probably live in the Robinson
house, though," Mr. Cable pointed out. "And the butler,
at least, is likely to be very loyal to the family—at least if
he's been in service with them for any length of time."

"Yes," I said, "but the man who paid the servants is
dead, and if what the cook says is correct, the widow may
not be as well-liked by the servants. That might make them
readier to talk, especially to help one of their own."

"I have an idea; let me think," said Mr. Clemens. He
paced around the room a few moments, then turned to face
us. "Why don't we start with Leonard's Aunt Tillie? If he
was close to her, he may have told her about Robinson's
giving him back his pay, which would back up his story. I
promised him I'd get word to her and tell her how he's
doing. She'll probably be glad to help us if she knows
we're working to prove his innocence. Maybe she can get
the butler and maid to come talk to us, away from the eyes
and ears of the family. She was your cook back when you
lived here, wasn't she, George? Do you still know where
she lives?"

"Of course!" said Cable. He jumped up and reached for
his hat. "She took Leonard and his brother in after their
parents died, and I believe she's still in the same house.
Come with me, and we'll see her this very evening!"

"Easy now, George," said Mr. Clemens. "You haven't
finished your drink, and neither has Wentworth. We've got
plenty of time. Sit back down and let's figure out what
we're going to say to Aunt Tillie. And while we're doing

that, I do believe I've got enough time for another drink, myself.''

Despite our leisure, it was still light when we went down to the street. We walked over to Jackson Square, where carriages were plentiful as usual, but the first two drivers we hailed claimed not to know how to get to the vicinity of First and Liberty, where Leonard Galloway lived with his aunt. I was surprised, since the area was clearly marked on my map—only a couple of miles away, north of Saint Charles Avenue. Had I not been with two older men, I would have thought nothing of walking it. Mr. Clemens began to frown, and I was in fear of an outburst of his formidable temper, when Mr. Cable hailed a jolly-looking Negro driver in a bright red vest, who looked down from the seat with a quizzical expression and said, ''It ain't really my business, but do you folks know that's sort of a rough neighborhood you're asking to go to?''

''I know it perfectly well,'' said Mr. Cable. ''We are on a mission of mercy, and do not fear for ourselves.''

''Sho 'nuff,'' said the driver, looking at Mr. Cable's sober dress, then at Mr. Clemens's white suit, and finally at me, towering over the two of them. ''Let me guess, now. You must be some kind of trump cards, to be goin' there and not worried about it. You's a preacher,'' he said, pointing at Cable, ''and he's a doctor,'' indicating Mr. Clemens. ''And maybe this here fellow's a lawyer.''

''No, no,'' said Mr. Cable. ''I am George Washington Cable, and this is Mark Twain, and the other fellow is Mr. Cabot, his secretary.''

''Hmmph,'' said the driver, looking us over more carefully. ''Well, maybe you is and maybe you ain't. That fellow *looks* like the picture of Mark Twain they got up outside the lecture hall. But you look more like a jockey than George Washington, besides which, you ain't near old enough. And maybe you'd best pretend this big fellow is a prizefighter so nobody messes with you, 'cause he sure don't look like no secretary I ever saw. Git on board. I'll take you there anyhows.''

It took us two or three minutes to get Mr. Clemens to stop laughing enough to climb on board, but eventually he did. The driver flicked his reins, and off we went.

We crossed Canal Street and drove southwest along Saint Charles Avenue, with the driver pointing out various places and sights. ''That's the Saint Charles Hotel, which is a mighty nice place to stay, if you got the money, and the Saint Charles Theater right next to it. You could get the streetcar here, but you'd have to walk a good piece at the other end, where you're going, so you a lot better off ridin' with me. I'll take you right there. This here's—Ho! Git that mule out the way! Folks ain't got all day to ride behind you!'' (This latter to another driver moving too slowly for his taste.) ''This here's Lafayette Square, and that's City Hall, where all the trouble starts. That statue over there ain't Lafayette, though—that's Ben Franklin. Lafayette was a Frenchman from France, and Ben Franklin was a Yankee, but I reckon they's both dead. Never saw no statue for a live man. Good *evenin'*, sister!'' (To a fashionably dressed young Negress.) ''And that's the Academy of Music, where they plays all kinds of concerts and operas—What you think you doin'? I had a rig like that, I'd look out where I was goin' 'fore somebody ran me down!—And up ahead we got Lee Circle, with a statue of General Lee, which is who they named it after.''

The driver kept up an endless stream of this sort of banter the whole way, commenting on the style and appointments of every other coach on the road and the competence or lack thereof of their drivers, not to forget remarking on pretty women we passed and generally making it impossible to get a word of our own in edgewise. Since I myself had no particular opinion on any of these subjects, I was content to let him babble on, but I could see that my companions were happy when he finally pulled up in front of the address we had given him.

The houses in this section were quite different from those in the Creole quarter we had come from: low, narrow buildings that our driver referred to as "shotgun shacks." There was no elegant ironwork here, nothing picturesque, and the streets were muddy, with wooden sidewalks and planks laid for pedestrians to cross at the corners. But the houses were well kept, and there was an air, if not quite of prosperity, at least of putting on a respectable face for the world. I wondered at the driver's having described the neighborhood as rough. Perhaps he took our dress and manner as an indication that we were used to more affluent surroundings. I had certainly seen less attractive neighborhoods in workingmen's sections of New Haven, although not with quite as heterogenous a mixture of races as here. And from some of the stories he told, I suspected that Mr. Clemens had seen far worse than I had.

We paid off our driver, and as we dismounted, he said, "Now, you ain't going to have much luck findin' a ride back downtown from here. That's why them other fellows didn't want to take you, like as not. I 'spose you could walk to the streetcar, but that's a bit of a hike on *these* streets. If you want, I can wait and pick you up when you're ready to go back."

Mr. Cable nodded his agreement to Mr. Clemens, who turned to the driver and said, "That sounds good to me. Tell you what. Go get yourself a drink somewhere, and come back in about an hour." He tossed the driver a fifty cent piece. "If we're not ready then, we'll let you know when we will be."

"Sho 'nuff," said the driver, looking at the coin with a surprised expression. "You finish up your business early, just send somebody down to the grocery store on the corner of Howard and ask for Henry Dodds—that's me—and I'll be here directly."

"We'll do that, Henry," said Mr. Clemens, and we walked up to the house.

Mr. Cable knocked on the screen door. A tall, slim Negro

50   man answered the door and peered out at the three of us
with a puzzled expression. He looked us up and down and
said, "Can I help you, gen'lemen?"

Mr. Cable stepped forward and put his hand on the door
handle. "Yes, we're looking for Matilda Galloway. Is this
the right house?" But Mr. Cable had barely finished speaking when a woman's voice came from within. "Is that Mr.
Cable? My lands, don't keep him waiting, Charley, let him
in!"

Charley stood back, and the three of us entered the front
room of the little house. There we found a heavyset Negro
woman wearing a shapeless flowered dress and waving a
paper fan as she greeted Mr. Cable. Another younger Negro
man stood behind her rocking chair, looking at us with
undisguised curiosity. "It's been a long time, Aunt Tillie,
but you don't seem to have changed much," said Mr. Cable.

"Well, it's a wonder I ain't withered away, worrying so
much about poor Leonard being in prison," she said, flut-
tering her fan. "But sit down, sit down. Can I get you
gen'lemen some lemonade? Charley, get another chair in
here. Don't make them stand up." After a few moments of
bustle and agitation, the three of us were seated, and Mr.
Cable had introduced us. Aunt Tillie remembered Mr.
Clemens from his previous visit to New Orleans, and was
obviously flattered that such a famous man took an interest
in her nephew Leonard's case. In turn, she introduced the
two young men: Charley Galloway, Leonard's younger
brother, who had answered the door, and Charles Bolden,
the son of her next-door neighbor. "Just call me Buddy,"
he said, with a crooked smile, clearly impressed to meet
Mr. Clemens. "No reason to get confused with two Char-
leys in the room."

I took a moment to look around the little room as the
woman went to the back of the building—presumably to
the kitchen—to fetch our drinks. While the house was small
and unpretentious, with kerosene lamps and bare floors, it

was clean and cozy, with bright wallpaper in a geometrical pattern. There were pictures on the wall: a watercolor sketch I recognized as a younger Leonard Galloway, a large photograph of a smiling Negro couple (relatives, I assumed) dressed in slightly old-fashioned clothes, and two or three framed colored pictures of landscapes—chromolithographs, from the look of them. Mr. Cable and Mr. Clemens were seated on a Turkish-style sofa along the side wall, and I sat in a straight-backed chair next to the window. Young Bolden brought a chair in from the kitchen and was shortly followed by Aunt Tillie carrying a tray with a pitcher of lemonade and six glasses.

When we were all seated and had our drinks, Mr. Clemens told of our visit to Leonard Galloway in the Parish Prison. "So far, they seem to be treating him decently," he concluded. "But jail's a rotten place, even with good treatment, and Leonard's taking it pretty hard." He shook his head, then fixed Aunt Tillie with a sincere gaze. "It'll take some doing to get him out of there, but if there's any way to do it, you can count on my help."

"Praise the Lord, that's the best news I've heard since the police came and took poor Leonard off," said the woman, raising up her hands in delight. "That boy wouldn't hurt a fly, Mr. Twain. He's a good churchgoing boy, and I told the police just that. And Mr. Robinson done took good care of him. He even paid him for the day he sent him home, and said he was sorry for yelling at him; Leonard gave me half the money that same day, bless his heart. Why on Earth would he try to poison a man like that?"

"That settles it," said Mr. Clemens. "I might have doubted Leonard's story up to now, but now I know it's true. Leonard is an innocent man. Cable, Wentworth, we're going to get him out of jail if it's the last thing we do in this town."

"I sure am glad to hear that, Mr. Twain," said Charley Galloway, smiling for the first time since we'd arrived.

52 ''You need any kind of help from me, just say the word.''
Young Buddy Bolden added his offer of help as well, and
with a broad grin, Mr. Clemens jumped up and shook both
their hands with great enthusiasm. ''Good, we've got a
team,'' he said.

Then he paused and looked around at the six of us in the
room, scratching his chin. ''Now, all I have to do is figure
out how to get Leonard out of jail. Does anybody here
know how we can manage that without using guns or ladders?''

~6

There was a moment of silence, and then Buddy Bolden laughed. "Well, if we was going to try and bust Leonard out of jail with guns and ladders, we wouldn't need Mr. Mark Twain to help us. Plenty of folks have ladders, and there ain't no shortage of guns, if it came right down to that. But I reckon you could count me out, if that's what you was planning, 'cause all you'd end up with is a bunch of colored folks being shot instead of just one being hanged. Still, I do have an idea that might work, if you don't mind listening."

"I sure don't mind listening," said Mr. Clemens. "There might be plenty of ladders around, but good ideas are in short supply just now."

"Well," said the young man, "we all know Leonard didn't kill this Mr. Robinson. But that don't seem to hold no water with the police. So what we need to do is prove who *did* kill him, and then getting Leonard out of prison is no problem at all. That make sense?"

"Makes plenty of sense to me," said Mr. Clemens, nodding his head. "Keep on talking."

"I reckon whoever killed Mr. Robinson, it has to be somebody he knew," said Bolden. "It don't make no sense any other way. Strangers don't go around putting poison in each other's food, 'specially not in big houses down in the Garden District. So whoever killed him, it was somebody he knew and trusted enough to eat or drink with."

"Yes, we've been thinking the same thing ourselves," said Mr. Cable. "A family member, or close friend, or a trusted servant would be my guess."

Charley Galloway shook his head. "Maybe family or a friend," he said, "but unless I miss my guess, it wasn't no servant." He paused, looking from Mr. Clemens to Mr. Cable, and finally at me; then, as if satisfied with what he saw in our faces, he continued. "I think the murderer has got to be a white person."

There was a silence; then, "Charley! Watch what you say!" said Aunt Tillie, clearly apprehensive at her nephew's statement.

"He doesn't have to hold his tongue for my sake, Aunt Tillie," said Mr. Clemens. "I've already come to pretty much that same conclusion, and I think George agrees with me. The police talk like they've solved the case, but I think they're going in the face of the facts. The important question is, which one of Robinson's friends and family is the killer?"

"Well, there's where my idea comes in," said Bolden. "One thing you learn pretty early, living this close to all those rich folks' houses, is that they'll go talking about anything in the world in front of the butler or cleaning maid, just as if there weren't nobody listening at all. They may think they've got secrets, but every one of them has got a houseful of servants that know more about their secrets than they do. You know that, Miz Galloway." He looked at the elderly woman who sat in her rocking chair, fanning herself and shaking her head. Outside the single window, the sky was turning darker, but it was still warm inside the little house.

"Well, I suppose it's true," said Aunt Tillie, after a pause. "But it's one thing to hear something, and another to tell about it. One thing for sure, if you work in the white folks' house, you best know how to keep what you hear to yourself. Maybe somebody in Mr. Robinson's house does

know who killed him, but even if they do, how you goin'
to get them to tell Mr. Twain about it?''

Bolden smiled. ''That's where my plan comes in, Miz
Galloway. Maybe they won't tell Mr. Twain about it, and
maybe they won't even tell you or me, but I reckon I know
somebody they *will* tell. All we got to do is convince her
to help us find out what we need to know, and then we can
use that to help get Leonard out.''

Aunt Tillie looked at Bolden with a suspicious expression. ''Who you talking about, boy? Who's this *her* everybody talks to?''

''You know who he means, Aunt Tillie,'' said Charley
Galloway, his face lighting with sudden comprehension.
''He's talking about Eulalie Echo.''

Aunt Tillie dropped her fan and clasped her arms over
her bosom. ''Lord have mercy!'' she said, shaking her
head. ''Poor Leonard ain't in enough trouble already that
now you want to go talking to a hoodoo woman!'' She
picked up her fan and began to ply it vigorously.

Bolden and Charley Galloway stood there with sheepish
grins, but Mr. Cable acted as if a poisonous snake had come
into the room. ''What a ridiculous suggestion! I know the
kind of superstitious nonsense these voodooists believe. I
witnessed some of their heathen rituals, back when I was
writing for the *Picayune*. How can you expect anything
useful from them?'' He stood up abruptly, as if ready to
bring the interview to an end.

''Hold your horses, George,'' said Mr. Clemens, furrow-
ing his brows and motioning Cable back toward his seat.
''One man's superstition is another's simon-pure gospel.
We've had this argument before. Let me hear Buddy's idea
before you try to convince me it's no good. We want to
prove Leonard is innocent and get him out of prison. And
as long as we accomplish that, I for one don't especially
care how we do it—short of murdering somebody on our
own, I suppose. Who is this hoodoo woman, and how do
you think she can help us?''

The two colored men looked at each other, as if deciding who was willing to risk Mr. Cable's wrath. At last, Charley Galloway swallowed, looking at Aunt Tillie, then turning to Mr. Clemens. "Her name's Eulalie Echo, and she lives at Fourth and Howard, right close by. A lot of folks know her—I mean a lot of folks that works in the white people's houses. She tells fortunes, and she gives advice, and they say she talks to spirits—"

"You mean to devils!" said Cable, with an agitated expression. I was somewhat surprised at how much the subject disturbed him. One of my friends at Yale had dabbled in spiritualism, and after dutifully attending a couple of his séances, I had no doubt that some people could talk to spirits. Whether the spirits ever said anything of interest back to them was another question entirely.

But Mr. Clemens cut Mr. Cable off with a wave of his hand and a look that threatened thunderbolts. "Let the fellow tell us what he has in mind, George. You can say your say when he's finished, but I'm not about to have you cutting him off after every three words. And if you want to argue religion, argue it with me, on our own time. How do you think this fortune-teller can help us, Charley?"

With hooded eyes, Charley Galloway looked back and forth between Mr. Cable and my employer, as if deciding which of them it was more dangerous to displease. Mr. Clemens's impatient expression apparently decided him, for he turned to face him and continued his explanation. "Like I explained to you, a lot of folks talks to her, and sometimes they tell her things they won't tell anybody else. And I reckon if she asks 'em questions, they'll give her answers they won't give anybody else. If she knows it's to help Leonard, maybe she'll ask some questions about what goes on in the Robinson house—and I bet she knows somebody who'll tell her what she wants to know."

Mr. Clemens nodded. "That's straightforward enough. No deals with the devil, no human sacrifices, no black magic—just asking the right questions of the right people.

Do you find anything objectionable in that, George?''

Mr. Cable still looked somewhat uncomfortable, although I wasn't sure whether it was more at the notion of dealing with a hoodoo woman or at being chastised by Mr. Clemens. But he nodded his head and said, "I suppose not, if that's as far as it goes. The object is to help Leonard, after all."

"That's right," said Mr. Clemens. "What about you, Aunt Tillie? Do you think Eulalie Echo can help us?"

Aunt Tillie rocked slowly back and forth. "Maybe," she said, grudgingly. "Maybe she can, and maybe she can't, and maybe she will, and maybe she won't. What I want to know is what she's goin' to want us to do for *her*. I never did hear that she was any special friend of Leonard, to be doing him favors. And I sure can't see her doing us no favors for free." She began rocking harder, as if to emphasize her opinion.

"That's a good question," said Mr. Clemens. "We probably need to know the answer to it before we start counting on this Eulalie Echo. Buddy, you're the one who suggested talking to her. Can you find out whether she'll help us, and what she might want in return?"

"Sure, I'll go see her tonight," said Bolden.

"I'll go with him," said Charley Galloway. He looked at Aunt Tillie and at Mr. Cable. "And maybe some folks ought to think about just how much Leonard's neck is worth. All I know is, if it was me sittin' there in Parish Prison, instead of my brother, I'd be mighty unhappy to find out my friends and family was letting me go hang because they didn't want to do business with Eulalie Echo."

"That's settled, then," said Mr. Clemens, slapping his hand down on the arm of the couch. "Can one of you bring me the answer at Royal Street tomorrow?"

Charley Galloway and Bolden looked at each other, and then Bolden said, "I'll do it. I don't got to work until tomorrow evening, anyway. Charley's got his barbershop to look after.''

"Good," said Mr. Clemens. "Now, what else can we do to try to clear Leonard? Aunt Tillie, do you know the servants in the Robinson home well enough to talk to them?''

Aunt Tillie thought a moment. "Only one I know to talk to is Arthur, the butler; he goes to our church, and Leonard brought him over a few times on his day off, when they was going to go out to the lake or to the park together. Arthur acted little bit stuck up at first, but he was friendly enough by the second or third time he came by. Now he nods his head and says hello when he sees me.''

"You say you see him in church," said Mr. Clemens. He leaned forward, closer to Aunt Tillie. "I'd appreciate it if you asked him if he'd be willing to talk to me, somewhere away from the Robinson house. Do you think he'd do that?''

"He always acted friendly with Leonard, so I think maybe he'd talk to you if he thought it could help the boy—seeing as how it's Leonard's own family asking,'' said the woman. "Day after tomorrow's Sunday, so I'll see him then and ask him.''

"Good. Ask him if he's free to come down to Royal Street to talk, the sooner the better. One more thing you may be able to help with, and then I'm out of ideas. I think Charley and Buddy are right that the killer is a white person. I think it's even more likely that it's one of Robinson's family or close friends, if that's the right word for somebody that poisoned him.''

"Poisoned him and let the poor colored man go to jail for it," said Charley Galloway. "There's lots of words for somebody like that, but I ain't going to say them in Aunt Tillie's house, 'cause she'd never let me in the door again.''

"I'll say 'em, if you want!" said Buddy Bolden, with a sly glance toward Aunt Tillie.

"I'd wash your mouth out with soap, Charles Bolden,''

said Aunt Tillie. Her voice was loud and stern, but she had a little smile on her face as she said it.

"That wouldn't do," said Charley Galloway, laughing. "Next thing you know, he'd be blowing bubbles through that cornet of his, and wouldn't that sound awful?" Everyone laughed, and some of the tension that had built up in the room began to dissipate.

"Maybe it wouldn't be so loud," said Aunt Tillie, and now her smile was bigger. "But Mr. Twain was saying something, and it ain't polite to go talking on without letting him finish."

Mr. Clemens was smiling at the exchange, but now his expression became serious again. "I think the murderer is one of Robinson's acquaintances, and so it would help me solve the case if I can talk to the people he was close to: his family, his close friends, maybe his business partners, if he had any. Now, Cable says to tell them I'm writing a book. He thinks that'll open the door and get them to talk to me. But Wentworth here thinks they'll be shy of the publicity, especially if one of them has something to hide. Leonard must have talked to you about them. How would you suggest going about getting in to see Robinson's family and getting them to talk to a stranger?"

"You want to go see Miz Maria Staunton, the widow Robinson's sister," said Aunt Tillie without even a pause for thought. "She can't hardly walk across the room without stopping to read a book halfway, or so says Leonard. He told me he heard her sister make fun of her for reading books right at the dinner table, 'fore she married Mr. Staunton. If she won't talk to two gentlemen writers, I'll be mighty surprised. And if you get her on your side, she's your way in to talk to the rest of the family."

"That's right; I hear she's active in the Lafayette Literary Society," said Mr. Cable. He jumped up from his seat and paced, evidently excited. "She writes a bit of poetry, holds literary salons, and wants to be a patron of the arts. Yes, I think she's our ticket, Clemens. Thank you, Aunt Tillie, I should have thought of that myself." He turned around and bowed to our hostess.

"Nothing to thank me for," said the woman, with a serious look. "It's Leonard's life we're trying to save, and anything I can do to make it easier is the least I can do." Then her expression changed, and she pointed to the place Mr. Cable had vacated on the couch. "We been talking serious business so much I like to forgot my manners! Now, you set right back down and make yourself comfortable, Mr. Cable. Is that glass empty? Charley, get that pitcher and pour the gentlemen some more lemonade."

When we were ready to leave, Buddy Bolden ran down to the corner to fetch our cabdriver, Henry Dodds, who drove up a few minutes later with Bolden on the seat beside him and a twinkle in his eye. "So, you wasn't foolin' when you said you was Mark Twain," he said to Mr. Clemens as young Bolden jumped deftly down to the brick sidewalk. "Maybe this other gen'leman's George Washington, after all."

"Yes, and the tall fellow's Abe Lincoln," said Mr. Clemens, climbing up to the passenger seat. "With two presidents on board, you ought to give us a free ride back to the French Quarter."

"Well, leastways I can see *you* ain't George Washington," said Henry Dodds. "Last I heard, he never told a lie, and that's more'n I can say about somebody else here."

"That's not a lie, that's artistic license," said Mr. Cable, hoisting himself up next to Mr. Clemens. "But you'll only have to take the two of them back to the Quarter. I'm staying down on Eighth Street, just below Coliseum. You can drop me there, then take these two gentlemen back to Royal Street."

"Eighth and Coliseum—sho 'nuff, Mr. Washington," said the driver, and I barely had time to seat myself before he snapped the reins and off we went, with Charley Galloway and Buddy Bolden standing on the sidewalk laughing.

We went past more of the double shotgun houses, but within a few blocks, the faces of the children playing on the street began to be predominantly white instead of the mixture of races in the neighborhood we had just left. The houses became larger and more affluent as we neared Saint Charles Avenue, and when we crossed it, we had clearly entered a very different realm. Even the children were better dressed, and the only colored faces to be seen were obviously those of servants.

Mr. Cable was staying with old friends—close to his former residence, as he told us—and there was still a fair amount of light when our driver dropped him off. Mr. Cable tossed Henry Dodds a twenty-five cent tip and suggested, "You might drive back along Prytania and point out the Robinson house—it's at the corner of Washington. I think Mr. Clemens would be very interested in that."

"Oho," said Dodds, as we turned and started down the street. "Now I'm beginning to see what you folks is up to. I thought it was mighty strange you had business up where I dropped you off. That ain't a neighborhood where a lot of white folks from out of town is likely to go visiting, if you get my meaning. But the boys down at the corner told me that was Leonard Galloway's house you went to, and ain't nobody in N'Orlins that ain't heard all about how he's in Parish Prison for poisoning Mr. Robinson."

"You're almost right, Henry," said Mr. Clemens. "Leonard Galloway's in jail, all right, but being arrested doesn't mean he's guilty. Never judge a man until you have all the facts." He paused for a moment, then added, "Just maybe, we have a few facts that the police don't have."

"Well, I'll be doggone!" said Henry Dodds, turning to look back at us. "I've been driving this old hack for twenty years, and I've seen just about everything you can think of, and a couple you probably *can't,* but this 'bout beats it all.

You sure this here tall fellow ain't Sherlock Holmes, instead of old Abe Lincoln like you said?''

Mr. Clemens laughed. ''Wentworth is a lot of things,'' he said, ''and a few of them have surprised even me when I found out about them. But one thing I can absolutely assure you—he isn't Sherlock Holmes.''

I wasn't certain how to take that statement, but just then Henry Dodds slowed his horse and pointed to our left. ''That's the Robinson house coming up, right there on the corner.''

The house in question was situated on a large corner plot and surrounded by a tall wrought iron fence. The grounds were attractively landscaped, and the house spoke of considerable affluence even for this neighborhood, where the evidence of wealth and power was plain to see. Although the sun was beginning to drop below the horizon, I could make out a two-story portico of wrought iron lacework, which stood out clearly against the pale color of the house—a light pink, or perhaps even lavender, if I could trust my sense of color in the fading light. It went entirely against all my instincts of the proper color for a home, yet somehow it was remarkably tasteful. ''What a pleasant place to live!'' I said.

''And just a short distance from the cemetery,'' said Mr. Clemens, pointing to the stone wall we had just passed. ''Very convenient, don't you think?''

7

The next morning was Saturday. Despite our having eaten a late and rather rich supper after our arrival back in the French Quarter, Mr. Clemens was up and about bright and early, full of enthusiasm about his chosen task of clearing Leonard Galloway of an apparently unjust murder charge. After his usual hearty breakfast—beefsteak, fried eggs, and strong coffee, not to forget the morning dram of whisky he took "on general principles"—we returned to our rooms. There we found a message from Mr. Cable, who had evidently made good use of his time after parting from us the previous evening.

"George has gone right to work," said Mr. Clemens. He tore open the envelope and nodded as he read, then turned to me. "The Lafayette Literary Society is giving a literary luncheon this very afternoon, and they've just learned of my visit to this fair city—thanks to George, no doubt—and would be honored and delighted to have me as their guest, blah blah blah. Of course, they'll expect me to say a few words after the meal, but that's no great imposition. The important thing, from our point of view, is that Mrs. Maria Staunton—the sister of Mrs. Robinson—will be present."

"Capital!" I said. "With any luck, we may even be seated at the same table with her."

Mr. Clemens shook his head. "The invitation is for me, I'm afraid. I could probably push them to find room for you, but what's the point? You'll have to stay here in any

64 case, to get the message we're expecting from the hoodoo woman.''

"Yes, I'd forgotten about that," I said, sinking into a chair. "Bolden will be coming to see us, so I suppose I have to stay here."

My disappointment must have shown in my face, for Mr. Clemens put his hand on my shoulder and said, "Don't feel slighted, Wentworth. It'll be a deadly dull literary luncheon, like hundreds of others I've been to: soporific speeches and self-congratulating literary talk by people who have less right than an Arkansas mule to an opinion on literature. I suppose the food will be good enough—this is New Orleans, after all—although the company will probably take the edge off my appetite. But I doubt I'll learn one thing of consequence about our murder case. All I can really hope to accomplish today is to wangle an invitation to Mrs. Staunton's home, and I'll be certain to get you included on that. I'll want you along when we meet the whole family, since they're our main suspects."

"I suppose I'll have to settle for that," I said. "What answer shall I give to the hoodoo woman—what was her name again?"

"Eulalie Echo," said Mr. Clemens. "Assuming that's her real name, not that it matters. Bolden says that everyone in the Garden District confides in her, so she could be our ace in the hole if she's willing to help us. Tell Bolden, or whoever comes to speak for her, that I'm out. You'll give me the message, and I'll answer directly when I'm back, although I can't say how long that'll be. George may want to talk about the case for a while after our luncheon. If Eulalie wants to talk with me, find out when's a good time for her. I can't think what else she might say. As long as she wants to help us free Leonard, I'm willing to work with her on any reasonable terms. Use your judgment, but don't put me out on a limb."

"Very well," I said. "I won't make any promises for you. I assume even a hoodoo woman can be reasonable."

"I certainly hope so," said Mr. Clemens. "It's not what **65** people usually want from witches and fortune-tellers, but I'm sure she's capable of it when it's to her advantage."

Around 10:30, Mr. Clemens left for the Garden District, where he would meet Mr. Cable and go with him to the literary luncheon. I spent some time on his business correspondence, then wrote a long letter to my parents back in New London. I walked out to post the letters, then lunched at a little gumbo shop just down the street from our pension, having left word where I was to be found in case someone came looking for me. Strange as the local cooking had seemed to me at first, with its unpredictable mixture of ingredients and hot seasoning, I was becoming accustomed to it—nay, actually taking a liking to it. Besides, a cool glass of lager went a long way to counteract the red-hot pepper.

After lunch, I was feeling lazy after the morning's work, and so, upon returning to our pension, I went down to the breezy courtyard with a cool drink and a book of stories by an English writer Mr. Clemens had recommended, a fellow named Kipling who wrote about India. The time passed pleasantly, in a tropical setting of potted ferns and a tall palm tree silhouetted against a square of bright blue sky, much as I imagined the skies of the Mediterranean to appear. Thus I spent the better part of the afternoon until our landlady (Mme. Bechet, a diminutive Creole woman reputedly of ancient family and impeccable pedigree) appeared to announce a visitor for Mr. Clemens. I looked at my watch and was surprised to see that it was nearly four o'clock.

"Well, Mr. Clemens is out, but I can talk to the fellow," I said. "Did he give his name?"

"Ah, m'sieur, he had no card. It is a colored boy with a suitcase. I told him to wait at the back door," she said. "Do you wish to receive him 'ere?"

"Why, it must be Buddy Bolden," I said. "Mr. Clemens

and I are expecting him. Send him in, if you please.''

The visitor was indeed Buddy Bolden, dressed in a good suit and carrying what looked like a miniature piece of luggage; I wondered where he might be traveling. ''Hello, Buddy,'' I said. ''Mr. Clemens had an unexpected appointment and won't be back until later—possibly not until after dinner. But come, sit down, tell me what the news is. Mme. Bechet will bring you something to drink. I could use another one, too.''

Buddy looked over at Mme. Bechet, who gave an audible sniff. ''M'sieur, I can bring *you* a drink, but I am not in the habit of waiting on servants and messengers.''

''It don't matter,'' Bolden said, with a shrug of his shoulders. ''I just have a message to give, and then I'll go.''

''Oh, bother,'' I said, remembering what part of the country I was in. ''At least come on up to my room, so we can talk in private. After you've gone, Mme. Bechet can decide whether she wants to fumigate.'' We climbed two flights of stairs and closed the door behind us. There were two chairs in the little room, and I waved toward them. Bolden put his case on the floor and sat in the one nearer the window. ''It may be beneath the landlady's dignity to fix you a drink, but if you'd like to wet your throat, Mr. Clemens won't miss a drop or two of his whisky, and I don't mind pouring it,'' I said.

''That sounds good,'' he said, smiling for the first time.

I went through the connecting door to Mr. Clemens's rooms, and returned with the whisky and soda bottle and poured us two drinks. When I'd given him his glass, and we'd both taken a sip, he said, ''You got to understand about these Creole ladies. She's got her pride, and she's got her French name. Her grandma may have been as black as mine, but that don't count, in her mind.''

''I suppose you're right,'' I said. ''But I don't have to like it.''

''What the hell, mister, I like it a lot less than you do,

but ain't nothing I can do about it, 'cept maybe have a drink and laugh about it.''

"I suppose you're right," I said. As boorish as Mme. Bechet had been, I had to admit that some of my friends at Yale were little better in their treatment of the lower classes. But there was nothing to be gained by harping on it, and so I brought the subject back to our business. "What news do you have for us? What does Eulalie Echo have to say?''

Bolden looked me in the eye, sizing me up with disconcerting frankness. After a moment, he said, "She won't say nothing without she sees you. You and Mr. Twain, both.''

"That's no surprise, although I can't see what she needs to talk to me for. I'm just Mr. Clemens's secretary, after all. But I'll give him your message. Did she tell you a time that would be convenient? Should we make an appointment?''

"No, man," said Bolden. "You don't need no appointment. Miz 'Lalie don't pay no mind to the time, least not *clock* time. Just go see her. She lives out at Fourth and Howard, real close to Miz Galloway.''

"That's a curious way to arrange things," I said. "What if we go to her place and she's not in? Doesn't she go out shopping or have other engagements?''

His face changed, and he glanced around him, although only the two of us were in the room, and the sky outside the windows was bright and clear. He picked up his glass and took a deep sip of the whisky. "I'll tell you something," he continued in a lower voice. "When me and Charley Galloway showed up at her house, it was like she knew we was coming and what we wanted. She was answering our questions before we finished asking them. I don't put a lot of stock in spirits, but 'Lalie Echo is scary, man. There's stuff goes on in that house of hers I don't understand at *all*. You and Mr. Twain go see her, and you'll see what I mean. And then she'll say whatever she has to say.''

I was surprised by Bolden's response, but I decided to reserve judgment until I had met the woman in question. "Do you think she means to help us?"

He laughed nervously. "If she didn't, you think she'd bother to talk to you? I don't know what she has in mind, but I don't think she'd be wasting people's time if she wasn't going to help out Leonard. And that's all any of us want, ain't it?"

"I suppose so," I said. "Well, I'll tell Mr. Clemens, and he'll decide what to do." Then, seeing that he still appeared somewhat anxious, I changed the subject, pointing to his little suitcase sitting on the floor. "Are you traveling somewhere?"

He grinned. "No, man, that's my cornet case. There's a dance at Odd Fellows Hall tonight, and I'm in the band."

"Oh, that's right. Charley Galloway said something about your cornet yesterday. I thought it was a joke."

"Well, it was, but it ain't no joke when I play it. Charley's in the band, too—guitar player and singer."

"I see. Well, it sounds like good fun," I said.

He laughed again, this time without a trace of nervousness or self-consciousness. "That ain't the half of it. By the time the dance is over, I'll have four or five pretty girls want to help me carry that little cornet case home." He finished his drink in one gulp, picked up the case, and stood. "Thank Mr. Twain for me. I sure do appreciate the taste of his whisky. Now I got to go. We been working on a couple of new tunes, and Charley's having trouble learning them, so we set up an extra rehearsal before the dance. You tell Mr. Twain what I said, and go see 'Lalie. I guarantee you, we'll get Leonard out of that jail if it takes all next week and a couple more days, too."

"I hope it doesn't take that long," I said, and shook his hand. "I'm sure Leonard doesn't want to stay there another day if he can help it."

"Amen to that," said Bolden, and I walked him down the stairs. As I let him out through the wrought iron door leading from the courtyard to the street, I had the feeling that unseen eyes were boring into my back. I closed the gate behind him and turned to find Mme. Bechet peering out at me through the curtains of her apartment, disapproval plainly written on her face.

Sometime after six o'clock, I went out to eat, Mr. Clemens not yet being back from the Garden District. Having seen a number of little restaurants in our walk down Decatur Street, I resolved to give them a try. The first place I walked into was full of Italians, and recalling Mr. Cable's stories of the Mafia and knife fights, I was about to leave, but the aroma of the food changed my mind. I ended up having a succulent chicken dish, cooked with tomato sauce and herbs, with thin noodles in the same sauce on the side, and a quite passable bottle of red wine. A pair of young men, with a guitar and a mandolin, began playing about halfway through my meal, and so I was fed and entertained quite adequately. It was nearly dark by the time I returned to Royal Street to find Mr. Clemens just alighting from a carriage, driven, much to my astonishment, by none other than Henry Dodds, who tipped his hat and sang out, "How d'ye do, Sherlock!" when he spotted me.

"Good evening, Wentworth," said my employer. "I reckon you've eaten. Have you heard from our friends out on First Street?"

"Yes, we have," I said, returning the coachman's salute. "Come on inside, and I'll tell you the whole story."

"Good. I have news of my own; we can swap stories," said Mr. Clemens. He tossed the fare up to Henry Dodds, and we went upstairs.

Up in Mr. Clemens's room, he insisted on my pouring us each a glass of whisky and soda, although I could have done without and I suspect he could have as well. Then he listened as I told him Bolden's message from Eulalie Echo. He only interrupted once, to say "Good man!" when I mentioned giving Galloway's neighbor a drink of whisky.

When I had finished, he said, "Well, I guess we'll have to pay Eulalie a visit. We may be spending more time out in the Garden District than here, by the time this is done. If I'd known that, I'd have had you get us rooms out there instead of down here by the river."

"You may have to," I said. "From the look Mme. Bechet gave me when I let Bolden out, she appears to consider me some sort of carpetbagger, or worse."

"Sticking her nose into our business is the quickest way for her to lose it," said Mr. Clemens. Then, seeing my expression: "Our business, Wentworth, not her nose. But let me tell you what I learned today. The Lafayette Literary Society luncheon was midway between a bore and a farce, as these things usually are. Why people who've never been to the moon insist on writing poetry about it is beyond me, but the woods are full of 'em. I suppose it would be too much of a challenge to them to write about something down-to-earth.

"Anyway, I met our pigeon, Mrs. Maria Holt Staunton, and a cute little bird she is, if a bit flighty. If her sister's anything like her, I doubt she can concentrate on one thing long enough to be a credible murder suspect. One minute she'd be talking about literature, the next about spiritualism, the next about the terrible murder in her family, and the next about who knows what? I think she almost welcomed the death, in a sense, because it gives her an excuse to dress up in black and go about with a mournful expression, which becomes her more than most, although it was never *my* taste.

"But I screwed my courage up, and sat next to her for the better part of an hour, playing the eminent literary gentleman and managing not to laugh inappropriately. For that alone I deserve this drink, Wentworth. And by careful attention, and not especially broad hints, I managed to get us a dinner invitation for Monday night. I had to represent you as a learned gentleman and a budding literary lion in your own right, but she'll never know the difference."

"Excellent," I said. "With any luck, we can parlay this into a chance to meet the entire family."

"Oh, I expect they'll be there," said Mr. Clemens, taking a cigar out of his pocket. "I've never known a literary lady who could pass up a chance to impress her whole family when she hooks a genuine author as a dinner guest. Maria Staunton has probably spent half her life being mocked as a bookworm and bluestocking. This is her chance to prove she was right all along, Wentworth."

"I suppose you're right," I said. "Meanwhile, when shall we plan on visiting Eulalie Echo?"

"We can decide that in the morning," he said. He snipped the end of the cigar and fished around in his pockets for a match. "Aunt Tillie may have spoken to the Robinson's butler, Arthur, by then. Possibly we can kill three birds with one stone and see them all on the same day. If not, perhaps we'll go out and visit Eulalie Echo tomorrow."

"There's something strange about visiting a hoodoo woman on the sabbath, don't you think?" I said.

Mr. Clemens found a match and struck it, then held the flame to the cigar until the pungent smoke came. When it was lit to his satisfaction, he looked up at me. "If you ask me, Wentworth, there's something mighty strange about visiting her at all. But anybody who can get Cable's back up the way it was the other night is someone worth meeting. If nothing else, I'll be able to pull his leg with hoodoo stories for as long as he lives. George is one of the best writers alive, and a fine man to sit at the dinner table with, but sometimes he needs the wind taken out of his sails." My employer chuckled. "I get the feeling that solving this murder case will be rewarding in more ways than one."

8

T he next morning was Sunday. Having spent most of the previous month and a half on board a steamboat, I took advantage of our being in a fixed location and went to church. Heads turned to see the stranger in a back pew, and the minister seemed to peer in my particular direction every time he made a salient point in his sermon. But the congregation sang some of my favorite hymns, and the service followed the familiar pattern. I returned to our pension feeling refreshed and glad that I would be able to report this attendance in my next letter home.

Mr. Clemens, who had stayed behind to read, was dressed and eager to be out and about his business. "You're back. Good!" He shut the book he'd been reading and stood. "We're going to see Eulalie Echo, and then Aunt Tillie. Come along. We can talk as we walk."

"It's still early," I pointed out to him. "They may not expect visitors. Besides, you told me when I left that you were going to organize your notes for the new book." I realized even as I said it that I was not at all enthusiastic about a visit to a hoodoo woman, who Mr. Cable's comments had led me to believe was a practitioner of some sort of heathen rites, this soon after visiting my own church.

But Mr. Clemens brushed aside my objections. "Sunday just after church is the best possible time to find people at home," he said. "Come on, Wentworth, we'll go down to Jackson Square and see if Henry Dodds wants to drive us out to the Garden District again.'' I picked my hat back up, and we headed downstairs.

"I've been working on the book all morning, copying over my notes and jotting down things from the last few days,'' he said, as we came out onto Royal Street and made a right turn toward Saint Philip. "I need a break to let the ideas ferment a little and to take my mind off my own troubles. Thinking about that poor cook sitting in Parish Prison makes me feel like the master of my own fate, in comparison. I'm more and more convinced he didn't kill Robinson. If I don't try to do my best to prove he didn't, and they hang him, I'll never forgive myself.''

We made our way down to Jackson Square, where the cathedral was just letting out worshipers from one of the services. Here was New Orleans at its most respectable and on its best behavior, and the square was full of bright dresses and well-cut suits. Young couples strolled arm in arm through the park, while their parents gathered in knots for conversation, and children ran after birds or each other. The few carriage drivers working today had their pick of fares. To Mr. Clemens's disappointment, Henry Dodds was nowhere to be seen. "Either he's got a fare, or he doesn't work Sundays,'' he said. "We can either go have coffee and beignets and wait to see if he shows up, or find another driver to take us out to Fourth and Howard. I want to talk to Eulalie Echo. Did you find out what her house number is?''

I suddenly realized that I had completely forgotten to ask Bolden this important question. "We'll have to find out before we can go visit her. Perhaps we should go to Aunt Tillie's first, and see if she knows.''

Mr. Clemens laughed. "If I didn't know better, I'd think you didn't want to meet this hoodoo woman. But we'll manage. Maybe the driver will know, or one of the neighbors. I do want to see her before Aunt Tillie.'' He sent me to look for a driver while he sat down to light his pipe. Soon I found one who was free, and signaled to Mr. Clemens. The driver, a thin fellow with a big nose, which had once been broken, and long, stringy blond hair starting to turn gray, looked down and favored me with a grin more professional than sincere. "You don't mind my askin', that's a funny neighborhood for a couple of white fellows to go to. Nothing in the way of entertainment, if you get my drift."

"I get your drift," said Mr. Clemens, who had just come up. "Maybe our idea of entertainment is different from yours. Will you take us there or not?"

The driver shrugged, although the fixed grin never left his mouth. "I think your money's as good as the next man's," he said. "Climb aboard."

Once aboard, it was easy to figure out why the driver had been willing to take the fare when all his fellows were busy. His cab badly needed a painting, the upholstery on the seats was badly worn, and there was a broken spring sticking through at one point. One of the wheels creaked annoyingly, as well, and wobbled more than I would have considered safe, had it been my rig. As for his horse, the swaybacked nag looked as if he was long overdue to be turned out to pasture, although I feared the poor creature was more likely to end up at the knacker's.

The driver took us across the broad expanse of Canal Street and out Saint Charles Avenue as far as Lee Circle before he spoke again. "Where exactly did you say you wanted to be set down, mister?"

"I didn't, because I don't exactly know," said my employer. "We're going to meet a woman named Eulalie Echo. We know she's at Fourth and Howard, but we forgot to find out which house she lives in. Do you know?"

"You best ask somebody when you get out there," said the driver. "I don't know nothing about that hoodoo woman." He turned pointedly to his driving, giving the reins a snap and clicking his tongue to tell the horse to pick up his speed.

Mr. Clemens laughed. "If you don't know anything

about her, how do you know she's a hoodoo woman? But that's all right. I guess you don't know anything that would help us, anyway.'' He leaned back and puffed on his pipe again.

The driver pulled his horse to the side as the streetcar came past, then sped up again. He looked back at us over his left shoulder, still grinning rigidly, but the twinkle was back in his eye. He said, ''I guess maybe I know more than some folks, but I know when to keep quiet, too.''

''Would this help you remember things?'' Mr. Clemens held up a fifty-cent piece.

The grin got wider. ''Why *sure,* boss, that's just the thing to put my mind in order. I've heard things to make your hair turn white, if it wasn't already.'' By now, the horse had slowed to a walk again. The reins were slack in the driver's hands.

''Well, I guess I've come by these white hairs honestly,'' said Mr. Clemens. ''I've seen plenty of strange things in my own time. But hoodoo is a new one on me. Is that different from regular magic or just some kind of Louisiana word?''

The driver looked around to both sides, then crossed himself. ''Hoodoo . . . voodoo . . . gris-gris . . . people call it lots of things. It's African devil worship, is what it is. The slaves done brung it with 'em. Some of 'em claimed to be good church people, and I reckon a lot of 'em was, but a few of 'em still kept up the old ways. And some of 'em still do. Marie Laveau was one of the voodoos. I seen her once, when I was just a tad. She went walking down the street, and more than one white man stepped off the banquette and let her pass. She was the queen of voodoo, my old daddy told me.''

The driver's voice had fallen until it was barely audible over the sounds of the street, and both Mr. Clemens and I leaned forward to hear him as he continued. ''She was a hundred years old, and couldn't nobody touch her. She wanted something done, she'd go to the mayor, or the judge, or the chief of police, and tell them to do it, and they *did*—no back talk. She would make policemen get down on all fours and bark like a dog, if they was crazy enough to bother her. There's a tombstone for her in old Saint Louis Cemetery, but there's plenty that'll tell you she never died.'' By now, all the driver's air of bluster had departed. He was clearly sincere in his statements, although I found them hard to credit. But his face showed a mixture of fear, and awe, and respect as he spoke of the mysterious voodoo queen. He glanced around as if someone might overhear him, even in a moving cab on a busy street in the middle of a modern city.

"That mostly tallies with the stories I've heard George tell," Mr. Clemens said to me. "And what about Eulalie Echo?" He locked eyes with the driver, who crossed himself again.

The horse turned right onto Fourth Street, and the driver continued. "I hear she's mighty strong, but not as strong as Marie. And some say she ain't evil like Marie, but I don't know 'bout that. Devils is devils, and ain't none of 'em any good, if you ask me." And with that, the driver shut his mouth again, and said not another word until he dropped us at the corner of Fourth and Howard. When Mr. Clemens paid him and added a twenty-five-cent tip, his grin flashed again, but it was obvious that he was glad to be rid of us. He gee'ed up his horse and was headed back toward Saint Charles Avenue almost as soon as our feet were on the banquette.

Mr. Clemens and I found ourselves at a street corner much like the others we had passed in this neighborhood. The houses were low and of wooden construction, and while many of them sported window boxes full of flowers and other decorative touches, the overall impression of the neighborhood was a far cry from the French Quarter, let alone the millionaires' rows south of Saint Charles Avenue. The building we were directly in front of housed a small grocery store, which was of course closed for Sunday.

"Well, we still don't know which house we're going to. I suppose we'd better ask somebody," said Mr. Clemens, looking around. As I followed his gaze, it became obvious that all the faces on the street around us were black, and that most of them were turning a wary eye on the two well-dressed white men who had just been set down in their territory. I suddenly felt very uncomfortable and out of place.

The nearest of the locals were three rough-looking youths lounging on and around a bench outside the closed store, smoking cigarettes. They had been talking loudly when we arrived, but now they were silent. Two of them had knives out, ostentatiously whittling on scraps of wood and pretending to ignore us, but one of them, a big fellow with his shirt unbuttoned nearly to the waist to display a bright red undershirt, was staring directly at us. Mr. Clemens spotted them, and before I could say anything in the way of warning, walked right over to them.

"Howdy, fellows," he said.

"I think you done come to the wrong part of town, mister," said the tough. "You best leave 'fore things get nasty. There be some mighty bad folks 'round here." He shifted in his seat.

One of the whittlers giggled. "Yeah, and we be some of 'em."

They all laughed in a very ominous way, exchanging meaningful glances. I found their manner disconcerting. I looked around, realizing that there was a silence on the street that hadn't been there a moment earlier. What had been a busy corner had come to a stop, and all eyes seemed to be turned our way. I stepped up into a protective position at Mr. Clemens's side, wondering what I would do if the situation turned violent. About all I could really hope for was to delay them while Mr. Clemens got to safety, and if the knives came into action, there would be hell to pay.

"Oh, look, mister got hisself a big friend. Now we better play nice," said the giggler. He looked up at me, a crooked smile on his face. The knife took a very long, very thin shaving off the wood.

"Shut up, Diggy," said the big one. He stood up, and I saw that he was nearly my height, with a stocky build that bespoke hard muscles. He was very young, but that would not necessarily make him an easy opponent if it came to blows, even assuming the other two didn't interfere. He glanced at me, then, apparently deciding that Mr. Clemens was in charge, looked my employer straight in the eye. "We ain't looking for trouble," he said.

"That's mighty good, because neither are we," said Mr. Clemens. "We just want to know where Eulalie Echo lives."

" 'Lalie!" said the whittler, in a half-whisper. Now all of the youths turned to look directly at us.

"You don't look like cops to me," said the red-shirted one, eyeing us suspiciously. "What you want with her?"

"That's my business, Joe Jackson," said a new voice— a woman's voice—from behind me. I turned to see a tall, slim woman with light brown skin standing by a doorway I hadn't previously noticed. She could have been almost any age; her face was unwrinkled and her hair dark and full, but there was a hint of vast experience in her eyes. She wore a simple white dress with no jewelry, but from the way she stood on the banquette, stock-still with her hands on her hips, looking coolly at the gang of toughs, she could have been a queen. " 'Lalie!" said another voice, this time just barely audible.

"Miss Eulalie Echo, I presume? Sam Clemens at your service," said my employer, with a sweeping bow. "And may I introduce my traveling secretary, Wentworth Cabot? Buddy Bolden said you wanted to see us."

"I was expecting you, Mr. Clemens," she said. Her voice was quiet and deep-pitched, with rich overtones like some woodwind instrument. "Come on upstairs, where we can sit and talk without the whole parish knowing our business . . . ah. Hold on one minute." She turned a meaningful glance at the youths on the bench, who were suddenly behaving as if their Sunday school teacher had caught them making irreverent remarks in church. I realized that the oldest of them was probably no more than fifteen. They avoided meeting her eye, but she wasn't about to let them off so easily. "You boys!" she said, and the red-shirted one, Joe Jackson, looked up at her.

"Ma'am?"

"This is Mr. Mark Twain. I invited him out here to talk business. If I hear one word about you and your friends causing him any trouble, you're going to be in trouble with me. You understand me?"

"Yes, *ma'am!*" said Jackson, and the others nodded eagerly.

She looked them up and down, then nodded her head as if satisfied. "Good, then. Come on in, Mr. Clemens. It's a whole lot cooler in the house."

I turned and followed her and Mr. Clemens through a door and up a dark flight of stairs. There was absolute silence from the street behind me. It was a warm summer day outside, but as I climbed the stairs, I found myself wondering whether it might not be getting altogether too cool.

9

A t the top of the stairs, Eulalie Echo led us through a beaded curtain separating the nondescript foyer from her front room. Watching her, it occurred to me that I had seen very little in her appearance or demeanor to account for the reaction her name had inspired in the boys. She was neither strikingly beautiful nor remarkably grotesque, and her dress was such as to suggest simple dignity, no more. Although her posture and bearing clearly suggested that she was a woman of some importance in her circles, they gave no hint of any supernatural powers. Not that I put any credence in hoodoo—no educated man could—and yet, one always wonders.

But if she left a great deal about herself unsaid in her personal appearance, a close observer might have learned much from her living room. The windows at either end were curtained, excluding the bright sunlight outside. There was a heavy aroma of patchouli, masking some other unfamiliar sweetish odor. The center of the room was dominated by three large sofas, arranged in a U shape, with a comfortable-looking armchair on the fourth side of the rectangle, and a low, round table in the middle; a black cat stared arrogantly at us from the central cushion of one of the couches. The ceiling bore a gas fixture, currently dark, but two large candles on the central table supplemented the dim light from the windows.

The walls were covered with religious images, not all of

them Christian. To one side was a small altar, bearing an elaborate floral arrangement and half-burned candles of three or four different colors: red, white, dark blue, and green. At the back of the altar was a framed picture of a man with a white beard—Saint Peter, perhaps. Not far from the altar was a small bookcase, holding what to me seemed a surprising number of volumes of various sizes and ages. Among them I recognized a well-thumbed Bible, but neither the titles (some in French) nor the authors of most of the others were familiar to me.

At various points around the room, on little tables or on the top of an ancient sideboard, were carved wooden boxes. One of them was open to show an enormous amount of costume jewelry, or so, from its sheer quantity, I assumed; I was surprised to see it, since Eulalie Echo herself was not wearing any ornaments. Several colorful jars and small urns were also spaced around the room. Most curious, to my thinking, was the presence at several apparently random places of ordinary drinking glasses, partly full of water or some other clear liquid, as if a group of people had been in the room sipping drinks, and had abruptly left. I had the same feeling I sometimes had when entering a gathering that suddenly fell silent upon my arrival.

Eulalie Echo sat in the armchair at the end and motioned for us to sit on a couch. As we took our seats, the cat gave us an annoyed look and stalked away. At the same moment, I caught a hint of motion from the darkened hallway behind Eulalie and a soft sound like muffled footsteps—someone barefooted, perhaps? I shook my head and looked back at the hoodoo woman. She and Mr. Clemens stared at one another for a moment; then she picked up a paper fan from the table in front of her and began to ply it. "Well, I didn't ask you here to waste your time," she said. "Buddy Bolden tells me you think Leonard Galloway doesn't belong in jail, and you want me to help you free him. Is that right?"

"Pretty much," said Mr. Clemens. "We have a couple of ideas how you might be able to help us."

"First, let me ask you something," she said, laying the fan on her lap. "What if I told you that I know a way to free Leonard Galloway and force the real murderer to confess?" She stared down at us, and the challenge in her look was unmistakable.

"If you have something like that, fire away," said Mr. Clemens, sitting upright on the sofa next to me. "I'm all ears."

She picked up her fan, smiling. "First you have to get a live rooster, a good fat one. I will sew a little suit of clothes for it: a coat and pants, a hat, even a necktie. Bring me the chicken, and we'll dress it in the suit, and tie its legs with string—one hundred yards of strong twine. Then I'll sing some chants, and you'll take the cock to Lafayette Cemetery and tie it near the murdered man's tomb." She leaned forward and fixed Mr. Clemens with her gaze. I ran a finger around the inside of my collar, glad that her eyes were not on me. "Now, the important part. You put some food and water just out of the chicken's reach, and put three coins on top of the tomb. As long as the cock suffers, so will the guilty man."

She stood and walked slowly toward the back hall, from which I could barely make out a low wailing sound. When had it begun? I looked at Mr. Clemens and gestured toward the exit; now was our chance to escape this madwoman, while her back was turned. But my employer gave me a nod, laid a finger against his lips, and motioned for me to remain seated. Just then, Eulalie Echo whirled to face us. Her hair, which before had been neatly groomed, was now disheveled, and there was a wild look in her eyes. "After three days, if he can last that long, the murderer will confess, and Leonard will go free." She raised her hands high and laughed a low, unsettling laugh that sent shivers up my spine. I looked at my shoes; when I looked up, there were two large, dark-clad figures on either side of her. I had not heard them enter. She pointed at Mr. Clemens. "Will you do this? Do you believe in my powers?" Her arms dropped to her side, and she fixed us with her gaze, daring us to question her.

"Good Lord, no!" I said, without waiting for Mr. Clemens to speak. I had never heard anything so barbaric in my life. What kind of evil sorcery did this woman practice?

Mr. Clemens, for his part, looked Eulalie Echo straight in the face, then shook his head. "If that's the best way you can think of to free Leonard, I don't think I can do business with you. Even if I were convinced it would work—and I've seen some mighty strange things in my time, so for all I know it *will* work—I'd still rather try something else first." He stood up and took a step in the direction of the door. "Come on, Wentworth, we won't waste any more of Miss Echo's time. Let's go see if Aunt Tillie's home from church yet."

But Eulalie Echo barred his way. "Good," she said. "And if you had wanted to do the rooster spell, I would refuse," she said, slapping the fan down on the table with a loud report. "The police do not appreciate such things." The taller of the two dark attendants escorted her to her seat; then, at her gesture, the two faded into the dark hallway behind her. I still was not sure whether they were male or female, old or young. "Sit down, Mr. Clemens. I am not a savage, whatever you may have heard about me. Many people would value a man's life above that of a poor animal, and indeed, sometimes circumstances justify it. But we are not at last resorts yet, and I would not try that spell unless we were. Mr. Clemens, I hope we understand each other now."

"I believe we do," said Mr. Clemens. I knew him well enough by now to see that he had the bit in his teeth, and there would be no stopping him. "I suppose I could make a fuss about your putting on that charade to test us," he said, "but I have a pretty good idea why you felt you had to do it. My objection wouldn't accomplish much besides advertising my own self-importance. Let's skip all that and

84 talk about how you may be able to help us, and what you'd want in return.''

"You are not easy to lead off the straight road, I see," said Eulalie Echo, smiling. "But I agree; let's talk about this business now. How can I help the famous Mr. Mark Twain?"

Mr. Clemens leaned forward. "Young Bolden tells me that you have many clients, white and black, from all over the city, and some of them could have useful information about the Robinson murder case, maybe without even knowing it. Maybe they tell you things they won't tell anyone else." He smiled at her; he could be quite a flatterer when it suited him.

"That is true," said Eulalie Echo, fanning herself. She sat tall and straight in her seat. I suddenly realized that her furniture was designed to let her visitors sink low into the soft cushions of the couch while she towered above them from her armchair at the end. Even I, tall as I am, had to raise my head to look her in the eye. I began to understand that she had raised herself to the esteem in which she was held as much by simple artifice as by any superhuman powers. At the same time, I realized that her voice and accent had changed. She sounded more like an educated woman than before. It was as if she had taken off a mask. Clearly, Eulalie Echo was a far more complex person than I had at first believed.

Mr. Clemens continued. "Now, it seems to me that you're in a good position to find out things I need to know. You might even be able to make the opportunity to speak with certain key people: the servants of families close to the Robinsons, their friends and business associates, possibly even the victim's relatives. Some of them might turn out to be prime suspects, once we see the lay of the land— always assuming we can prove that Leonard Galloway is innocent.''

She listened carefully, nodding occasionally, as Mr. Clemens outlined how she might pass on pertinent information gathered in the course of her occupation or ask questions designed to elicit secrets from her clients. Gradually, a cloud came over her expression, and at last she raised a hand to silence him—something I would never have dared to do—but Mr. Clemens stopped in mid-sentence and waited for her to speak.

"None of that should be hard to do," said Eulalie Echo. She leaned forward, her eyes flashing. "But why should I do it? I don't want to insult you, but are you really trying to help Leonard, or are you playing at being a detective as a way to gather a few more stories? Many people trust me where they would trust no one else, because I have a true gift and a calling to help them. How do I know you will not put me in a book for people to laugh at as an ignorant woman, or worse yet, hold me up to scorn as a fraud who preys on superstitious people? If you do that, I might lose everything, while you can simply go on your way and never face the consequences of what you have done. Your friend Mr. Cable learned the hard way what New Orleans people think of those who call attention to their failings. He was born here, but now he lives in the North. You can also return to the North, or to Europe, or wherever you want to go. But I will have to stay here in New Orleans, where everyone will know I have betrayed them to an outsider, a northern white man who has put them in a book for the whole world to stare at. What do you plan to offer me that is worth that risk?"

"We're both risking something," said Mr. Clemens. "You've been frank with me; let me be frank, as well. I am known as a man who tells the truth, who sees through shams and charlatans. Many of my enemies—and I have made my share—would welcome the chance to paint me as a gullible old fool who believes in magic and fortune-telling. Just by visiting you, I open myself to their ridicule. But you know, I don't particularly care what those varmints say about me. Not compared to what I'd think of myself if an innocent man is hanged and I know I could have saved him, if I'd tried a little harder. An author's reputation for fair play is his whole stock in trade, and I am willing to risk that for Leonard Galloway. You have my word that neither I nor Wentworth here''—and he gestured in my direction—''will do or say anything to hurt your standing with your own people, or to reveal your role in this to anyone who would use the knowledge to harm you. All we need is enough information to point ourselves in the right direction. We don't even need to know the name of anyone you've talked to, unless you decide to tell us. Are those conditions satisfactory?''

"Fair enough," said Eulalie Echo. "I believe you are a man of your word. And I think that you sincerely wish to help Leonard. I will take the risk."

"Good! Now, the question remains: what do you want from me in exchange for your help?"

She shrugged and said, "Would it make it any easier if I told you in advance that I don't want your money?"

"That's good, because I don't have very much of it," said Mr. Clemens. "Being a famous author has its points, but a full bank account ain't necessarily one of them." He paused a second, as if in thought, then leaned forward and looked her straight in the eye, saying, "I don't suppose you happen to know anything about good investments, do you? I mean, anything the average person might not be aware of."

Eulalie Echo laughed long and heartily, a startling contrast to her demented-sounding cackle of earlier. For a moment, another mask seemed to have dropped, and I caught a glimpse of a woman with a rich sense of earthy pleasure. Finally, she said, "Ah, Mr. Clemens, there I am as much in the dark as you. My guiding spirits do not tell me very much about getting money. Oh, they make sure that I can live in comfort, but they have no useful advice on finance and investments. It is good I am so easily contented, otherwise I might have second thoughts about my gift."

Mr. Clemens sighed. "I guess it's just as well. Being

content may be a more valuable talent than the ability to make money." He lifted his hand to his chin and thought a moment. "I suppose I might even be convinced of that, in my weaker moments," he said at last.

She laughed again. "You are a wicked man, Mr. Clemens. But seriously, there is something you can do for me. My stock in trade is knowledge, and there are many things I can only learn from books. I have a small collection, as you can see. But there are books I cannot find in New Orleans. You go to many places, and as a writer you must know many booksellers. If I tell you what I need, will you find it and send it to me? This would be worth more to me than money."

"Easily done," said Mr. Clemens. "It'll be a distinct pleasure, in fact, and any books I can find will be my gift to you. Do we have a bargain, then?"

"I think so," said Eulalie Echo, gravely. "And to prove it, let me tell you a few things I have already learned. First, you should know that the murder victim's marriage was not at all happy. I think you should take a very close look at Mr. Robinson's wife. I think perhaps Mr. Robinson was not faithful to her, nor she to him. Also, Mr. Robinson's political ambitions put him in debt to some very unsavory people. I think it will be worth your while to talk to Tom Anderson."

"Who is Tom Anderson?" said Mr. Clemens, making writing motions at me. I pulled out my pocket notebook and began to jot down the particulars as Eulalie Echo spoke.

"Tom Anderson is a saloon owner," said Eulalie Echo. "He has made himself useful to the police and to the people who tell the police what to do. He is deeply involved in politics, although he hasn't been a candidate for any office—yet. I think that will change, someday. He has his finger on the pulse of the vice district, which has a great deal of money and power behind it. He is a man on his way to the top, and Mr. Robinson recognized his importance. I think they had many interests in common, whatever their differences at first glance. You will learn things by talking to Tom Anderson that you won't learn elsewhere.''

"I'll talk to him," said Mr. Clemens. "What do you know about Arthur, the Robinsons' butler? Leonard suggested I talk to him.''

"He's been with them for years," she said, waving her fan slowly. "A stiff-necked man. He is the sort who feels that what he does is less important than who he does it for; he may be only a servant, but he served a powerful master. He was very loyal to Mr. Robinson, and I think he may be just as loyal to the widow Robinson. He will want to stay faithful to his master's memory, and will not want to talk about family secrets, but if you convince him that talking is the way to avenge his master, I think he will have something to tell you.''

"Is he friends with Leonard?''

"He was, before Leonard was arrested. I don't think they were very close friends, but they sometimes did things together. You may need to convince him of Leonard's innocence before he will cooperate with you. Tillie Galloway has spoken to him, and she will be able to tell you more. And I will be able to tell you more in a few days, when I have spoken to certain people.''

An odd sound came from the back room. Eulalie Echo paused, as if listening to something we couldn't hear; then she stood. "And now I am afraid I must ask you to leave. There are things I must tend to that I have already left for too long. I will let you know when I have news.''

For his part, Mr. Clemens promised to keep her informed of his own progress, and on that amicable note, he and I took our leave of this strange New Orleans voodoo queen. She showed us to the door, and we made our way down the dark stairs to the street. I had the impression, as the door to her front room closed behind us, that a low conversation had begun. It was as if somebody had been waiting for us to leave and had returned to the room as soon as we had left. Was it one of the mysterious assistants we had seen? Had they been listening to our whole conversation? Or was the noise simply the cat reclaiming its favorite seat?

When we came out onto the banquette, the summer sun still shone brightly, although there were a few small, fluffy clouds in the sky that hadn't been there earlier in the day, and a pleasant breeze had picked up. That seemed wrong; the weather should have been dark and stormy, to match the atmosphere inside the voodoo woman's parlor. There should have been thunder and lightning and hard, driving rain. Instead, two young women were wheeling baby carriages along the banquette, followed by a lazy-looking hound dog. On the bench by the little store, three old men sat in the shade and argued good-naturedly about baseball. I shook my head and adjusted to a world that had suddenly become ordinary again.

It made the most sense for us simply to walk to the Galloway home, a mere three blocks away from Eulalie Echo's house. Someone had laid a series of planks across the street to preserve the boots of pedestrians from the mud, and we crossed from one wooden banquette to the next. Before we had gone half the block, a voice called out behind us: "Mister! Where you going?"

I turned to see two of the local boys who had been loafing on the street corner when we had arrived at Eulalie Echo's door. Mr. Clemens had also turned, and it was he who answered them. "Why, we're just walking over to the Galloways' house on First Street. Do you want to show us the way?"

"Sure, mister," said the larger one. I recalled that his name was Joe Jackson. "It ain't too hard to find." He strutted up to join us and pointed down Howard Street. "This-away," he said, and off we went to see Aunt Tillie, with the other boy bringing up the rear.

"I sure appreciate the favor," said Mr. Clemens to Joe Jackson's back.

"Thank 'Lalie Echo, not us," said the youth. "She told me and Diggy to keep an eye out for you, and make sure you didn't fall into no trouble."

Mr. Clemens followed along at his usual unhurried pace, and after a bit, leaned over and confided to me. "Now, Wentworth, you see the advantages of consorting with a voodoo woman!"

I myself was not about to forget that our two young escorts had just a short time previously reacted to our presence in their neighborhood with unfeigned hostility, and I resolved to remain on my guard. Perhaps a good word from Eulalie Echo had gained us the respect of Joe Jackson and his cohorts; but how quickly would respect turn again to hostility if one of us said or did something that met with their disapproval? It was while I was contemplating the latter issue that we turned the corner onto First Street to find Buddy Bolden lounging on a front porch, with an open shirt and no jacket.

A smile spread across his face as he took in our little group. "Well, I didn't know we was going to have a parade today," he said. "You got everything but the band."

"Hello, Buddy," said Mr. Clemens. "If I'd known we'd have an audience, I'd have sent out for a couple of elephants and a troop of cavalry to put on a real show for you. But I'm afraid you'll have to be content with just the four of us. Joe and Diggy are taking us to Aunt Tillie's house. You want to come along, too?"

"Why not?" said Bolden. And he stood up and joined us as we marched the remaining half-block to our destination, whistling jauntily as he walked with us.

At Aunt Tillie's, Mr. Clemens promised to send for Joe Jackson if he needed any errands run in the neighborhood, and we went inside.

Aunt Tillie was delighted to see us, and she bustled about, getting us settled and insisting on bringing us refreshments before she would join us to talk. She chattered and smiled, but as she listened to Mr. Clemens describe our visit to Eulalie Echo, I had the sense that something was bothering her. She looked more strained than when I had seen her two days earlier, although she did her best to hide it. She seemed genuinely pleased that the voodoo woman was willing to help, and readily agreed not to tell anyone of Eulalie Echo's involvement. But when Mr. Clemens asked about her conversation with the Robinson's butler, her face fell. "Oh, Mr. Twain, there's bad news. Arthur don't want to talk to nobody," she said. "Not me, not you. I begged and pleaded, and told him it was to save Leonard. I 'bout broke down and cried, right there in front of the church, but he just shook his head, sad-like. I don't know what's the matter with that man. I thought he was friends with Leonard, but now I just can't understand."

Mr. Clemens frowned. "I knew we'd hit a snag of some kind sooner or later," he said. "I didn't expect it to be the butler, though." He took a sip of the lemonade Aunt Tillie had brought us and leaned back on her couch, lost in thought for a moment, staring up at her ceiling. Finally, he looked around the room with a curious expression.

"Maybe this isn't as bad news as it seems," he said. "If the butler won't talk to us, maybe we can figure out what his silence means. Why wouldn't he talk to me if he knew it might help clear his friend?"

I pondered for a moment. "Perhaps he's shielding someone else," I suggested. "But whom?"

"Very good, Wentworth, that's the same conclusion I'd drawn," said Mr. Clemens. "Now all we have to do is figure out who that could be."

"Humph," said Buddy Bolden. "You don't suppose ol' Arthur killed Robinson himself?"

I had thought exactly the same thing, and nodded to him. He crossed his arms on his chest, nodding at me with a conspiratorial air.

"I don't suppose anything," said Mr. Clemens. "Especially about a man I've never met." Bolden's smile faded, and I was suddenly less certain of my suspicions of the butler. Mr. Clemens continued, "I'm trying to get invited to the Robinsons' house, if only to meet this butler who doesn't want to talk. Maybe he still thinks Leonard's guilty. Or maybe he's hiding something. We'll see. Meanwhile, we've plenty of other lines in the water, and one or the other is bound to get a nibble before long. I hate to think of poor Leonard stuck in that damned Parish Prison an hour longer than he has to be. I'm not a patient man, Aunt Tillie. But I'm afraid all we can do at the moment is wait."

"Lord have mercy," said Aunt Tillie. "If I knew anything else to do, I'd have done it long ago. I just can't understand why that man won't talk."

"He may not be talking now," said Mr. Clemens. "But he will. I guarantee you: he *will* talk to me, by the time I'm through."

≈ 10

Mr. Clemens spent most of Monday doing research for the book he was writing about our journey down the Mississippi. Even though he had been a pilot before the war, he had not kept abreast of the more recent history of riverboat travel, and he felt the need to check his facts. "It doesn't matter if you know more about boats than Noah himself," he said. "You can write five hundred pages of absolutely bulletproof facts, and if there's one little slip on page five hundred and one, somebody is guaranteed to find it and hold it up to prove you an ass in front of the whole world. The great problem of getting older is that your memory fills up with all sorts of nonsense, and just when you think you know something, it turns out to be dead wrong. So I have to double-check everything, and then see it all with my own eyes, before I dare believe it."

I accompanied him to the Custom House, from the roof of which there was a fine panoramic view of the city. We spent half an hour picking out various landmarks and looking at the course of the river both upstream and down. After satisfying himself that he had a good mental picture of present-day New Orleans and environs, he went for a look at some older maps of the city in the Howard Library on Lee Circle. Henry Dodds had pointed out the Romanesque building as he drove us out to the Garden District, and my Baedecker identified it as one of the last works of the noted Louisiana-born architect Henry H. Richardson. But I had

94 spent more than my share of time in libraries while at Yale, and Mr. Clemens had no need for my assistance. I decided instead to pass the afternoon in walking about the city, sightseeing.

I walked along the levee from Canal Street to Jackson Square, enjoying the ever-changing spectacle of the river and the boats. There was far more commerce on the water than I would have expected, to hear Mr. Clemens's tales of how the steamboat business had declined from thirty years ago. But even before his comments on the fallibility of memory, I had learned that when a man of advanced years speaks of the things he knew in his youth, a prudent listener should allow for some margin of error.

In fact, there were more kinds of steamboat than I had ever seen before, from small packets that offered cheap transport to minor river ports, to the Streckfus excursion boats catering to holiday crowds, and the cargo boats bringing cotton and sugar into New Orleans to be reloaded onto oceangoing ships bound for dozens of ports both domestic and foreign. One of the excursion boats had a steam calliope on the texas deck, and it was playing a cheerful (if a bit out of tune) version of "Dixie" to greet the passengers as they boarded.

The wharves along the river swarmed with half-naked men glistening with sweat as they wrestled crates and barrels and cotton bales on and off the boats. Here were larger ships, as well: steamers from Veracruz, Havana, Port of Spain, Rio de Janeiro, others bound for Portugal and France and the coast of Africa. Shouted orders, angry curses, and hearty work songs filled the air, not only in English, but in Spanish, Italian, Creole French, and other, even more exotic, languages. By one recently arrived boat, a group was gathered around a man with three creased playing cards atop a barrel—a game I had learned the hard way to avoid. At another spot, a group of young colored boys were diving into the river to wash off the dust and escape the heat, whooping and laughing and splashing. I remembered my own days of swimming in the river at New London, and I envied them their innocent fun.

The riverfront was the best free show in town, I decided. Half the loafers in New Orleans seemed to agree with me; everywhere along the docks I saw men sitting contemplatively on pilings or bales, watching other men at work. Here a slim Negro strummed a banjo; there an old fellow in a straw hat flipped through the pages of a newspaper; another dozed, his back against a piling, waking intermittently to spit a stream of tobacco juice through his mustache and into the river. As a veteran of a long river journey on the *Horace Greeley*, I watched it all with an appreciative eye, until the summer sun drove me indoors for a cool drink and something to eat.

I had lunch (little bits of tender veal braised in red wine with garlic and spices, served with hominy grits) in a restaurant near the French Market, whence I heard the melodious cries of the vendors—almost a sort of music in themselves, with the words marvelously distorted. Then I decided to explore the Roman Cathedral of Saint Louis, which the guidebook informed me was built in the Spanish-Creole style of a century before, but refurbished in 1850. It was cool inside the church, and quiet, although a few solitary worshipers knelt in the pews, counting their rosaries, or brought candles to light in little niches by statues of the saints. According to my guidebook, the large mural behind the altar (of the French king Louis XI) and the frescoes painted on the ceiling were of newer vintage than the rest, but I found them impressive, nonetheless.

The cathedral is flanked by twin buildings of colonial vintage, the Presbytère (or parsonage) and the Cabildo, the seat of government during the city's Spanish era, both now courthouses. In the center of the large square in front of the cathedral, surrounded by greenery, stands a large equestrian statue of Andrew Jackson, reportedly the first of its kind in America. Whether the rider is an accurate portrait of Old Hickory is apparently a constant subject for debate in New

96   Orleans, although few still living can have laid eyes on its
subject; not that the citizenry allows the shortage of eye-
witnesses to curtail its enjoyment of a good argument. The
horse is unquestionably a fine piece of work.

I wandered about the streets adjoining the square an hour
or two longer, then returned to our Royal Street pension
where I found Mr. Clemens, back from his day at the library, smoking a pipe and nursing a drink. "How did it
go?" I asked.

"Not as badly as I expected," he drawled. "Half the
things I want aren't to be found anywhere in Louisiana,
and another half is unreliable, and another half is flat-out
lies."

"That's three halves," I said.

Mr. Clemens snorted. "Yes, but I told you that the first
half isn't to be found, and the third half is a pack of lies,
so neither of those ought to count at face value. You can't
apply mathematics to literary research, Wentworth. I'm surprised they don't teach you these things at Yale. I may have
to give them back that honorary master's degree they gave
me."

We spoke a bit more about his work in progress, in particular two or three details of his research that I would need
to follow up for him, then went to our separate rooms to
change for dinner. Tonight we were to dine with the family
of the murder victim, John David Robinson, at the home
of his sister-in-law, Mrs. Percival Staunton. Mr. Clemens
reminded me that the entire family were suspects in the
murder; he and I would have to put our powers of obser-
vation to good use.

Mr. Clemens had arranged for Henry Dodds to drive us
to our dinner party, and the coachman was waiting with his
cab when we walked out to the street. "How d'ye do,
gen'lemens, hop on board," he said. Then, surveying our
formal outfits, "Looks like y'all dressed fit to kill. Whose
funeral is it goin' to be?"

"Yours, if we're late for dinner!" said Mr. Clemens,

climbing to his seat. "But if you don't get us lost, we should be there in time." Then, he leaned over to me and added, sotto voce, "Not dressed fit to kill, but maybe fit to catch a killer!"

Henry Dodds clucked at his horse and edged our cab out onto Royal Street, as Mr. Clemens laughed at his own joke. "Hang on, Wentworth," he said as we headed toward Canal Street. "If Henry doesn't break our necks, we'll soon get a look at how the other half of New Orleans lives!"

Dodds took us along the now-familiar route to the Garden District, out Saint Charles Avenue past the statue of Henry Clay, City Hall, Lee Circle, and the Howard Library, where Mr. Clemens had spent the day working. But when we reached Jackson Avenue, instead of turning to the right, toward the working-people's homes on the lake side of Saint Charles, we turned left into the Garden District proper, where some of the finest homes in the city were sited. The houses and the lawns grew larger and more magnificent, and the people we saw on the street were better dressed than in the French Quarter. Even the servants seemed to be wearing their finest outfits. We passed several carriages with parties dressed as if for an evening on the town. A few of them recognized Mr. Clemens, or perhaps it was merely the famous Southern spirit of hospitality that made them wave to us.

I had visited many of the finer homes in Connecticut and Massachusetts, belonging to my father's family and social circle; and, if I may say so without boasting, I had grown up in a rather fine house myself. The ancestral Cabot home in Boston, in which my grandparents still resided, was perhaps even more impressive. But very few of them could match the magnificence of the houses we passed on the streets of the Garden District, each of them seemingly grander and more impressive than the last.

The Staunton residence was a substantial prewar mansion in Greek Revival style, at the corner of First and Chestnut. The house was painted a pale lavender color, setting off two tiers of elegant white columns at the front; Ionic on the ground-floor porch, Corinthian on the balcony. The galleries and the fence around the neat front yard were of the wrought iron lacework characteristic of New Orleans architecture, a baroque touch contrasting with the more restrained Grecian lines of the house itself. A pair of live oak trees planted on the strip between the banquette and the road made a picturesque frame for the visitor approaching the front of the house.

No sooner had Henry Dodds pulled his rig to a halt in front of the Staunton house than the front door opened. A little lady in a dark blue dress with a white lace shawl fairly danced out onto the porch. "Mr. Clemens! You've come!" she cried, as if there had been some doubt about it. This, I took it, was our hostess.

"Mrs. Staunton," said my employer, as I helped him down from the high seat of Henry Dodds's cab. "Of course I came. Have you ever known a writer to turn down a chance for a free dinner?" He tipped his hat and bowed, and our hostess skipped back and forth from one foot to the other, all but overcome with delight.

A vigorous, dark-haired man appeared on the porch beside her and strode down the walk toward us. "Good evening, gentlemen," he said in a deep voice with a thick Louisiana accent. "Tell your driver to take the cab 'round back, and he can tie up his horse. Louisa will give him something to eat in the kitchen." He dismissed our driver with a gesture toward the back of the house.

"Why, I surely 'preciate it, sir!" said Henry Dodds, raising his cap. He flicked the reins and disappeared around the corner.

"Mr. Clemens, welcome," said our host. "My wife has hardly spoken of anything else since she invited you, so I'm glad to make your acquaintance at last. Percival Staunton at your service." He was a remarkably handsome man, with chiseled features and penetrating blue eyes over a thin moustache. I judged his age to be somewhere in the vicinity

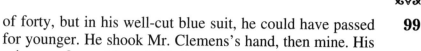

of forty, but in his well-cut blue suit, he could have passed for younger. He shook Mr. Clemens's hand, then mine. His grip was firm, although his hand was somewhat cold and clammy.

"Come on inside," said Staunton. "We're still waiting on two of our guests, but most of the party came early, in anticipation of you."

Mr. Clemens formally introduced me to Percival Staunton and his wife Maria, and Mrs. Staunton declared herself delighted to welcome us to her home. She wore her dark hair in a Psyche knot, and her oval spectacles gave her a distracted look. Her silk dress was slightly old-fashioned, cut high at the neck and bustled, but of excellent material and workmanship. She beamed at Mr. Clemens, favoring him with a crooked smile, then shook my hand very gravely, peering at me through her spectacles. "I must say, I envy you, Mr. Cabot, spending your days in the company of such a famous writer. Welcome to our home."

"Pay no attention to her, Wentworth," said Mr. Clemens. "She talks that way to all the writers' secretaries she meets." He laughed, and so did her husband, but I thought I detected an edge of strain in Mr. Staunton's laughter.

Our hosts led us inside, where we gave our hats to a servant and stepped into a large formal parlor, lit by twin crystal gas chandeliers, where the other guests awaited us. In short order, we were introduced to Dr. Alphonse Soupape, an old Creole gentleman with a fatherly expression, a generous waistline, and silvery hair. I remembered that he was the physician who had first suspected foul play in the poisoning of Robinson. Standing with the doctor as we entered was his wife, Camille, a little birdlike thing with an almost impenetrable Creole accent. Next to Mrs. Soupape was Gordon Dupree, a sharp-featured, almost completely bald gentleman of about the same age, whom Mr. Staunton introduced as the family lawyer. "And a good one," said Dr. Soupape, smiling. "Percy keeps him busy."

"Far better to keep the family lawyer busy than the family doctor,'' Dupree riposted, and they laughed like old friends who had gone through this exchange more than once before.

Camille Soupape, however, frowned at their amusement. She touched her husband on the elbow and rebuked him gently: "Watch what you say, Alphonse. It is too soon to make such jokes." There was an awkward silence as the doctor and the lawyer remembered that there had been a recent death—and an untimely one—in the family of their hostess. Both men looked sheepish, and Dr. Soupape cleared his throat and said, "Ah, yes, well . . .''

But the momentary embarrassment ended as Mrs. Staunton returned to the group. With her was a middle-aged couple: the wife short and plump, with a studious expression; the husband tall, with thinning hair and a rumpled suit. Both squinted through thick spectacles. "Mr. Clemens," said our hostess, "I would like you to meet Professor Laurence Maddox, of Tulane University."

Professor Maddox beamed at my employer. "An honor, Mr. Clemens!" He pumped Mr. Clemens's hand vigorously.

"And this is his wife Elaine, my dearest friend," said Mrs. Staunton. "The president of the Lafayette Literary Society, and a devotee of all the arts." She smiled fondly at her friend while Mrs. Maddox made a fuss over Mr. Clemens. He responded in his usual public style, with broad compliments on both the lady and the literary luncheon he'd attended two days previously.

Mr. Dupree proclaimed himself a longtime reader of my employer's writings. "You should do more of your travel books," he said. "Best thing in the world to take a man away from his troubles."

"I'm glad to hear you say that," said Mr. Clemens. "I'm working on a new one right now, in fact. It's all about my recent journey down the Mississippi on a riverboat, and it's chock-full of exciting incidents and local color. If you and all your friends will undertake to buy two or three hundred

copies each, you'll make a great contribution toward taking **101**
me away from my own troubles.''

Everyone laughed again; then a smartly uniformed colored servant arrived, bringing drinks for Mr. Clemens and
me. A tall blonde woman with a matronly figure wrapped
in beige silk and displaying a small fortune in jewelry came
up and took Mr. Dupree by the arm. "Now, Mr. Twain,
don't you go giving Gordon any ideas," she said in an
exaggerated drawl. "He just might go ahead and do it."

"Mr. Clemens, my wife Pamela," said the lawyer.

Mr. Clemens bowed and said, in an even more exaggerated drawl, "Madam, I had just made up my mind to persuade your husband to purchase the entire print run of my
next book, but seeing that you're opposed, I'll confine my
efforts to selling him a single copy. I promise you only the
finest quality, every page guaranteed full of words from top
to bottom, all spelled correctly or your money back."

Mr. Clemens was in fine form, as I'd seen him before in
the company of literary well-wishers backstage at his lectures. He played the part of the famous author to the hilt,
dropping little quips and compliments suited to the audience with the ease that comes of long practice. I suspected
he could do it in his sleep. My usual function, lurking on
the edge of the conversation and prying my employer away
from boring conversational partners, seemed superfluous in
this cultured company. I wandered away from the little
group, better to examine the paintings I had noticed hanging at one end of the room. I must confess a fondness for
art, one that occasionally provoked mirth from my com-
rades on the Yale football team. Despite their ridicule, I
never passed up an opportunity to admire a collection.

I walked to the far end of the long room, where two
large portraits at the north end were warmly lit by the evening sun shining through four full-length windows on the
western side of the room. In this light, the colors in the
paintings stood out brightly. I stood, sipping my drink, and
examined them. Nearer the windows hung an oil painting

of our hostess, Maria Holt Staunton. It was a full-length seated portrait, and showed her as younger and slimmer, without the spectacles, but not so changed as to be unrecognizable. Her face held a distant expression, as if contemplating something inspiring, and around her neck was a silver cross. But my eye went to the portrait's hands, which were very gracefully drawn. They were holding a book, the left index finger between pages to mark a place, as if she wanted to waste as little time as possible in posing and return to her reading.

"I hate that picture," came a voice behind me, and I turned to see in the flesh the very person I had been contemplating in the portrait. Mrs. Staunton smiled. "Everyone tells me it's a remarkably good likeness, but I was *so* uncomfortable sitting for it. I was seventeen, and Percy and I were engaged to be married. The portraits were a gift from his father." I glanced back at the other painting, which showed a young Mr. Staunton, although one would have had to look twice to see what differences time had wrought to its subject. He was shown in riding clothes and boots, cradling a hunting rifle and smiling easily—the very picture of a gentleman at his rural retreat, I thought.

"Mr. Staunton looks at ease in his," I said. "He could step out of the painting and into the party, and nobody would be the wiser."

"Ah, but then there would be two of him," said Mrs. Staunton. She laughed lightly. "One is quite enough, I assure you."

I was not quite certain how to reply to this pronouncement, but I was spared the necessity as Mrs. Staunton's eyes focused on someone behind me and she said, "Oh, good, Eugenia and Reynold have arrived. Come, Mr. Cabot, let me introduce you to my sister and brother. I was so afraid that Eugenia would not feel up to coming out this evening. I don't know if you have heard that she recently lost her husband, John. Our dear brother Reynold has been trying to get her to come out into company a bit more, but this is her first time with anyone other than family present.''

I turned to see the new arrivals. There could not have been more contrast between a brother and sister. Mrs. Robinson was dressed in mourning, but no amount of dark cloth could have disguised her rare beauty. Her hair was of a light blonde color, her eyes were large and blue, and her complexion flawless. She might have passed for twenty-two or twenty-three years old, although I knew she had to be at least fifteen years older than that. Despite her recent bereavement, she smiled graciously as she kissed her sister.

As for Reynold Holt, had I not been informed that he was Eugenia Robinson's brother, I could easily have taken him for her father. He wore a gray beard in the style of General Lee, his hair was a stringy gray, and his complexion pale and unhealthy looking, but he stood erect and tall—just under six feet—and his shoulders were broad. He walked with a cane, holding his left leg very stiff. His expression was best described as severe, although he did allow a brief smile to cross his lips as he greeted Mrs. Staunton.

''I'm so glad you could come,'' Mrs. Staunton said to her sister. ''I know it must be hard so soon after your loss.''

''Thank you, Maria,'' said Mrs. Robinson. Her voice was low and full of rich overtones, like a violoncello. ''I wish John could be here; it seems so unfair he can't meet Mark Twain. He always looked forward to his new books.''

Her words suddenly reminded me of what Mr. Clemens and I were doing at this gathering. This group was made up of the murder victim's closest acquaintances. If we were correct in our belief that Leonard Galloway was falsely imprisoned, odds were that one of the people in the room with us this very minute was a cold-blooded killer.

11

At dinner, Mr. Clemens was seated directly to the right of our hostess, while I was near the middle of the opposite side of the table, between Mrs. Maddox and Mrs. Dupree, and opposite Reynold Holt, who was flanked by Mrs. Robinson and Mrs. Soupape. I was pleased, because this arrangement would give me an opportunity to observe the murder victim's widow, and perhaps gain some information relevant to our investigation.

The dining room was as elegantly decorated as the parlor, lined with well-executed colored engravings of hunting scenes mounted on ivory-colored paneling above dark walnut wainscoting, and lit by a sparkling gas chandelier. We were seated at a long mahogany board with twelve chairs that Mr. Staunton declared to be genuine Chippendale, imported from England by his grandfather, "before the War." Mr. Clemens had half-jokingly told me, earlier that day, that when a southerner talked about the War (there was only one of any consequence, to them), you could practically hear the capital letter on the word.

As it happened, the three older men among the present company had served in that terrible national conflict. Mr. Dupree, Dr. Soupape, and Reynold Holt, as I learned, had all served in the same volunteer regiment, the famous Washington Artillery of New Orleans. Having grown up in Connecticut, I had often listened to men of my father's generation tell their stories of war. Now I was curious to hear the experiences of men who had seen action on the other side.

But Mrs. Staunton adroitly deflected our conversation to literary topics, saying, "I can hear you gentlemen talk about the War any time I wish. But tonight, our guest is Mr. Clemens, and while I'm at the table, we'll speak of other subjects, if you please." A glance at her recently bereaved sister, Mrs. Robinson, made it clear that it was not only for herself that she wished to turn the dinner conversation away from bloodshed. I consoled myself with the possibility that the veterans would tell a few war stories after the ladies had withdrawn.

This was the first time I had dined in a private home in New Orleans, and I was mightily impressed. The chef started us off with a rich turtle soup with a dollop of dry sherry in each serving. Then came a shrimp cocktail on ice, full of delicate flavor. Then followed a salad with a Roquefort cheese dressing, which was the prelude to our main course. That was baked trout in a tomato, mushroom, and pepper sauce, which Mrs. Maddox told me was one of numerous varieties of Creole sauce handed down from one generation of New Orleans cooks to another. On the side were sweet potatoes, carrots, and string beans cooked with almonds and covered with cream sauce. Mrs. Maddox expressed regret that the Stauntons' cook had made white dinner rolls instead of the corn bread for which she was apparently famous throughout the district, but I must confess I found no fault in her choice. An exceptional dry white burgundy accompanied the meal; and when dessert finally arrived—pecan pie—I was ready to declare myself in culinary heaven.

During the meal, Mr. Clemens continued to flatter our hostess and the other ladies while telling tales of his days on the river and of his travels overseas and commenting on famous writers, especially those associated with the South. I was surprised to hear him speak highly of Joel Chandler Harris, whose Uncle Remus stories I had always considered to be nothing more than children's tales. "Harris has the best ear for the language of the old-time plantation Negro I've ever encountered," he said. "The man is a national treasure and ought to be revered."

"Well, sir," said Professor Maddox, "I don't doubt the accuracy of his imitations, but are they of a worthy object? Shouldn't the business of a writer be to elevate our thoughts, rather than to copy something commonplace and crude?"

"Humani nil a me alienum puto," replied Dr. Soupape. "Nothing human can be alien to me. I'd say that if that was a good enough philosophy for the Romans, it ought to serve an American as well, Professor. You're a bit young to recall the old plantation days, but those of us who saw those times think them worth the remembering."

"Hear, hear," said Mr. Dupree, raising his wineglass. "The old days and the old ways, long may they be remembered."

"Yes indeed, let them be remembered long and well," said Mr. Clemens dryly. "That may be the only way to keep a new generation from making all the same mistakes."

"Which mistakes are those, sir?" said Reynold Holt. His face was unreadable, but there was a challenge in his tone, and I heard his sister, Mrs. Robinson, draw a sharp breath. Mrs. Staunton was about to say something as well, but her husband broke the tension with a laugh.

"Why, Reynold, don't you know Mr. Clemens is a famous humorist? You can't go quizzing our dinner guest about every little jest he makes, now. That's the whole reason Maria invited him, after all." He picked up the wine bottle with a flourish. "I do believe your glass is empty, Mr. Clemens. Some more of this excellent burgundy?" My employer nodded; a servant took the bottle from Mr. Staunton and filled the empty glasses around the table, and the awkward moment passed.

* * *

The ladies lingered a bit longer after dinner than the normal custom, listening to Mr. Clemens spin tales. Mr. Dupree, the lawyer, was especially interested in Mr. Clemens's impressions of New Orleans. "I know you spent some time here in your piloting days," he said, "but as far as I'm aware, you've been back only once before this visit. What would you say is the biggest change in the city?"

Mr. Clemens leaned back in his chair and thought for a moment. "Actually, New Orleans has changed less than most cities up North. Especially in the old part of the city, there aren't as many new buildings as in Chicago or New York. Partly this is good luck; you haven't had a big fire in the city since before I was a cub pilot. Oh, you've had some fine buildings burn down, like the Saint Charles Hotel, but not whole blocks."

"A tribute to the courage and effectiveness of our firemen," murmured Dr. Soupape, and several of the company nodded their heads in agreement.

"Certainly," said Mr. Clemens, "but to look at the other side of the coin, you've been denied the opportunity to start fresh and put up modern buildings in the center of town. Chicago has, and the city's economy is a hundred times better off for its chance to rebuild."

"A curious way of looking at it," said Mrs. Robinson, toying with her wineglass. She had not spoken much during the evening, and I looked at her with some curiosity as she spoke. "My husband had considerable real estate holdings in the city, and he often spoke of replacing some of the older buildings with modern construction. But that would have been planned for, and well known in advance, and even so, he was concerned that it would have caused people to lose their homes. I would think the suffering of those who lost their homes in a fire or some other great disaster would far outweigh the material benefit of rebuilding the commercial district."

"I don't discount the suffering," said Mr. Clemens. "And I don't recommend burning down your city just to get a few fresh building sites. But remember, a whole new generation has grown up in Chicago since '71. I doubt the fire means much more to them than any other story of their parents' time, while they go in and out of the new buildings every day of their lives.''

''I wonder,'' said our hostess. She looked in my direction and smiled. ''Mr. Cabot, pardon me if I am in error, but I would guess you to be one of the generation born since the War. Is the past so meaningless to modern youth?''

I was conscious of every eye at the table turned toward me. ''I can't pretend to speak for all my generation,'' I began. ''I'm probably more aware of history than many of the fellows I knew in school.''

''And where was that?'' asked Mrs. Staunton, gazing intently at me.

''I was at Yale,'' I said, somewhat self-consciously. I had sometimes encountered those who took my education as an invitation to quiz me or as a sign that I might hold myself superior to the common run of mankind.

''Really,'' drawled Professor Maddox. ''I am surprised that the scholars at such an illustrious school have so little regard for the accomplishments of their forebears. But perhaps I judge them by too high a standard.''

''Pay no mind to Laurence,'' said Mrs. Maddox with a laugh. ''He is a Harvard man, and he can be terribly snobbish about it.''

''Beware, Professor, I'm a Yale man myself,'' said Mr. Clemens, a twinkle in his eye. *''Honoris causa,* of course— still, I'll have to stick up for Wentworth and my fellow sons of Eli.'' There was general laughter at this, with Professor Maddox loudly declaring his allegiance to good old Harvard against any New Haven upstarts. It was the familiar sort of banter I'd often traded with my relatives, most of whom had gone up to Cambridge.

Mrs. Robinson seemed somewhat befuddled at the good-natured exchange of intra-university invective, until Mr. Clemens leaned over to her and explained, ''This is an academic rivalry old enough and deep enough to make the War seem but a passing incident, and I must stand up for my side.''

''I don't like your comparison, sir,'' said Holt, in a tone that cast a chill over the company. ''There are those present to whom the War is not a joking matter.'' He glared belligerently at Mr. Clemens, and his visage showed no trace of humor.

But Mr. Clemens was not about to be cowed. ''Mr. Holt, I understand the importance of the War as well as anyone at this table. I'd be surprised if we had the same opinions on the subject, but I am not such a fool as to belittle a struggle in which so many good men fought and died. You may not know how much of my own time and energy I invested in the publication of General Grant's memoirs.''

At the mention of Grant's name, Mr. Holt rose to his feet. His eyes bulged, and his face turned red. ''Don't mention that butcher's name in my household,'' he said.

The widow Robinson began to pull at her brother's sleeve. ''Sit down, Reynold, please,'' she said. ''This is neither the time nor the place to refight the War.''

Mr. Staunton's face took on an expression almost of boredom, as if he had gone over the subject many times before. ''You forget yourself, sir,'' he said in a long-suffering tone. ''This is not your household, but mine, and it ill becomes you to pick quarrels with my guests. The War is long since over; take your seat.''

At these words, Mr. Holt seemed suddenly confused. His anger disappeared as quickly as it had arisen. He dropped back into his seat and picked up his wineglass while his sister fussed over him, leaning close and whispering in his ear. Although I was almost directly across from them, I could make out only a few words. There was a flutter of relieved conversation as the tension left the atmosphere.

Still, I kept a close eye on Holt, fearing that his anger might return. He seemed subdued for now, but if he were suddenly to turn on Mr. Clemens, only his sister was be-

110   tween them. Would I be able to intervene in time to save my employer from harm?

As if she could hear my thoughts, Mrs. Dupree leaned over and confided to me, "Poor Reynold. He has never been quite himself since the War. Pay him no mind; he really wouldn't harm a fly."

Meanwhile, Mrs. Staunton, recalling her position as hostess, turned to her guests with a smile. "My apologies, Mr. Clemens. I am sure I speak for all of us, especially my brother"—she shot him a glance—"when I say that we are honored to have you as our guest, in our city and in our home. We are not provincials here, as much as the North may think of us as such. An honest difference of opinion is the only true spice of civilization and culture. Your beliefs may differ from ours, as one flower in a garden does from another, but each has its own place and its own beauty."

Our hostess might have gone on in that vein for some time, but Professor Maddox, sitting to her left, chuckled and said to Mr. Clemens, "What Maria means to say, Mr. Clemens, is that you and Mr. Cabot might be Yankees, but we still like you. I spent the best years of my youth at Harvard, and learned, contrary to what I'd been taught at my mother's knee, that many of you Northerners are actually quite human."

There was a general murmur of agreement, and Mr. Staunton signaled to the servant to refill the wineglasses.

"So, Mr. Clemens," said Mr. Dupree, "what were you going to tell us about General Grant's book? I spent most of '64 and '65 trading fire with his men, right up to the end. Nobody likes losing, but there's no denying he knew his business. What was your part in his book?"

The other men nodded and leaned forward, eager to turn the talk back to the universal subject of southern talk. The women exchanged glances and seemed to heave a collective sigh, resigning themselves to the fact that the conversation was back on its inevitable course.

"It was pretty much an accident," said Mr. Clemens, **111** "though I'll concede that it could only have happened to someone who knew the general to begin with. I'd heard that he was planning to write his memoirs, and I went to his apartment to offer my congratulations. As it turned out, he and his son were looking over a contract for that very book. I knew as much about publishing as he did about fighting a war, so I volunteered to look over the contract to make sure he was getting a fair offer. Well, one look was enough to convince me that it would have been a mistake for him to sign it. I told him I'd publish the book myself and give him seventy-five percent of the profits."

"That sounds like a very generous offer," said Professor Maddox. "Did you ever have any qualms about making it?"

"No, because I took it as my patriotic duty to erect a monument to the man who brought the War to a conclusion and ended four years of bloodshed. I am as proud of having helped that book come into the world as of anything I have written myself, if for nothing else, because I made certain that the author got fair value for his labor. Only a fool could have lost money on the contract I gave him. I could have spent the same amount of energy on my own writing, lining my own pockets, but I have never once regretted publishing that book."

Mrs. Staunton listened with interest to my employer's story of how he published Grant's memoirs, smiling and nodding. "So, Mr. Clemens, I see you have done your part to make certain that our youth know what their forebears have done," she said. Mr. Clemens beamed to hear her words of praise. "So that," she continued archly, "they may learn from their mistakes."

My employer, who had just taken a mouthful of pecan pie, nearly choked. Finally recovering his composure, he laughed heartily, and said, "A palpable hit, Mrs. Staunton! Let it never be said that southern ladies don't know how to turn the tables on us poor Yankees!'' Everyone laughed, including (I was glad to see) Mr. Holt.

Then she turned to me, still smiling. ''Mr. Cabot, did you say this was your first visit to New Orleans? What do you think of our city?''

''It has its own character,'' I said, trying to choose my words carefully. ''I haven't traveled as widely as Mr. Clemens, of course, although I hope to, but I can't say I've ever seen the like of New Orleans. New York may be more cosmopolitan in its way, but the exotic elements there are of more recent origin, and not as well blended into the whole. One isn't aware of the Dutch origins of New York at all, whereas the French roots of New Orleans are plainly visible.''

''And visibly beautiful,'' Mr. Clemens interrupted, nodding in the direction of Mrs. Camille Dupree, who blushed slightly and called him a flatterer. ''Of course I am,'' he replied, nodding graciously. ''It is one of my favorite pastimes.''

Mrs. Staunton laughed, then turned to me again. ''Mr. Clemens told me that you are planning a career as a writer, yourself,'' she said. ''Have you decided on which genre you will strive to conquer?''

''Watch yourself, young fellow,'' said Mr. Dupree, chuckling. ''Maria has never been able to resist new writers and poets. Before you know it, she'll be spoiling you rotten and making you totally unfit to be anybody's secretary.'' He gestured with his coffee spoon toward my employer. ''Mr. Clemens, if I were you, I'd keep a close eye on him before he gets out of hand.''

''Oh, he can get out of hand if he wants to,'' said Mr. Clemens. ''Best thing in the world for a young fellow, every now and then. As far as Mrs. Staunton's spoiling him, I reckon I can prevent that by getting there ahead of him and letting her spoil me, instead. Why should the young get all the attention?''

There was a general round of laughter, and Mrs. Maddox

said, "Oh, you're hardly worth Maria's effort. She could never take any credit for your success, but Mr. Cabot is a blank slate, and if she plays her cards right, she can chalk everything he writes to her own account." Everyone laughed again, but again I noticed that Mr. Staunton's laughter seemed a bit forced.

We sat conversing in this amiable way, touching on literature, history, and current affairs, for over an hour. Then, around nine o'clock, the ladies went into the parlor, and our host brought out a fine old cognac and a box of Havana cigars. I took a small snifter of the former but declined the cigars. Mr. Clemens took one enthusiastically, and after the ritual preliminaries, lit it up and declared it excellent.

Mr. Staunton smiled. "Well, Mr. Clemens, I have heard that you were in the habit of buying a box of the best Cuban cigars and setting aside the contents, then replacing them with cheap cigars to offer your guests. Is this true?"

"Slander, downright slander," said Mr. Clemens. He blew a smoke ring, then continued. "Although I knew a steamboat captain who used to pull that trick. He swore that nobody ever noticed. But that's still running a risk, because there *are* people who can tell a good cigar from a bad one, and some of 'em don't have a sense of humor. If you're looking to save money on cigars but still smoke the best, the reverse trick is the one to try." Here he leaned forward and pantomimed opening a box, then turning it upside down. "What you do is buy a box of cheap cigars, the kind made up of sweepings off the factory floor, empty it out, and fill it with good Havanas. Pass *that* box around, and watch your guests turn up their noses. Then you can light one up with a clear conscience, knowing you've offered them the best. And you'll save money, even counting the cost of the ones you throw away, because you can keep refilling the same box for years."

"Aha, and have you employed this stratagem?" Professor Maddox asked in a mock accusatory tone.

"Why would I admit it, even if I had?" said Mr. Clem-

114 ens, and there was another round of laughter.

Mr. Holt joined in the laughter, but at the same time he shook his head. "Only a Yankee would take pride in such tricks," he muttered. I noticed his brother-in-law give him a hard glare at this, but Holt only snorted and took another drink. I began to suspect that Holt was somewhat too fond of his bottle.

Without our hostess's limitation on conversational subjects, the talk inevitably came back around to the War. This was fine with me, because there was much I wanted to know. What had made them fight so long and hard against superior numbers, in support of a cause they must have known was hopeless? Even I had heard of the Washington Artillery, which had played a role in every battle fought by the Confederate Army of Northern Virginia, from Bull Run to Appomattox. Here were three veterans of that regiment, and I listened in fascination to their reminiscences.

"Fredericksburg was where we gave the Yanks their medicine," said Mr. Holt, who had been an artilleryman at the age of sixteen. "We watched 'em come up the hill with bayonets fixed, while our riflemen picked holes in their ranks. The Federals' cannon were across the river, where they couldn't hurt us, but the infantry kept on coming. When the fools got close enough, we gave 'em a taste of canister, and sent 'em to the devil." His face shone with a fierce light, and I was glad I wasn't among the men who'd had to charge his position atop Marye's Heights more than thirty years ago.

"Yes, it was a cold, grim day," said Mr. Dupree. His face was less excited than Mr. Holt's, and in his voice I sensed compassion for the boys who'd been on the receiving end of the Confederate cannonade. "General Lee was somber as I ever saw him, even though it was a clear victory for us. The only time I recall that he looked worse was at Gettysburg, when he apologized to the men he'd sent into the Federal guns."

"And at Chancellorsville, when Stonewall was shot,"

said Dr. Soupape, shaking his head. "I was at headquarters when the news came. I think that was the worst." He shook his head sadly, and his eyes had a faraway look, as if he were seeing that bloody battlefield of thirty years ago, instead of the elegant Garden District dining room in which we sat.

"At least Old Jack had a clean end to his pain," said Mr. Holt, and a chill fell over the room again, although I wasn't quite sure why. His face was still fierce, but the light had gone out of it.

I thought he was about to speak again, but Mr. Dupree put a hand on his shoulder. "Now, Reynold, we're among guests, and this is not a time to reopen all the old wounds."

"It's all very well for you to say that, Gordon," said Holt. "God knows, there aren't many others I'd listen to it from, but you have your badge of honor, too. I'll say no more." I looked at his face, a dark mask of untamed pride, and wondered if he had begun drinking earlier in the day, before coming to dinner.

"As long as a man has his honor, that is sufficient," said Mr. Staunton dogmatically. He thumped a fist on the table. "Nobody can say that Reynold Holt has given up his claim to honor, and I'll defend that statement with my life."

I was completely at a loss what to make of the last few speeches, other than to ascribe them to a superfluity of liquor at the table. Earlier, Staunton had seemed at odds with his brother-in-law Holt, but now he backed the man's boorish behavior. As for the "badge of honor," I could guess what that meant. Detective LeJeune had informed Mr. Clemens and me that Mr. Holt had been wounded, captured, and held prisoner by the Union after Chancellorsville. I had no idea what sort of treatment he had received, but it seemed a long time to hold such a grudge. The War had ended before I was born, and questions of honor were long since settled, it seemed to me. But these Southerners evidently had long memories.

So I was even more startled when Mr. Holt glared at his

116   brother-in-law, Mr. Staunton, and said, "I am glad to hear you speak in favor of honor, sir. Would that your actions always matched your words."

Mr. Staunton's face went through several changes while he struggled to find words. Dr. Soupape raised his hand as if warning him against continuing, and Mr. Staunton looked at him uncomprehendingly for a moment. Then he pulled himself together and said in a very quiet voice, "I will overlook what you have just said, Reynold. I have defended my honor more than once, as you will no doubt realize upon reflection. But the hour is growing late, and the ladies will be waiting for us in the parlor. I suggest we go and join them." He stood and gestured toward the door leading into the next room.

With that, the dinner came to a most perplexing end.

12

When Mr. Clemens and I arrived back at our pension on Royal Street, it was well after midnight, and the air had cooled enough for even a native of Connecticut to feel comfortable. I had wined and dined in a manner to which I had previously aspired only in my dreams, and a good night's sleep seemed the only thing remaining to bring the evening to a fitting end. But Mr. Clemens had other ideas. He loosened his tie, poured himself a drink, and started to fill a pipe. I began to excuse myself and head for my room, but he glared at me and said, "Where the hell are you going, Wentworth? This is no time to be crawling into bed."

"I beg to differ with you," I said, somewhat grumpily. "I can barely keep my eyes open."

"Differ all you want," he said, "but I need you to stay awake a little longer. Leonard Galloway's neck may depend on it. Too many things went on at that dinner party tonight for me to keep track of by myself, and unless you help me remember them, I'm likely to miss something important. Splash some cold water on your face if you have to, and have a seat."

I was tempted to protest further, but his logic was inescapable, and in any case, his expression brooked no dissent. So I poured myself a tumbler of soda water and sat down opposite him while he finished loading his pipe. At last he looked up at me and said, "Quite a passel of suspects, ain't they?"

"Good Lord!" I said. "I thought I was going to have to jump over the table to keep that Reynold Holt from attacking you when you mentioned General Grant. Don't these people know when they've lost a war?"

Mr. Clemens chuckled. "Yes, Holt must have been a real fire-eater when he was young. Percy Staunton isn't any kind of lamb, either. That detective said that Staunton's fought a couple of duels, if you can imagine that. So he's no stranger to killing, or at least not to the idea of it." He struck a match, and held it to the tobacco.

I shook my head in amazement. "Well, I think we can safely put both of them right at the top of our list. I wonder what they had against Robinson?"

He had the pipe well lit by now and took a couple of fragrant puffs before answering. "Who knows? We'll have to find that out somehow, if we're going to prove somebody besides Leonard Galloway killed Robinson. Motive is one of our key points, along with method and opportunity. The courts always want to know all three of those."

"The method isn't any puzzle, at least," I said. "Robinson was poisoned."

"Yes, but we need to know how he was given the poison. Especially if the cook didn't do it—how did someone get him to take a dose of something everybody supposedly knows is deadly poison? And the stuff he took, jimsonweed, is fairly obnoxious stuff. You wouldn't have much luck trying to pass it off as an exotic variety of cabbage."

"That means we have to look to opportunity, then," I said. "Which of our suspects had the opportunity to give him the poison in an undetectable form? It would have to be someone who visited him that day, or shortly before, I'd think."

"That may be," said Mr. Clemens. He took a sip of his whisky and rubbed his chin, thinking. "I don't know enough about jimsonweed to say how it could have been disguised, how long it keeps, how much of it you need.''

''I'll bet Dr. Soupape would know,'' I said. ''He'd be a suspect, in my book.''

''True, but if he'd done it, I doubt he'd have called attention to it. He could have declared Robinson the victim of some common ailment and sent him to the undertaker without a question being asked.''

''But he might have feared being found out, if he'd done it,'' I said. ''Perhaps he wanted to throw suspicion on someone else.''

''Well, that brings us back around the circle again,'' said Mr. Clemens. ''Which of our suspects had the opportunity to poison Robinson—and the knowledge to do it without suspicion? What we really need to know is who visited the house that day, and maybe the day before. Arthur, the butler, could tell us that. Leonard seems to think he'd know something that might clear him.''

''I wonder what it could be?''

Mr. Clemens shrugged. ''For all I know, poor Leonard is grasping at straws. But I'll keep on trying to corner the butler, and I'll see what I can find out. I have a pretty good idea who could tell us what we need to know about the poison and how it could've been given. I'll have to go see Eulalie Echo again. Meanwhile, we can speculate on motives. Not knowing a great deal about Robinson, it strikes me that almost anyone at the dinner table could have had some reason to kill him.''

I was surprised. ''Really? The majority of the company struck me as honest, unexceptional people. What motives do you impute to them?''

''For most of them, I'd put my money on politics,'' said Mr. Clemens. ''Robinson was going to be a serious candidate for mayor next election, running on a reform platform. We'll have to talk to George Cable about exactly what that means in New Orleans politics, but wherever there's a reform candidate, there's an establishment that stands to lose something if he's elected. Staunton and Holt

120   are from families with old money, and old money is usually
dead set against reformers. So maybe that's the direction
we need to look in. Dr. Soupape and the lawyer, Dupree,
could have political motives, too.''

I frowned. ''Do you really think that his death is a political assassination? I suppose I can't deny the possibility,
but even granting the assumption that some political rival
is the killer, I'd suspect someone like that saloon owner
Eulalie Echo mentioned, Tom Anderson, rather than these
respectable citizens.''

Mr. Clemens chuckled. ''Poor Wentworth. I wish I had
your faith in respectability, but when you've been around
as many years as I have, you'll put respectability and politics in separate categories. Even the reform candidates have
to crawl into bed with the likes of Anderson if they want
to win any elections. Of course, they don't always *want* to
win. Sometimes all they want to do is stand up and wave
the flag for their principles and go down to defeat satisfied
that they've fought the good fight. Southerners are particularly prone to that kind of noble futility. John David Robinson may have been one of that kind. Or he may have
been a pragmatist, in which case you can bet he'd have
swapped horses with the devil himself if it improved his
chance to be elected mayor. He'd have made enemies either
way. That's what politics is all about. But you're right. We
may have to look beyond our dinner circle for possible
suspects.''

I was hardly pleased at this prospect, and I said so.
''Why, if you cast a wide enough net, you'll have half the
grown men in New Orleans as possible murderers. We can't
quiz all of them.''

''Not unless we want to spend Christmas in a warm climate,'' he agreed, and took another long pull on his pipe.
''So, first of all, we need to find out who was going to be
hurt if Robinson actually managed to win the election. We
need to know what promises he'd made and what political
IOUs he'd left around town that somebody might have

called in at an inconvenient moment. If Robinson was willing to undercut his own class to win the election, he could have made enemies even among his own in-laws. In fact, a lot of people consider their in-laws enemies just by virtue of the relationship . . .''

I laughed. ''I suppose you're right,'' I admitted. ''So we need to find out as much as possible about Holt and Staunton.''

''And everybody else,'' said Mr. Clemens. He leaned back in his chair, puffing on the pipe. ''Our two hot-headed southern gentlemen aren't the only likely suspects, although they're well up on the list. But for one thing, I'd think either of them would be more likely to take the direct approach if they were going to kill a man—a pistol, rather than poison. In a way, I wish the killer *had* shot Robinson. If it hadn't been poison, they probably wouldn't have arrested the cook for it.''

''Who could it be, if not Holt or Staunton? None of the others seemed like murderers to me.'' I tried to imagine the kindly old Dr. Soupape or the scholarly Professor Maddox as a cold-blooded killer and failed. Nor did bookish Maria Staunton seem a likely poisoner to me.

Mr. Clemens stood up and paced around the room. ''Don't be so certain. You can't expect the murderer to sneak around like the villain in some melodrama, Wentworth. Almost any of the people at that table could have had a motive to kill Robinson. It could be money, or some kind of insult, or a check to someone's ambition, or infidelity. You never know what might send a person over the edge. The doctor would certainly know about poisons, for example, and the family lawyer might have a political ax to grind or a finger in his client's business. And if, as Eulalie Echo hinted, the marriage wasn't quite what it ought to have been, even our bookish Professor Maddox might have had a motive for doing away with Mr. Robinson. Suppose Maddox learned that Robinson had made unwelcome advances to Mrs. Maddox? Or conversely, suppose the professor and Mrs. Robinson were secret lovers?

"The widow Robinson does nothing to allay suspicion by coming out into company two weeks after her husband's untimely death, even though it is only a small dinner party at her sister's home. LeJeune says she has an iron-clad alibi. Still, was she so lightly affected by her bereavement? Could it be that it wasn't all that unwelcome an event?"

"It seems a monstrous suggestion, but I suppose we have to consider it," I admitted.

"I'm afraid so," said Mr. Clemens. "On the other hand, she's not completely ignoring propriety. For one thing, I didn't manage to wheedle an invitation to her house, as I'd hoped to. That's a line of inquiry to follow up. It would have given me a chance to see the scene of the crime and possibly to talk to Arthur. Meanwhile, we need to explore other avenues into the Robinson's circle. I think you should allow Mrs. Staunton to take you under her wing and foster your literary ambitions."

I was astonished at the suggestion. "Surely you don't think she is a suspect!"

"I don't think she's the main one, no," said Mr. Clemens. He pointed the stem of his pipe at me. "That doesn't mean I can't imagine motives for her. Suppose Robinson was making advances to her? Suppose she knew him to be mistreating her sister? Suppose he was blackmailing her husband? Maria Staunton's bluestocking facade could be hiding a warehouse full of long-held grudges and secret passions. Trust me, Wentworth, I've seen plenty of these would-be literary Southern ladies before."

I thought back to Mrs. Staunton's curious expression as she responded to my offhand remark about her husband stepping out of his picture. "Perhaps you're right. Though it still seems a bit far-fetched to me."

"To tell you the truth, it does to me, too, but that doesn't mean we can ignore the possibility," he said. He took a sip of his whisky, then continued. "More likely, to my way of thinking, is the chance that she knows something about who killed Robinson, especially if her sister or her husband is the guilty party. And she just might let it slip. Even if she doesn't, you'll have a chance to see how she and her family act when they're not on their best behavior for dinner—if what we saw this evening fits that description.''

"I certainly hope not," I said, shuddering. "Holt was bad enough, trying to fight the war all over again. I think he had more than his share to drink, as well."

"It's not just the drink, Wentworth." Mr. Clemens's face took on a grave expression. "That man saw his share of terror at firsthand. I know what it's like to fire a gun and see a man fall dead; to do it over and over for the whole course of the war must be far worse."

"You were in the war?" I asked. "I hadn't known."

"I wasn't in it for long. Part of a Confederate irregular company in Missouri—the Marion Raiders, we called ourselves. We spent a few weeks skulking in the woods and learned more about retreating than the man that invented the maneuver. Then about half of us deserted. There's no way to paper over the bare truth of it. I lit out for Nevada with my brother and ended up becoming a writer. But before the company broke up, we shot down one fellow, some poor stranger who'd blundered into our territory. It was simple murder, nothing more. I was one of maybe a dozen who fired our rifles, so I can't claim any *credit* for the kill, if such an absurd term applies to it, but I have as good a sense as anyone what it means to kill a man, and I wouldn't wish it on my worst enemy."

"Good Lord," I said. "I had no idea."

"I don't tell the story too often," he said after a long pause. He took a sip of his whisky. "It's hardly an asset to my reputation, especially considering my later support for the Union cause. But I got off easily in comparison with some. Holt stood with the Washington Artillery at Fredericksburg, mowing down men whose only crime was following a damn fool's orders to attack an impregnable position. So he knows better than I do what it's like to deal out mass murder and see the victims fall dead in front of your eyes. What's more, that detective told us that Holt was wounded and captured at Chancellorsville and spent half a year as a prisoner at Fort Delaware. I've heard a few stories from prisoners of war on both sides, and none of them are pretty; even the strongest man might break under that sort of distress.''

"Poor fellow! I suppose one has to make allowance for his pain. It might have unbalanced him, don't you think?''

"Of course it might have," said Mr. Clemens. "Murder isn't the act of a balanced mind." He stood looking out the window, and took a couple of puffs on his pipe, then turned to face me. "Then again, I doubt whether there's a completely balanced mind among the entire dinner party." He paused again, a little too long for my liking, then added, "Present company excluded, of course."

He winked at me, and made a shooing motion to indicate that our discussion was finished. I stood and bid my employer a good night, and went quickly out before he had a chance to think of another topic to explore.

It occurred to me, as I closed the door to his rooms, that in spite of his initial reluctance to make himself part of this murder investigation, Mr. Clemens was enjoying the challenge immensely, even though it was a matter of life and death for poor Leonard Galloway. Then I smiled, as I realized that despite my exhaustion, I was having almost as much fun as he was.

⤳ **13**

The next morning I was sorely tempted to sleep late, but it was not to be. The sun came shining strongly through my curtain, accompanied by the crowing of a neighbor's rooster. After the tenth or eleventh iteration of his morning cry, I began to think that perhaps this bird would be a proper subject for a trial of Eulalie Echo's voo-doo ritual for making the guilty confess. Then, just as he ceased his vocal exercises and a blissful silence fell, a large dray came down the street and stopped just opposite my window. I heard loud thumps and curses as two or three men proceeded to unload some dozen large barrels, which sounded as if they were full of tin and broken crockery. The driver cursed continually at the teamsters, and they swore back at him in viva voce. After about five minutes of this, a window went up on the floor below me and Mme. Bechet began a series of high-pitched imprecations in Cre-ole, to which the driver, showing his versatility, replied in the same tongue.

I tried to pull the pillow over my head and ignore them all, until Mr. Clemens threw up the window in the next room, and joined in the slanging contest. Mme. Bechet knew when she was in over her head, and presently I heard her cry *"Merde!"* and slam her window shut. The drivers tried to pay Mr. Clemens back in his own coin, but Mme. Bechet's closed window allowed him to pretend that there were no ladies' ears present to be offended, and he lit into the offending parties with added gusto. My employer had spent enough of his life aboard steamboats and on the wild frontier to have the advantage over any city-bred man. Still, it was several minutes more before the teamsters realized that they were up against a crackerjack in the art of invective, and abandoned the competition. By then, it was amply clear that I was not likely to get any more sleep that morning.

I sat up and wiped the sleep out of my eyes. I was in better condition than I had any right to be, considering the amount of wine I'd drunk the night before—and, to judge from Mr. Clemens's display of temper, far better off than he was. I listened to him stamp around for a few minutes, thinking he might go back to bed and leave me free to close my eyes a little longer. But soon enough I heard him tapping on the connecting door. "Wentworth! Are you up yet?"

"Yes, sir," I said, and hastened over to open the door, revealing him standing there in his nightshirt.

"Read this," he said, and thrust a piece of paper at me. On the outside was his name and the address of our pension. I unfolded it and saw in neat writing, *Come see me this evening. I have news. E. E.*

"Eulalie Echo," I said, looking up at him. "When did it come?"

"During the night, I suppose," he said. "It was on the floor just inside the door, and as sure as my name's Sam Clemens, it wasn't there when we came in."

"I certainly didn't see it," I agreed. "Then again, I was tired enough when we got in that I won't swear to my eyesight at the time. Could Mme. Bechet have delivered it while we were still sleeping?"

He pointed toward the floor. "Did you hear her just now? That wasn't the voice of a woman who's been awake for any length of time. Those jackasses downstairs woke her up, or I'll eat my hat. In any case, it looks as if I'll have to go see our voodoo woman sooner than I had planned. I wonder what her news is.''

"We shall learn this evening, I suppose.''

''Yes, certainly,'' he said, putting his hands behind his back and pacing back and forth a few steps, thinking. "But I'd also like you to call on Mrs. Staunton. You can talk about literary things—make something up, she won't know the difference—and see what you can learn about the household and the family. With any luck, she'll talk her head off when she has a budding author all to herself.''

"Yes, but I should do that this afternoon and go with you this evening,'' I protested. ''Surely you don't want to go to Eulalie Echo's neighborhood by yourself, and after dark.'' I remembered all too well that on our trip downriver, Mr. Clemens had been in need of my protection more than once. I was loath to let him wander off alone, especially in such a dubious neighborhood.

''Oh, that'll be no problem.'' He dismissed my concern with a wave of his hand. ''I'll get Henry Dodds to drop me at her door. Don't worry; she's not going to cast any spells on me. And when I'm done, Eulalie will surely be able to whistle up some of the local boys to walk me over to Aunt Tillie's. Then Henry can pick me up there, and I'll pick you up at the Stauntons'. Besides, I have other plans for the afternoon, and I'll want you with me for certain, where we're going.''

''And where's that?'' He was full of plans for a man who hadn't even had his morning coffee.

''We need to pay a visit to Tom Anderson's café,'' he said. ''They say politics makes strange bedfellows. I want to find out who some of John David Robinson's political bedfellows were; if there's a political angle in this murder, that's the place to find it out. George Cable tells me that Anderson's café is where the dirty work is done. And from what I've read in the papers, Boss Tweed's reign at Tammany Hall was a Sunday school picnic compared to what these Louisiana politicos do every day.''

128   "You don't make the place sound very attractive," I said.

Mr. Clemens turned a wry smile on me. "I suspect it's attractive enough, to a certain sort of scoundrel. That's exactly why I want you along. There are times when an ex-football player is a handy fellow to have at your side, and I reckon this might be one of them. Tom Anderson may be still a young man, but he comes with a reputation for dirty business I'd hate to drag around after me at *my* age."

He paused for a moment, looked toward the sunlight pouring through my window, and continued, "But let's stop gabbing and get dressed." He went back through the connecting door and began to rummage through his wardrobe. I saw his formal suit from the previous evening carefully folded over a chair near the window. "Damnation, I've only one good shirt left clean. We'll have to remind Mme. Bechet to have our laundry done today." He turned and looked through the open door at me, still standing there in my nightshirt, half-asleep.

"Act alive, now, Wentworth! If you hurry up, I'll have time to write a few pages of my book after breakfast."

In fact, Mr. Clemens wrote for the entire morning. I spent the time catching up on my secretarial duties. I started with a visit to the post office to dispatch his letters (to Henry Rogers, his backer in New York, and to his family in Vienna, Austria) and to pick up incoming mail being held for him. He also sent me to the local typewriter dealer to find a ream of typing paper and a supply of the ribbons for his machine, on which he did all his writing meant for the press. After one last stop, just off Canal Street, at a newsstand that carried good Havana cigars and a selection of out-of-town newspapers, both hands of my watch were beginning to home in on the vertical. I walked back to our apartments on Royal Street, where Mr. Clemens was busily typing away. When he saw me enter with my arms full of paper and other supplies, he glanced at his own watch and declared it to be lunchtime.

"I second the motion," I said. "I've walked up enough of an appetite for both of us. Where shall we eat today?"

He looked at his manuscript, raised a finger to indicate I should wait a moment, and typed a few more words before replying. "Well, if you're up for a little more walking, I thought we'd kill two birds with one stone and take our lunch at Tom Anderson's," he said, looking at the page in his machine. "It's supposed to have a pretty decent spread—at least, all the police and politicos eat there, and I suspect Anderson knows better than to skimp on the refreshments when he's catering to that crowd. The cops can usually eat free of charge anywhere they want to. In New Orleans, that presents a real challenge to somebody who wants to keep their business." He typed the end of his sentence, pulled the paper from the typewriter, and added it to the small stack growing on the table.

"So perhaps we'll get a decent meal as well as a few clues in our murder case," I speculated.

"I certainly hope so," he said, standing up. "I'd hate to give my business to a low-class restaurant just to save some poor fellow from the hangman. Come along, Wentworth."

We walked up Saint Philip Street to North Rampart and made a left, heading toward Canal. Rampart was a broad street, but not a prosperous-looking one. Yet there were a number of colorfully dressed young ladies to be seen strolling about or standing in twos and threes on the street corners, talking. Several of them waved to us, smiling and calling out, and at first I thought they must recognize my employer. I was surprised, for nothing in their appearance suggested that they were of a class where one would ordinarily assume a familiarity with literature.

Then, at the corner of Saint Louis, we walked past a group of them on our side of the street, and I heard clearly what they were saying. Mr. Clemens laughed nervously, saying, "No, thank you," but I was completely speechless.

130   When we had gone a few steps farther, he turned to say something to me, and laughed again, louder this time. "Why, Wentworth! You're red as a beet. Don't tell me you've never been in this kind of place before."

"These are hardly the sort of young women I am used to associating with," I sputtered. Not only had they made the most improper suggestion, but I noticed on closer examination that their dress, which at first appeared merely to push the boundaries of fashion to an extreme, was in fact well over the border into questionable taste. After a few more strides, I recovered my composure enough to continue. "Why, that one in red is young enough to be your daughter!"

He looked back over his shoulder at the young woman in question, and replied, *"All* of them are young enough to be my daughters, more's the pity."

"Pity is barely an adequate term to describe the plight of these poor women," I said, still angry. "Don't the police know what's going on here?"

"I'm sure they do," said Mr. Clemens, matter-of-factly. "I suspect that's why the police have made Tom Anderson's their regular meeting place, just to keep a close eye on matters of interest." He pointed toward the block just ahead, where I could see a sign for the very restaurant we were planning to visit.

"How peculiar that someone like Mr. Robinson would frequent such a questionable establishment," I said, suddenly thoughtful.

"I wondered when you were going to think of that," said Mr. Clemens. "Come on now, Wentworth, let's see how Tom Anderson feeds his customers."

From what I had seen of the neighborhood, I came to Anderson's expecting a squalid, tawdry place, filled with the sort of shameless demimondaine we had seen on the nearby streets and the pathetic men who seek out their company. Much to my surprise, the place was sparkling clean, full of rich mahogany and bright brass, and brilliantly lit with dozens of electric bulbs. The customers, in outward appearance at least, were no less respectable than those at other New Orleans restaurants in which we had eaten. Anderson's was obviously popular, as well—almost all the tables were occupied by groups clearly enjoying a hearty luncheon, with a good many more lined up at the bar.

A well-built fellow, nearly six foot tall, with reddish blond hair and a large mustache, saw us enter and came bustling over. "Oho, Mr. Mark Twain!" he said loudly, taking my employer's hand and shaking it vigorously. Conversations stopped and heads at all the nearby tables turned to observe us, and I realized that this was precisely the effect the man intended. "Tom Anderson at your service," he continued, with an exaggerated bow. "You've come to the best eating and drinking place in New Orleans, and I can guarantee you won't regret it! What's your pleasure, gentlemen?"

"Well, it's my pleasure just to meet you, Tom. I've been hearing about Tom Anderson's café practically the whole way down the Mississippi," said Mr. Clemens. (This was blatantly untrue; I had never heard it mentioned before Eulalie Echo's suggestion that we talk to the owner.) "I said to myself, no place could possibly live up to that kind of reputation, so here I am to see for myself whether it's true. Just find a table for me and my secretary, Mr. Cabot, here, and we'll see what's on the bill of fare."

"Nothing easier," said Anderson. He led us to a private booth toward the rear of the restaurant, away from the noise and commotion of the front room, although he kept up a stream of talk evidently calculated to let as many of his customers as possible know that he was entertaining none other than Mark Twain. When he finally got us seated, he said, "There'll be a boy along to take your luncheon orders in a moment, but first, it'd be my great honor to buy you both a drink. What'll you have, gentlemen?"

Mr. Clemens ordered his usual whisky and soda, and I decided on a lager. Anderson signaled to a waiter, who scurried off and soon returned with our drinks, plus one for our host, who had taken a seat with us. Anderson appeared to be in the prime of life, perhaps thirty-five years old, with bright blue eyes and a jovial expression suitable to his trade.

Mr. Clemens and Anderson lit up cigars and chatted about trivialities after the drinks arrived. Then Anderson asked, "And how long do you plan to be here in New Orleans?"

"It'll take me a little longer—maybe a week or two—to finish the research on my new book," said Mr. Clemens. "Once that's done, I can do the writing any place I can find a table and chair. I plan to take the train back to New York, with a few stops along the way for lectures. Then I'll see if I can afford a boat trip over to visit my family in Europe. I'm trying to raise some cash to recoup a couple of bad investments, and the best way I know to do that is to put together a book that everybody wants to read. I hope to get back on my feet fairly quickly." He sipped his drink, a contemplative expression on his face, then his eyes lit up and he turned to Anderson.

"You know something, Tom? I bet you're just the man who could give me pointers about some of the stuff I ought to be putting in the New Orleans sections of the book. After all, what would a book about New Orleans be without Tom Anderson in it?"

"Oho, now wouldn't that be something?" said Anderson, a broad smile on his face. "Tom Anderson in a book by Mark Twain!" Then his expression became serious, and he lowered his voice. "But a man doesn't get the class of customer I do by talking about everything he hears. There's stuff I could tell you would make your hair stand on end, and be the making of your book, for sure. But the next thing you know, my place would be half-empty. And I've got waiters and cooks to pay, and a band in here every night, and if I close the doors, they're all out of work. So maybe I'd best decline the honor."

"There's ways around that," said Mr. Clemens, leaning forward. "If I change the names and a few of the circumstances, nobody knows who told me what. Or if a fellow drops a little hint where I might find out certain details for myself, I can do all the real legwork. I've done it before, you know. And the name of the man who helped me is nowhere in the book, but I make sure he's got a copy of it with a great big *thank-you* written in the front, over my signature."

"I see your drift," said Anderson. He took a puff on his cigar and blew a smoke ring, then another smaller one. "Still, there's things it's healthier for all concerned not to say too much about. What kind of stories would you be wanting for your book, now?" He leaned forward, a predatory look on his face. The expression reminded me that he was far more than simply the jovial tavern keeper he appeared to be.

"Scandals and crimes are what sell books," said Mr. Clemens, looking Anderson straight in the eye. "Your average reader wants to think he's getting the truth about things nobody else knows, even if there are half a million others reading the exact same book. But of course, that's just the kind of thing you probably can't talk about. Like this fellow Robinson, who was running for mayor before he got killed. Was it really the cook who poisoned him, or was it somebody with a political axe to grind? I reckon he didn't get his poison salad in *your* place. From what I hear tell, he probably thought he was too good to set foot in here, anyway."

"Oh, don't be so sure of that," said Anderson. "I saw him in here more than once. He came in here with that lawyer, Gordon Dupree."

"Now there's a surprise," said Mr. Clemens. He sat up straight, took a puff of his cigar, and continued. "I thought Robinson was one of those reformers that acts as if there's something dirty about real politics. Usually they've never worked a day in their life."

"Aye, I know the type," said Anderson, nodding. "They sit out in the Garden District and look down their noses at the workingman, except when they get the notion to go passing laws against him having a little fun on a Saturday night. Robinson wasn't a bluenose, I'll grant him that, but he came here more for business than for fun, I'd say."

At this point, the serving boy approached the table again. Anderson gave him an irritated look, motioning him away. The lad turned to an empty table nearby and began to swipe his towel across the top, acting as if that had been his purpose all along. But it was clear that his attention was turned toward us. I noted that patrons at the other tables would occasionally glance our way, as well. Clearly we were the center of attention for the whole room.

"Politics, I take it," said Mr. Clemens. He leaned toward Anderson and lowered his voice in a conspiratorial manner.

"Sometimes politics, but as often as not it was real estate," said Anderson. "Robinson had a fair amount of money invested in this part of town. Every now and again, he and Dupree would ask my advice about properties they were interested in. But you'll pardon me if I don't go into any more detail. I'm a man who knows when to talk and when not to. Robinson's not here to object, but there's others who might, and it's not my place to tell their business."

He stood up and extended his hand to Mr. Clemens. "A pleasure to see you here, Mr. Twain. Go ahead and order anything you like. Your money's no good here today. And maybe next time you're here, we'll talk a little more about that book idea of yours. I just might know a few stories you'd like."

Mr. Clemens shook his hand, thanking him profusely. "I'm giving a couple of lectures before I leave town," he said. "I'll make sure to leave a couple of tickets at the box office for you, if you'd like. You look like a man who enjoys a good laugh, and I think I can promise you a fair share of that."

The tavern keeper chuckled and said, "Many thanks, Mr.

Twain. I may do just that, if I can find a way to get out of work. But this place is a full-time job.''

Anderson walked away, and Mr. Clemens looked at me and muttered, ''Well, the son of a bitch may know some stories I'd like, but it looks like he's not about to tell the only one I'm interested in today.'' He stubbed out his cigar and picked up the bill of fare.

''That may mean there really is a political motive to the Robinson murder,'' I said, glancing around to see if anyone was listening. ''Too bad Anderson didn't want to talk.''

Mr. Clemens peered at me over the menu, his eyebrows bristling. ''Yes, but now we know there's smoke, which means we can be pretty sure there's fire somewhere,'' he growled. Then his expression lightened up. ''And if nothing else, we've gotten ourselves a free lunch out of our visit. I wonder if their T-bone steaks are good today?''

14

After our discussion with Tom Anderson in his Rampart Street café, Mr. Clemens and I enjoyed a leisurely luncheon, surrounded by a crowd that, if one could believe the rumors, included half the dishonest politicians and unconvicted felons in New Orleans. Then, as we had previously arranged, we met Henry Dodds and his cab at the corner of Rampart and Canal. Dodds greeted us in his usual colorful style, and we climbed aboard for the ride out to the Garden District, traveling the by-now-familiar route along Saint Charles Avenue. On the way, my employer and I compared notes on the interview with Anderson.

"Anderson's hiding something," said Mr. Clemens. "I can't tell you what, but I know there's more to the story than he was willing to talk about."

"I suspect you're right," I answered. "Perhaps Anderson was afraid of being overheard. Half the other customers were staring at our table the whole time we were there."

"Yes, that's part of the price of having my picture plastered all over the country. You can hardly blame the rascal for not wanting to tell me anything in front of the crowd; he might as well have been on stage. In a way, he *was* on stage—promoting his business by letting everybody see that he was having a drink with Mark Twain. The man has no more shame than Barnum, although at least he had the decency to give us a free lunch in exchange for the publicity.''

My employer chuckled, then leaned forward to address our driver. ''Let's ask Mr. Dodds his opinion. Henry, you must have driven a lot of men coming to and going from Anderson's place. Any bits of hearsay you can pass on to us?''

Henry Dodds turned halfway around, chuckling. ''Tom Anderson's a slick one, all right. Knows how to keep his mouth shut, and makes sure the folks that works there does the same. I know a couple boys works in his kitchen. They say you're likely to see almost anything in the world in that place, but you ask 'em what they mean and they just roll their eyes.'' He turned back to his horse and flicked the reins. ''Watch it now, you stay off them streetcar tracks!'' The horse pulled to the right, tossing his head, but obeying his driver's signal.

Mr. Clemens nodded. ''I reckon you're right, Henry. Maybe if Anderson comes to my lectures, I'll ask him up to the dressing room for a drink and see if he'll talk any more in private. Meanwhile, I'll just have to put together what few hints he dropped and see where they lead. I wonder what kind of real estate Robinson had in that part of town, and why he went to Anderson's to discuss it.''

''Perhaps it was merely a convenient meeting place,'' I suggested, thinking of how my father's legal practice often took him to out-of-the-way places. ''If he were dealing with someone from that part of town, he might very naturally have suggested meeting at Anderson's. Don't you think so, Mr. Dodds?''

''Sure, he might,'' said Henry Dodds, turning around again and grinning. ''Just like a bullfrog might natcherly set down and take his afternoon nap in a gator's nest.''

Mr. Clemens burst out laughing and clapped our driver on the back. ''And with just about as much chance of coming out in one piece, I'd bet!''

We spent the rest of the journey discussing what needed

to be done to complete Mr. Clemens's research book he was working on. I made a few notes on places he still wanted to visit in New Orleans and people who might have interesting anecdotes or information about the old times in the city, but my mind was not entirely on my employer's business, I must admit. I was more concerned with how I was to proceed in my meeting with Mrs. Staunton. Winning her confidence and getting her to tell me her family's secrets seemed an impossible task.

Mr. Clemens sensed my preoccupation and said, "Don't worry, Wentworth. You'll do all right. Just jump right in; she'll be sure to follow you. You're enough of an innocent that she'll never suspect you're up to anything."

Dodds looked back at us when Mr. Clemens said that, but he said nothing. But after he dropped Mr. Clemens off on the corner of Fourth and Howard, he headed back toward the Staunton residence at First and Chestnut, and turned around to look at me. "You watch yourself, young feller," he said, wagging his finger. "I reckon you ain't up to nothing funny, but that cook of theirs, Louisa, tells me that Mr. Staunton has a nasty temper, 'specially when he's been drinkin'."

"Don't worry, Henry," I said. "I'm not up to anything funny."

The driver shook his head, a serious expression on his face. "I reckon you ain't, if you say you ain't. But some folks might take it wrong if they thought you was prying into family business, not that a nice young feller like you would do that sort of thing. I just thought you might want to know where the bear traps was before you stepped in 'em."

I met his eye and nodded slowly. "I appreciate the warning, Henry. Thank you. I'll be careful."

At the door, I presented my card to the butler and waited on the shady veranda. A dozen objections to Mr. Clemens's plans for me to pry Mrs. Staunton's secrets out of her leapt

into my mind in the interval of perhaps two minutes. What **139**
if Mrs. Staunton turned out to be unwilling to talk to me
about her family, especially about the recent murder, on
such brief acquaintance? What if she had other plans for
the afternoon? What if she had company? What if she were
indisposed? All this raced through my imagination, and
then I heard a light footstep inside the door, and she threw
it open, an eager expression on her face. "Oh, Mr. Cabot!
What a delightful surprise! Please do come in!"

She took me through the large parlor where we'd had
dinner the night before to a more intimate room lined with
bookshelves. "You didn't see our library last night," she
said. She took her seat in a sofa under a pair of bright
windows overlooking the garden and made a motion that I
should sit beside her. "I'm sure this is nothing in comparison to Mr. Clemens's collection, but we do our best to
keep up literature."

I was about to protest that I had never laid eyes on my
employer's library, but thought better of it. Best not to diminish whatever prestige I had as Mr. Clemens's personal
secretary by admitting that I knew less of his writings or
of his taste in literature than the lady in whose home I was
sitting probably did. Instead of sitting, I walked over to
look at what was on the bookshelves.

Her collection was surprisingly complete, featuring beau-
tifully bound copies of both classic and modern poets:
Homer, Virgil, Dante, and Milton, as well as Byron and
Scott, Tennyson, Longfellow, and Browning. Nor were the
novelists neglected. I saw Fielding, Austen, Dickens,
Thackeray, Eliot, and Trollope, as well as several French
writers: Sand, Balzac, Hugo. There were other less familiar
names: Sidney Lanier, Thomas Holley Chivers, Lord
Bulwer-Lytton, and the *Southern Literary Messenger.*
There were two or three books by George Washington Cable, undoubtedly by virtue of his being a local author, and
several by Mr. Clemens, under his pen name of Mark
Twain. And I was especially struck with the presence of

140   several modern writers who had been the talk of the more
advanced literary set at Yale: Edward Bellamy, Oscar
Wilde, George Bernard Shaw, and Stephen Crane.

"Why, I'd say you've put together a remarkable collection, Mrs. Staunton," I said, quite sincerely. "This is a fine
library, as good as I've seen in a private home."

Mrs. Staunton leaned forward and smiled brilliantly.
"You flatter me, Mr. Cabot. But please, do sit down. And
I wish you would call me Maria. Would you like something
cold to drink? Or perhaps a cup of coffee would be more
to your liking?" She touched a bellpull by the side of the
couch and motioned again for me to sit beside her.

"I think I would like iced tea," I said. The room felt
warm and somewhat stuffy, although a bit of breeze was
stirring the lace curtains. Perhaps I had drunk one lager
more than I should have at luncheon; I thought I would be
more comfortable on my feet than sitting. Then I remembered that I was supposed to be pressing Mrs. Staunton for
information that might help clear Leonard Galloway of the
murder of her brother-in-law. Maintaining a proper distance
might be comfortable, but it would hardly encourage her to
talk freely, and that was what I was here for. I took my
seat beside Maria on the couch.

"I'm simply *delighted* that Mr. Clemens came to visit
us," she said. "And I'm very pleased that he brought you
with him. I know you must be hard-pressed to find any
time when you're not doing things for him. That's why I'm
so glad you were able to come see me today. Tell me, what
is it like to work for such a famous writer as Mark Twain?"

I put on my biggest smile. "Well, I spent most of this
morning running errands, and that gave Mr. Clemens the
freedom to work on his new book. And we spent most of
the midday talking to a man who may be able to contribute
material, but that was mostly Mr. Clemens's doing. He
asked the right questions, and the fellow we were inter-
viewing supplied the answers, and I took notes. One thing
I've learned from watching Mr. Clemens is that the research

behind a book can be the hardest part. Get your facts, and the rest falls into place very naturally.''

''You make it sound very easy,'' she said. ''Though I suspect there's far more to your work than just running errands or taking notes. Mr. Clemens wouldn't need a Yale graduate for his secretary if that's all there were to the position. And don't I recall that you are a writer yourself?'' She leaned forward and smiled in a way that made me feel very important—and at the same time, a bit uncomfortable.

I cleared my throat and answered. ''I've done a few things. Nothing really important yet, though I expect that people will eventually know my name.'' I was surprised at how nonchalantly I said it, never having written anything more challenging than my college examination papers. But I did intend to remedy that deficiency as soon as I had time.

''I expect they *will* know your name,'' she said, her eyes glowing. She turned to face me directly. ''You are very modest, Mr. Cabot, but I see more behind your facade than you may think. Why, I believe you have the soul of an aesthete!''

''Excuse me?'' I wasn't quite certain what to make of her last statement, but it seemed unlikely to lead to the kind of information my employer wanted me to extract from her. I resolutely tried to change the subject. ''I suppose a writer must bring something of himself to his subject, but the choice of a suitable subject is still the most important ingredient. A writer must choose something that arouses the reader's passions—''

I was interrupted by the arrival of a servant, whom Mrs. Staunton told to bring a pitcher of iced tea; then she turned her gaze back to me and said, ''Please go on, Mr. Cabot. I completely agree with what you say about arousing the reader's passions.'' She put her hand on my elbow. ''Don't you think that should be the goal of every worthy artist?''

''Yes,'' I said, ''but to reach that goal, a writer must use the strongest material possible. The man who never ventures out of his drawing room may compose a fine sentence,

142   but the man who has traveled the world and taken part in
great events will have something to *say*. That, I suppose,
is why Mr. Clemens was so proud of having published
General Grant's book. I suspect that your brother, Mr. Holt,
would have stories worth the writing down, as well."

"Poor Reynold!" she said, sitting up straight again. "It
may be just as well he keeps most of his memories to himself. What details he has let slip from time to time . . . I
have come to dread those moments, Mr. Cabot." She shud-
dered, then stood up, walked to the nearby window, and
pulled back the drapes, letting a shaft of light and a pleasant
breeze enter the room. There was an awkward silence as I
groped for something to change the mood. But then my
hostess turned and seemed to shake off the depression that
mention of her brother had brought upon her. She came
back and sat beside me, and smiled sadly.

"If there is some great literary work buried within my
brother's mind, I am afraid it must remain buried. It may
be just as well; I think it would be too terrible to read."

"My apologies for broaching a painful topic," I said. "I
did not realize it was so difficult for him—or for you."

"Do not apologize," said Mrs. Staunton. "Eugenia and
I are very lucky, compared to the unfortunate women
whose brothers and husbands never returned at all. I have
understood just how lucky we are, these past few days, after
Eugenia's husband . . . *died* so suddenly; you must have
heard the story. Reynold has been a pillar of strength for
her, Mr. Cabot. He has taken over the management of her
household and seen her through a most difficult time. I feel
he must have been preserved for just this occasion."

"Perhaps he was," I said, inwardly congratulating myself on having brought the conversation so quickly around
to the subject of the murder. "Was he on good terms with
Mr. Robinson?"

"Well, of course he felt closer to Eugenia than to John,"
said Mrs. Staunton. "That is perfectly natural; blood is
thicker than water, as the saying goes. But John and Rey-

nold were good friends, even before they served together in the War. When they came home, I think that John felt responsible for Reynold, and he tried to give him projects to occupy his interest, helping John with his business. Not that Reynold needed money—he has an independent income, thank goodness. But Reynold was glad to be useful, and it would be unnatural if he didn't feel very grateful to John.''

"Yes, certainly." Her wording left certain things rather ambiguous. If the murdered man had felt it necessary to find work for his war-shocked brother-in-law, I wondered how that same brother-in-law had been qualified to take over the management of the business, as he evidently had. What was Mrs. Staunton leaving unsaid? I forged ahead, trying to elicit information without appearing to be an inquisitor.

"It must have been convenient, as well, that he was familiar with Mr. Robinson's business, when he suddenly had to take it over. What sort of business was Mr. Robinson in? I don't think I've heard."

"Oh, John wasn't *in business,*" she said, with a dismissive wave of her hand. "He would buy and sell land from time to time, or make investments. He owned a good deal of property around town. And of course, the last few months, his plans to run for mayor took up a great deal of his time. I can't say I paid much attention to the details. John always went to Mr. Dupree if he needed advice on business or politics."

"Yes, Mr. Dupree seems a very sound fellow. An old friend of the family, I take it?"

"Yes, he was Reynold's commanding officer in the artillery. He's been ever so much help to us. I think he feels guilty about poor Reynold's being captured, although nobody could hold him responsible for the fortunes of war." She stopped, and then her expression changed. "But here we are going on and on about my family and their troubles. It must be dreadfully boring to you. Tell me about your writing. I'm so interested in what you're working on.'' She laid her hand on mine and looked me in the eye. I started back a little, then made myself relax. If I were too stiff in her presence, she might not be as willing to unburden herself to me.

"Oh, nobody with any feeling could find your stories boring," I said, trying to keep the subject of her family alive; I felt that I had just now come within range of possible leads to the murder, and I wanted to stay on track. The chance might not present itself again. "The fortunes of war, and what they've done to a family like yours, are the very essence of dramatic material. Why, any writer worth his salt would do almost anything to know your family's story in its entirety.'' As I said the words, I realized that they were actually true. Her family history contained the germ of high drama. Perhaps I ought to record her story for Mr. Clemens's book—or possibly (dare I aspire to it?) my own. I found myself warming to the subject, and laid my other hand on top of hers to emphasize the sincerity of my interest.

"Do you really think so?" She moved closer to me, her eyes wide. "I can't imagine that a man of your experience would be so interested in my story. I must say, I find it very flattering."

I was not quite certain the discussion was headed in the direction I wanted. "Why, Mrs. Staunton, flattery was the last thing on my mind . . .'' I began. She lifted her chin, looking directly in my eyes, and suddenly the door burst open with a sound like thunder, and we both jumped. Mrs. Staunton lost her balance and fell against me, her face pressed against my chest. She tried to right herself, but her hands and mine were entangled. I pulled my hands free and reached out to steady her. All this happened in the space of an instant, before I had a chance to wonder what had made the sound that startled us.

Gaining my composure at last, I looked toward the door.

Her husband stood there. His face was contorted with anger, and she leapt to her feet.

"Percival!" she said. "I didn't expect you so soon!"

"I can see that, madam," he said, in a chilling voice. "Go to your room. I will speak to you later."

"But, Percival—it is not what you think. You cannot believe that—"

"*Go!*"

She fled. Meanwhile, I had struggled to my feet, prepared to defend myself. Mr. Staunton might be willing to listen to reason, but so far, I had seen no sign of it. "Mr. Staunton, you are making a mistake," I began.

"No, sir, you are the one who has made a mistake. I don't know whether you have any sense of honor or not. I can't say I've seen evidence of it." He had stepped back into the doorway, blocking it. His face was twisted into a hideous mask, so that I might not have recognized him. Was he drunk? His anger seemed all out of proportion to anything that had happened.

"On the chance that perhaps you are a man of honor, and not just a Yankee coward, I will send my representatives to see you and arrange to settle this matter man to man; dawn tomorrow. I suggest you put your affairs in order, Mr. Cabot. Now, get out of my house, sir!" He stepped aside and pointed at the front door.

"Mr. Staunton, I can explain," I said again. Surely the man was willing to listen to reason. Surely he could not deny the simple truth. "Maria—Mrs. Staunton and I were merely talking. Nothing happened until—"

He cut me off abruptly. "You will have your chance to explain it to my seconds, sir." I could see that he was having great difficulty keeping himself under control. He fairly shouted at me: "I will see you at dawn, or I will hunt you down and shoot you like a dog. *Out of my house!*"

15

As much as I wanted to defend myself against Mr. Staunton's accusations, I realized that it would be unwise to stay in the Staunton house a moment longer. I had been perfectly correct, both in my behavior and in my intentions, at least as far as his wife was concerned. But I knew from my student days what kind of trouble could arise from imaginary insults, especially when a woman was involved. And while the disputes usually died down of their own accord, ending in handshakes and wry jokes, I had also seen them degenerate into shoving and fisticuffs. A fellow in such a truculent mood would but rarely listen to reason, and then only from a close friend. I thought it best to give Mr. Staunton time to reconsider his hasty words. So, with as much dignity as possible, I collected my hat and left the premises.

I was in a bit of a quandary what to do next. Mr. Clemens had said that he would come with Henry Dodds to pick me up after his meeting with Eulalie Echo, but I could hardly stand waiting on the street outside a house from which its enraged master had just ejected me. I walked briskly to the corner so as to take myself out of Staunton's immediate view. Once there, I stopped to think.

The Staunton mansion was not much more than a mile from Eulalie Echo's. I could easily walk the distance. But if Henry Dodds decided to drive Mr. Clemens by a different route than the one I walked, we might easily miss one another, and I did not wish to speculate on the scene that might develop if Mr. Clemens appeared at Staunton's door asking for me, only to learn that I had been sent away. Still, I could think of no better plan. I set off at a brisk pace, backtracking the route Henry had brought me on that afternoon.

After walking a short distance, I found my mood much improved by the serenity of the fine houses of the Garden District. The spacious green lawns and gorgeous flowers shone with brilliant colors in the late afternoon light. Still, I found it hard to forget that Percival Staunton had issued a challenge to meet him at dawn, presumably with weapons at hand. It seemed likely that he would retract it when he had time to hear his wife's side of the story. After all, nothing had really *happened.* It was absurd to think that he would carry through his threat to hunt me down over an affront that existed only in his imagination. And yet, Mr. Staunton might be an Othello, easily aroused to jealousy. Perhaps his wife's past conduct had given him reason, although I had seen nothing untoward in her conduct concerning me. Or maybe he was an untrusting man who kept his wife on a short leash because he knew no other way to handle her. None of these possibilities encouraged me in my belief that his anger would be short-lived. I kept remembering Mr. Clemens saying that the man had supposedly fought two duels.

The walking was easy in the Garden District proper, where the streets were well kept up and the crossings paved. But on the lake side (northwest, by the compass) of Saint Charles Avenue, the condition of the streets deteriorated. The wet climate, with a rain shower almost daily, meant that the unpaved streets had little chance of drying completely, however brightly the sun shone the rest of the time. Often the crossings were merely a few boards laid over the mud, and it was difficult to negotiate them without soiling my shoes. The banquettes were dry but narrow, and I found myself picking my way from one dry spot to an-

148   other. At last I arrived at the corner where we had dropped off Mr. Clemens earlier, and much to my relief, there was Henry Dodds's rig tied in front of the little grocery store. I sighed. Now I was on familiar ground again. Mr. Clemens would tell me what to do.

I stuck my head in the door, and there was Henry himself, sitting with a tin cup of beer in his hand and carrying on an animated conversation with two other Negroes. "Hello, Henry," I said. "No sign of Mr. Clemens, I take it?"

"No sir, no sir," he said, getting to his feet abruptly. Then he looked at me sharply and said, "I thought you was goin' to be down on Chestnut where I left you. Lord a mercy, Mr. Wentworth, you didn't *walk* all the way here, did you?"

I managed a sheepish grin and said, "I'm afraid so. Things didn't work out as expected—or at least, not as I expected. Mr. Staunton put on quite a display of temper."

"I heard he can get mighty hot," said Dodds. Then he winked at me. "But it can't be all that bad, if you had the time to walk away. He was mad enough, you'd've been *runnin'!*" The other men with him laughed, and I joined in.

I was relieved at having found our driver, although I really needed Mr. Clemens. He would be able to advise me on how to handle the unpleasantness with Mr. Staunton; perhaps he would even take it on himself to act as an ambassador to smooth things over. On the other hand, his own temper was mercurial enough that he might not be the best choice for a peacemaker. But he would undoubtedly know how to handle the situation and rectify the misunderstanding between me and Mr. Staunton.

I decided to wait for my employer on the bench outside the store, so as to enjoy the little bit of evening breeze that had sprung up. The street was busy, with horse carts rumbling by and men and women returning from a day's work. Many of them nodded pleasantly when they saw me sitting there. Still, late summer in New Orleans was considerably warmer than I was used to, and I hoped Mr. Clemens wouldn't be much longer. I wondered what news Eulalie Echo had for him. It must be something important to our murder investigation, or she could have simply sent a written message, or even a verbal one.

My mind kept racing back to my interview with Maria Staunton and its unfortunate conclusion. I realized that Mr. Staunton's irrational behavior this afternoon might elevate him to the status of primary suspect. Of course, merely being angry did not make one a murderer, or the whole human race would be at each other's throats. But there was an edge to Staunton's anger, something beyond the normal. Had he been drinking? Or had I somehow walked into the last act of an ongoing drama, innocent of all the motives and passions that drove the characters I was seeing for the first time? In any case, it now seemed to me all too possible that Staunton could have gone over the border into homicidal rage over some imagined injury from his brother-in-law. Hadn't the New Orleans detective told us that a high proportion of murders were domestic affairs?

Of course, I still needed to account for the fact that the victim, Mr. Robinson, had been poisoned. Poison implies planning and premeditation; it is not the weapon of a man in a sudden rage. But perhaps, after the rage had passed, Staunton had nursed some insult or slight over a period of several days or even years, until his anger built to a homicidal level. That might be sufficient explanation. I wondered how easily the poison could be obtained. The poisonous plant had apparently been growing near Leonard Galloway's home, but how much could one deduce from that fact? Was jimsonweed a common garden weed, or was it rare and confined to certain spots? Would someone picking it be noticed and remarked upon? Eulalie Echo might know; a voodoo woman might be expected to have some knowledge of herbs and the like.

The thought of Eulalie Echo reminded me of the curious

150   change in her speech during our interview. At first she had
sounded much the same as the other New Orleans Negroes
we had met. But something Mr. Clemens had said—I tried
to remember what—had made her change from the broad
southern speech patterns to something more refined. Did
she habitually speak to white men in a cruder accent? What
possible advantage was there for her in being believed more
ignorant than she really was? And what made her drop the
pretense while speaking to Mr. Clemens? Perhaps Mr.
Clemens could explain it to me.

I suddenly looked up and realized that the sky was beginning to darken. I pulled out my pocket watch and saw
that it was after eight o'clock. My stomach also reminded
me that it had been some time since our luncheon at Anderson's café. I decided to knock on Eulalie Echo's door;
after all, my question about the poison would justify the
interruption. Even more importantly, Mr. Clemens didn't
know what had happened at the Staunton home; my news
would place the murder investigation in a new perspective,
which Eulalie Echo might also need to know about.

I stood up, shaking my leg, which had begun to fall
asleep. Across the street stood Henry Dodds's horse, plac-
idly chewing on some weeds growing along the banquette.
A group of small girls were skipping rope, accompanying
themselves with an incomprehensible rhythmic chant.

I walked to the voodoo woman's door and raised my
hand to knock, but before I could do so, it opened. I started,
then looked up to see a tall, powerfully built black man.
His face was impassive, his manner quiet but commanding.
The fellow looked somehow familiar, although I couldn't
quite place him. "Mr. Cabot," he said, in a deep voice,
almost without inflection.

"I am here to see Mr. Clemens," I said. "I am his secretary, Mr. Cabot."

"Yes, I know," he said. "Mr. Clemens left a message
for you. He and Eulalie Echo went away—on important
business. He might be back tomorrow, or maybe the next

day. He said to wait for him at Royal Street.''

"What—when—" I stammered, then managed to frame a coherent question. "Where have they gone?"

"Eulalie didn't tell me, so I can't tell you. Don't you worry; he's with Eulalie. She will protect him." I recognized the man now. He was one of the two assistants Mr. Clemens and I had seen in Eulalie's apartment during our visit.

"But it is absolutely vital that I get a message to him," I said. "It is a matter of life and death!" The words sounded overly dramatic even to my ears, and yet I knew them to be true.

The man looked at me with an impassive face; he might as well have been carved from ebony or some other rich, dark wood. "Eulalie deals with life and death all day long. Now she's gone away and taken your master with her. You will have to wait."

"But—" I should have saved my breath. The man closed the door in my face, his message delivered. I stood there speechless, alone in a strange town and in imminent peril, without the faintest notion how to go about extricating myself.

Henry Dodds drove me to the pension on Royal Street, shaking his head over Mr. Clemens's disappearance. "I could have told you 'bout that hoodoo woman, but didn't nobody ask Henry Dodds, no sir. But I 'spect she ain't goin' hurt Mr. Twain. Don't make sense she'd do anything to him." This last may have been meant to reassure me, but it had the opposite effect.

All manner of possibilities ran through my head. How genuine was the message from Mr. Clemens? Had Mr. Clemens really gone away with Eulalie Echo on his own accord? Or might it have been under duress? Was Eulalie Echo working for herself, or was she the puppet of someone else—Tom Anderson, or some of his criminal associates? Mr. Clemens had insisted on my discretion, but he himself had spoken freely about wanting to solve the Robinson murder case and free the colored cook. Could someone have decided to remove a troublemaker from the scene?

And yet it was perfectly in character that Mr. Clemens would go haring off on some errand that caught his interest. Perhaps Eulalie Echo had material for his book or a clue to the Robinson murder case. Had it not been for my own dilemma, I might not have seen anything at all sinister about it. But my own predicament made it essential that I find him.

Of course, it was possible that he needed my help more than I needed his. He might be a prisoner in Eulalie Echo's house, guarded by the very man who had just told me he had gone away. My mind conjured up still wilder possibilities: that Staunton and Anderson were in cahoots, and that the scene with Mrs. Staunton had been staged to frighten me. Or perhaps I was meant to go off hunting for Mr. Clemens, leaving the poor cook to rot in prison. All this and more went through my fevered brain as Henry Dodds's horse clip-clopped his way back toward the French Quarter.

I did not tell Henry Dodds about Mr. Staunton's challenge, as I understood it to be. I would have to try to put it off until Mr. Clemens had returned; was it not the custom for the parties to bring seconds with them? I could think of no one else in the city to whom I might appeal for this service. Mr. Cable I barely knew; and the only other men with whom I had more than a nodding acquaintance were Dodds and Buddy Bolden, neither of whom seemed likely to offer to stand with me on a so-called field of honor. A staunch southerner such as my challenger might indeed take their very presence as a calculated insult. Besides, I was not about to engage in something so barbaric as a duel. No modern, civilized man could take the notion seriously!

I stopped by the room briefly, hoping Mr. Clemens might have sent some message, but there was nothing there. I more or less forced myself to go out and eat. I had very little appetite, but I knew I had best get some nourishment in my body. I returned to the little café just around the corner where Mr. Cable had taken us to meet the police detective, ordered up a bowl of gumbo, and surprised myself by finishing it and ordering a second. I washed it down with two large glasses of iced tea; this was no time to drink anything stronger.

When I returned to the pension, Mme. Bechet met me at the entryway. "There are two gentlemen here to see you," she said, and my heart came to my throat.

They were waiting for me in Mme. Bechet's little front room, which doubled as her office. The two were Reynold Holt, Staunton's brother-in-law, looking as stiff and fierce as he had when first I met him, and another man whom I didn't recognize: a slightly built fellow with a long face and thick side whiskers, whom I guessed to be a little younger than Staunton. Holt and the other man stood when I entered, and Holt said, "Mr. Cabot, may I introduce Marcus Keyes? I suggest we go to someplace private where we can talk."

I took them upstairs, hoping that perhaps Mr. Clemens would have returned, but the dark windows quickly disabused me of that hope. Holt and Keyes declined my offer of a drink, and we took seats around the table in Mr. Clemens's sitting room. There was tension in the air, but Holt came directly to the point of their visit. "Have you appointed seconds, sir? The usual process would be for us to negotiate with them and allow you time to prepare yourself for the morning."

"I'm afraid not," I said. "As you know, I'm a stranger in town; the only person I could really call on is Mr. Clemens, and he has unexpectedly been called away on business. If there were any way to postpone things until his return—"

"That would be most irregular, sir," said Holt. "My principal is very disturbed. He wishes to resolve this matter without delay."

"I understand that he is disturbed," I said, "but I have

not been given the opportunity to explain myself, and I wish that I could. I am certain that once he knows the facts of the matter, Mr. Staunton will recognize that nothing untoward took place. Is there any way you gentlemen could persuade Mr. Staunton to give me a chance to defend myself?'' Mr. Keyes chuckled, and I suddenly realized that my words could be taken differently than I had intended.

"Pardon me, Mr. Cabot, I surely don't wish to make light of your situation," said Keyes, his expression now solemn. "If the whole affair were in my hands, I would be the first to urge a postponement, in hopes that the parties would accept some less drastic means of settling the dispute. But Mr. Staunton is most insistent; I've known him since we were boys, and he can be stubborn. But he might listen to you, were you to appear tomorrow and offer an apology. In fact, in your circumstances, I believe I would do exactly that."

I didn't think I had done anything to apologize for, but I decided not to press the issue. "And if I were to appear and he insisted on fighting? I have to tell you, gentlemen, I have no experience with this kind of thing. For me to stand up against an expert pistol-shot would be suicide."

There was a moment of silence as the two men digested this fact. It was, I realized, in some ways an admission of fear on my part. But it was also a tacit indictment of Mr. Staunton's issuing a challenge to a man untrained in the use of weapons; no gentleman would wish such an unfair advantage.

After a moment, Reynold Holt shook his head. "I am afraid that failure to appear tomorrow would be even riskier. I have seen my brother-in-law in many circumstances over the years, and I would not care to risk his forbearance. He told me in so many words that if you didn't appear, he would come find you and shoot you where you stand. I tried to reason with him; he is risking enough trouble simply by issuing the challenge. Whatever you may have heard, the law in Louisiana does not turn a blind eye on dueling, sir.

"But here are your choices, as I see them. If you are really afraid of Percival Staunton, leave town, and quickly. Take him at his word; if you are in New Orleans, he will hunt you down. But if you are a man of your convictions, and know in your heart that you did no wrong, I urge you to appear on the field. He may have cooled off; he may accept an apology; or he may consider his honor satisfied, and delope."

"Delope? I don't understand the term."

"Fire into the air," said Keyes. "It is a way of satisfying one's honor without shedding blood. If we can convince Percival that the injury was inadvertent, and that you sincerely regret it, it would be a way for him to salvage his pride without returning an injury for an injury. But I agree with Mr. Holt. You must either agree to meet Percival, or you must depart the city as quickly as possible. I know which is the honorable course, but it would be inappropriate for me to advise you how to conduct yourself. Are you certain you don't know anyone to stand up with you?"

"Unless Mr. Clemens returns by morning, no." I thought a moment and decided to press my case with Staunton's seconds. Perhaps they were more inclined to reason than he. It seemed strange that Mr. Holt, who just yesterday evening had been moody and quick to take offense, was today playing the diplomat for his brother-in-law, who yesterday had been the one to pour oil on troubled waters. Now the roles were reversed. I didn't know what to believe, but I had best take advantage of the chance to speak my piece. The two men were becoming restless, and it was clear they were eager to be off.

"Tell Mr. Staunton that his wife will corroborate this, that nothing improper happened today. She and I were in the library for half an hour at the most, with servants coming and going. Other than a few polite generalities, our conversation was entirely about literary matters."

Reynold Holt snorted in derision, and the more formal Mr. Keyes said, "That's not how Mr. Staunton told it to me. He walked into his own library and found his wife in your arms."

The injustice of this accusation enraged me, and yet I had no ready reply. How to refute the accusation? Staunton was obviously ready to believe me guilty; he had evidently come home unexpectedly and upon learning that I was in the library with his wife, had assumed the worst. To tell him that what he took for an embrace was merely the result of an accident—that the surprise of his own sudden entrance had caused his wife to lose her balance and fall against me—would brand me as naive. The two men sat with stony faces waiting for my explanation.

"She stumbled and fell," I said. Holt and Keyes exchanged glances, and I could see that they believed nothing I said. "When Mr. Staunton entered the room, his wife stood to greet him, and she stumbled and fell," I repeated. It did not sound convincing, even to me.

"Come to City Park, on Metarie Ridge," said Holt, standing up. "Our party will be at the entrance near Esplanade Street, half an hour before dawn; I believe that sunrise tomorrow is shortly after five. Come there with your seconds, or alone, if you have no friends. Or, if you are a coward, take the next train north; I don't care. It would simplify things for all concerned."

"I am no coward," I said, coming to my own feet. "Tell Mr. Staunton I will be there, by myself, if necessary. But I have no desire to injure him or anyone else."

"Then let us hope that Mr. Holt and I can persuade Percival to overlook the matter under contention," said Mr. Keyes. "Because I can assure you that, unless he has changed his mind during the last hour, he has every intention of injuring you."

⇒ 16

It should surprise no one to learn that I slept very little that night. I spent a good deal of time mentally turning over the different ways I could imagine the events of the next day turning out, and trying to prepare myself for everything I could foresee. Alas for my mental composure, the majority of my imaginings found me facing Staunton on the field, gun in hand.

I realized I knew almost nothing about the code of honor by which duels were supposedly fought. Vaguely I recalled that the challenged party could dictate choice of weapons, not that I had enough experience with any sort of weapon to make a difference. The code almost certainly did not permit the parties to settle their differences by fisticuffs, which was the only style of fighting in which I might have an advantage over Percy Staunton. I had never fired a pistol in my life, and the closest I had ever come to fencing was in my boyhood, swinging a length of cattail stalk at another boy, similarly armed. My mother had put a stop to it with the admonition "You'll poke each other's eyes out."

It was tempting to believe that in the clear light of dawn, when I gave my word as a gentleman that nothing had happened between me and Mrs. Staunton, and then apologized, that Mr. Staunton would give up his grudge. I could imagine myself in months to come, telling my old friends about my "duel" in New Orleans, and laughing at it all. Yet I could still see the livid face of Percival Staunton, ordering me from his house. My only real hope was that his seconds were correct in their belief that they could talk him out of it.

I did spend the better part of an hour writing to my parents. My conscience reminded me that my letters had been getting shorter and shorter as the distance from home increased, and I made up for it with a long letter. On the final page, I told them of the possibility that tomorrow might be my last day, and tried to say such things as I thought might be comforting. I wrote another note to Mr. Clemens, informing him of the events of the day, of my intimations concerning Staunton's possible guilt in the murder of his brother-in-law, Robinson, and other information I thought might be of use to him in following up the case. In the event of my death, I asked him to forward my letter to my parents. Should I survive, I would send it myself, sans the final page.

I thought at first of making out a will, but then realized that in the absence of witnesses it would be without force. In any case, I had little enough property to be concerned with—really, little more than my clothes and the small amount of money I had saved. At last, I simply added a line to my note to Mr. Clemens, asking him to forward my personal effects to my parents. I had a moment of regret that there was so little to pass along, and no one besides my parents to pass it to. I felt I should have made more of an impression on the world than I had so far. But it was a bit too late in the day for such self-recrimination; should I survive the morning, it would be time enough to consider such things.

I did at last extinguish the light and try to sleep. For the first time in longer than I could remember, I knelt by my bedside and said my prayers. I had not prayed more sincerely since I was a little boy, yet I felt like a hypocrite. Surely God would see through my sudden return to piety. I could only pray that he would not hold me guilty for my falling away from regular prayer. But raised as I was in the heart of New England, I had been given plentiful reminders of the fate of sinners in the hands of an angry God, and only occasional hints of divine mercy. Still, I felt that if I were destined to meet my maker the next morning, I would be remiss not to renew my acquaintance with him. I prayed a long while.

I closed my eyes for a very short time; when I opened them again, my watch told me it was nearly four o'clock. I splashed cold water on my face and dressed hurriedly. I was surprised to find myself wondering about the proper dress for such an occasion; was it customary to appear in one's best clothes, or would that be taken as a sign of arrogance? At last I laughed at myself and put on my ordinary daytime clothes. I was going to the meeting place not to fight a man, but to talk him out of fighting. I could not allow myself to be drawn into the tawdry drama of dueling, with all its outmoded conventions.

The morning was pleasantly cool and slightly misty in our location a few short blocks from the river. I found a café open and gulped down a cup of hot black coffee. I had heard somewhere that it was best to avoid eating just before a duel, but I felt I needed at least a cup of coffee to have my wits at their sharpest—besides which, I did not intend to fight anyone. There were a couple of carriage drivers waiting by the river side of Jackson Square. I had a moment of regret that Henry Dodds was not one of them; instead, my driver was a short, chubby fellow with a sleepy-looking round face, who was not in the mood for talking. And once we were on the road, neither was I. I had made up my mind what I was going to do, and there was no reason to worry about anything else.

There were four men waiting in the shadows of the trees at the entrance to City Park. My driver looked over the scene and gave me a curious glance, but took his fare and drove away. I would worry about getting home when it was time. I stepped toward the waiting group, saying, "Gentlemen, I am here."

"Are you alone, sir? It is customary to bring seconds to protect your interests." I recognized the voice, full of concern, as that of Dr. Soupape, and stepped closer to the trees. I could see the other men with him, now: Reynold Holt, Marcus Keyes, and Percival Staunton.

Now I needed to put my plan, such as it was, in action. "I cannot assemble seconds on so short notice; in any case, I have not come to fight." I stepped forward again, holding my hands out, to show that I had come unarmed. I knew that I would not have been expected to bring my own weapon to a duel, but the gesture seemed important.

"Then have you come to apologize?" Reynold Holt stepped forward, limping slightly.

"If Mr. Staunton will accept it, yes," I said. Deep inside, I knew I had done nothing to warrant an apology; but my purpose was not to preserve some imagined purity of character, but to assuage Mr. Staunton's anger. As yet, he had said nothing, and so I could not gauge his mood. The success of my strategy depended entirely on whether he was willing to forgive an injury that existed only in his imagination.

"Mr. Cabot, I am glad to hear you say that," said Dr. Soupape. "I have seen more than my share of gunplay and killing, and would as soon live out my life without seeing any more." He turned to face my challenger. "Percy, you see. Mr. Cabot wishes to apologize."

Staunton stepped forward, slowly, not quite steady on his feet. "He wishes to evade the consequences of his actions," he said in a dreadful voice. "I believe him to be a coward, and nothing more."

"If he were a coward, he would not have come at all," said Marcus Keyes, laying a hand on Staunton's arm. "Hear him out, Percy. There's no reason to go through with the duel."

Staunton glared at him. "That is for me to decide. I am

the injured party, and I have a right to satisfaction. Don't try to force me into anything, gentlemen. My honor has been tarnished, and it will take more than a mealy-mouthed apology from a yellow-bellied Yankee to restore it to its proper luster.''

The devil take these Southerners and their honor, I thought, and then felt ashamed of myself. I could not afford to let my anger get the better of me. I knew myself to be no coward, whatever Staunton's benighted notions on the topic. I would make my apology and hope it was sufficient.

"Mr. Staunton, I have reflected on the events of yesterday and feel that I owe you an apology," I began. "While I must insist that no impropriety took place, either on my part or on that of Mrs. Staunton, I recognize that the appearance of improper conduct is also to be avoided, and I sincerely regret having in any way failed to maintain proper decorum in my visit to your house. What you saw was not what you believe it to be; I am sure that your wife will tell you the truth of the matter. But I am genuinely sorry for having caused you grief.''

All the time I spoke, I kept my most sober expression, and looked him frankly in the face, trying to read his response. But the waxing light revealed his face to be even more contorted and masklike in its anger than I remembered it from our confrontation in his library. Was the man ill? He seemed far different from the host I had seen at the dinner table only two nights before. As I finished speaking, I held out my hand and said, "I hope we can be on friendly terms again. I have never intended you any injury or insult, and I don't want to begin now.''

Staunton looked down at the proffered hand, an unreadable expression on his face. The corner of his mouth gave a twitch, and then he pointed his finger directly at me. "You lie, sir!" He practically shrieked the sentence, and I involuntarily fell back a step as he continued. "You think you can talk your way out of the trouble you have stirred up, but it will not be so easy as that. I'll listen to no more lies. My wife had a mouthful of them to feed me, too! Either stand up to me today, or take your cowardly hide out of my sight. But I promise you, sir, if you walk away without giving me satisfaction this morning, I will hunt you down wherever you stay within New Orleans." He turned on his heel and walked away, followed closely by Reynold Holt. I stared at him, stunned by his intransigence. The shadows in the park were lightening; dawn was almost here.

"My God, what does the man want?" whispered Dr. Soupape, his face pale. He turned to me. "Mr. Cabot, Percy is not at all himself today. I cannot say what he is likely to do. If he were to listen to me, he would be at home under medical supervision. Nor is it my place to advise you; but if it were, I would tell you to take his threats very seriously. I fear that he *will* attempt to carry out his promise to hunt you down. I know of a place across the river where you can stay, if you want. He will not look for you there."

Marcus Keyes had stayed behind with us, and now he stepped close, a strained look on his face. He cleared his throat and spoke hesitantly. "It may not be my place to say so, Mr. Cabot, but I think your best play right now is to offer to stand up to Percy. He's trying to bluff you, and I think if you call him, he'll fold."

"Fold? I'm not sure I follow you."

Keyes glanced over at Staunton and Holt huddled together, a little distance away, then said in a low voice, "I think Percy means to give you a good scare, but not to hurt you. I don't see a killing offense here, to be honest, and I've told him so. He might just try to wing you, but he can't do that without risking worse. I don't think his hand is steady enough. If he's smart, he'll delope and declare himself satisfied."

"I wish I knew that for certain," I said. "It is my life on the line, you know."

"Understood," said Keyes. "But I have only your word that you're not a crack shot, and that you hold no grudge against my friend. I'm bending the code of honor a good bit to tell you this. After all, you're supposed to have your own seconds to look after your interests. If you stand up, after what I've told you, and put a bullet through Percy's heart, I've as good as killed him myself. Do you follow me?'' His face was serious, and his voice insistent.

"Yes, I do follow you," I said. "Thank you for your advice. I will give it careful consideration.'' We stood there a few moments longer, none of us sure what to do next. The light grew, and a few birds began to sing. It struck me with sudden force that these might be the last birds I would ever hear singing. Until that moment, it had not occurred to me that I might really die.

"Let me try to talk to Percy," said the doctor. "My gray hairs may have some force with him still. I would dearly wish to see this day end with no shots fired.''

"As would I," I said. "Do your best." He and Keyes walked over and joined the other two men, and I heard them speaking in low voices, although I could not make out what they said. I was left to consider what my choices might be. Was Staunton serious in his threats? Could I safely elude him? I began to think about slipping off while Staunton was distracted, taking advantage of the dark underbrush to make my escape. But if I did so, how would I carry on my work with Mr. Clemens, if I were constantly looking over my shoulder for an assassin? And where was Mr. Clemens? For all I knew, he was back on Royal Street, reading my note to him at this very moment. And if not, where was he? There were too many imponderables for me to make a clean decision. If only Staunton would back down!

I must have stood there for ten minutes, listening to the voices, at first barely audible, then gradually swelling in volume. I began to make out snatches of the talk, first one, then another of them trying to persuade Staunton to call off the duel. There was no doubt in my mind that all three men were desperately trying to prevent the confrontation. At last I heard the doctor tell Staunton he feared for his health,

164 and Staunton roared out, "I am here for honor, not for
health, damn you!" He turned and pointed at me. "Are
you ready to stand, or will you run like a Yankee dog?"

I was about to reply when a large closed carriage came
rattling up the road at high speed. We all drew back somewhat, wondering who could be rushing to join us, for there
seemed no other reason for anyone to be approaching this
isolated spot so early in the morning. I thought for a moment that it might be Mr. Clemens, riding to the rescue.
But then the carriage stopped, and a slim woman's form,
dressed in black, descended from it. "Percival!" she cried,
and rushed toward him. It was Mrs. Eugenia Robinson, his
widowed sister-in-law.

"Eugenia! You should not be here," said Mr. Holt, obviously surprised at his sister's dramatic arrival. But she
brushed past him and confronted Mr. Staunton.

"It is you—*all* of you—who should not be here," she
said in a firm voice. "I have spoken to Maria. She has done
nothing to be ashamed of. This *boy* has done nothing." She
pointed at me.

"Words are for women, deeds for men," said Mr. Staunton in a toneless voice. The light was bright enough by
now for me to see his face clearly, and the sight was not
reassuring. His mouth wore a cruel smirk, and there was
something akin to madness in his eyes. "You have done
enough to make my life miserable," he said to her.

Mrs. Robinson threw her arms around him with a cry of
"No!" and for a moment I thought she might yet prevail.
But he steeled himself against her, and pushed her into her
brother's arms.

"Get out of the way and let a *man* defend your sister's
honor," he snarled. "Reynold, take your sister to her carriage and order the driver to take her home. She does not
belong here." Holt looked undecided for a second, but then
he stepped forward and grasped his sister firmly by the arm.
She tried to pull away, but was no match for her older
brother's strength.

"Percival!" cried Eugenia Robinson. "Go home to Maria while you still can. Better to die in your own bed than here on the cold ground!" Something in her choice of words disturbed me. Did she really believe that I would kill her brother-in-law?

But Staunton ignored her, staring into the distance as Mrs. Robinson was borne away. Then he turned and pointed directly at me. "Sir, will you stand up to me?"

So it had come down to two choices: I could either stand or flee.

There would be nothing cowardly about walking away from this encounter. The man was a practiced duelist, and I had never fired a pistol in my life. More to the point, I rejected the entire notion of settling points of honor by resort to weapons; no civilized man could see it as anything but a barbaric survival from an ignorant past age. Better to walk away without regrets, and leave him to brag about his victory to those who cared about such things. It was the sensible thing to do, and I longed to do it.

But if I fled the city, I left Mr. Clemens to pursue the murder case alone. Moreover, he needed me to run errands, to oversee his writing and lecturing schedules, and to serve as a buffer between him and the ordinary chores of daily existence. I would be leaving my employer without help at a time when he most needed it. And without my help, he would almost certainly have to abandon the search for John Robinson's murderer, leaving poor Leonard Galloway to face the hangman for a crime I was now certain he did not commit. I could not allow that to happen.

The risk was that I would receive a serious, perhaps fatal, wound by standing up to Staunton. His seconds thought he might deliberately shoot to miss me. And his evident illness might degrade his marksmanship sufficiently to make him miss, even if he were attempting to hit me. But the risk remained; no game played with live ammunition was without danger.

All this went through my mind in the space of perhaps

ten seconds. I stood looking at my opponent, more and more convinced that his mind had somehow snapped. I was gambling with my life to face him with a weapon in his hand. He seemed incapable even of standing entirely still; he would occasionally twitch, or lurch unexpectedly as if to catch his balance. It would be suicide to accept the\challenge. And yet . . .

"Bring out the pistols," I said. "We will settle this today."

Dr. Soupape heaved a great sigh, and looked at me with an expression I hope never to see turned my way again. "First let us take a little walk to a more private place," he said. We followed him farther into the park, along a path that might have been charming had I been in the mood for scenery, to a majestic grove of oak trees. There was a broad open space here, and the peaceful setting was in sharp contrast to the violent purpose to which we were about to put it.

Dr. Soupape stopped and gestured to Keyes, who brought forth a case that he opened to reveal two pistols. "They are a matched pair," said the doctor. "Are you familiar with firearms?"

"No," I admitted.

He shook his head. "I thought as much. Take either one, then. Each has one bullet; I loaded them myself. Pull the trigger and it will fire." I chose the one nearest to me, and watched Staunton take the other. He opened the mechanism, checked that it was loaded, and closed it with a loud metallic sound. He nodded at me, but I could not fathom his thoughts. He handed the pistol to Reynold Holt, who had returned, and Keyes said to me, "Take off your jacket. I'll hold the gun."

"Why?" I asked, handing him the pistol. I slipped out of my jacket and laid it on the grass, feeling the cool morning air for the first time.

"A bullet that hits a button makes a worse wound," he

said, handing me back the pistol, butt first. "No point in taking the chance."

Staunton had his jacket off, as well, and I noticed for the first time that he was wearing a silk shirt that buttoned in back. Dr. Soupape took us to a level spot of ground and measured off ten paces. "Mr. Cabot, you have the choice of ends." *Just like a football game,* I thought. I saw no advantage to either end, and chose the one nearest to the place where we had entered the oak grove. Staunton went to the other, and Dr. Soupape took up a position midway between us, but out of the line of fire. "Are you ready, gentlemen?" he asked.

"I suppose so," I said, and Staunton said, "Yes."

"Is there no way to prevail upon you not to continue?" said the doctor, peering at Mr. Staunton. "Surely honor has been satisfied by Mr. Cabot's willingness to appear."

Staunton was unmoved. "I've heard enough jabber. Get on with it, Alphonse."

Dr. Soupape then turned to me. "Mr. Cabot, you have many years ahead of you. Do not risk them here today. There is nothing to prove by your presence."

"I hear you and appreciate your concern, Doctor," I said. It was all I could do to hold my ground, quite frankly. "But I fear I'm out of choices. Please continue."

"Very well, gentlemen. May the good Lord have mercy upon us all." He took the white handkerchief from his breast pocket and said, "I will drop the handkerchief on the count of three. You may then take aim and fire at will."

Some thirty feet away stood Staunton, his white shirt clearly visible against the bushes behind. I thought I saw him wobble where he stood; he appeared to be seriously ill, I thought. His illness must have affected his mind; there was no other rational explanation for his insistence on actually dueling. "One," said the doctor.

I lifted the pistol and looked at it. I hadn't realized they were quite so heavy. It would be difficult to hold steady, especially for a novice. I hoped it would be even more

difficult for a man who was apparently having trouble staying on his feet. ''Two.'' A bird whistled, somewhere off to
the left.

I let the pistol fall to my side again. I supposed I still
had time to turn and run, if I were so inclined. Staunton
gave a lurch to the left, then caught himself upright, glaring
at me the entire time. The doctor hesitated until Staunton
was fairly on his feet again, then he said, ''Three,'' and
dropped the handkerchief.

I raised my pistol, and saw Staunton bring his up at the
same time—slowly and confidently, like a man who had
done this a hundred times. I deliberately lifted the pistol
straight into the air and fired upward. The report was louder
than I had expected, and the kick of the gun nearly tore it
from my hand. I had a sudden flash of horror, wondering
where the bullet would land. The harsh smell of gunpowder
assaulted my nose, as I lowered the pistol to my side again.

Staunton still had not fired. He stood pointing the pistol
directly at me; I could see the hole in the muzzle quite
clearly. I thought about a hole that size suddenly appearing
in my chest, and a chill went up my spine. Still he did not
fire. Was he testing my courage, seeing how long I could
look death in the eye without breaking and running? Somewhere behind me I heard a voice shouting something, and
running footsteps, but I dared not turn and look. Staunton's
arm wavered, and the muzzle lost its aim. He lifted his
head, then lowered it again to sight the gun at me. This
time his arm was steady. He held a direct bead on my heart
for a long count of three, his eyes boring into mine. Suddenly, he lurched, caught himself, tried to bring the gun on
target again, and then collapsed like a rag doll.

17

There was an almost imperceptible pause as Staunton fell to the ground, as if time were somehow frozen, and then everything seemed to happen at once. Dr. Soupape and Marcus Keyes rushed to the fallen man's side, while Reynold Holt stood as if thunderstruck, before starting over to join them. I bent to pick up my discarded coat, then began to walk toward the other end of the field to see if there were any way to help my stricken opponent, when a loud voice directly behind me said, "Drop the gun, mister. And put your hands in the air!"

I let the empty pistol fall from my hand and raised my arms above my head. I was about to turn to see who had spoken, but the voice said, "Stay where you are!" and reinforced the point by shoving a hard blunt object into the small of my back. It was all I could do not to fall forward, but I managed to keep my feet. A hand reached out and picked up the pistol, and then a big man in a blue uniform and a tall, rounded helmet came in front of me. A policeman.

"All right," he said, shaking his billy club in my face. He was clean shaven and broad shouldered; he had a bulbous nose, and bushy eyebrows over inquisitive blue eyes. "You're under arrest for dueling and for discharging a firearm in public. And you'd better hope you haven't killed that poor fellow there, or it'll be a murder charge. You can

170 bet the house on it, mister.'' He slipped the pistol into his pocket.

''I don't know what's wrong with him, but I didn't shoot him,'' I protested. I wasn't even certain of that; could my shot into the air have come down, by some evil stroke of fortune, and hit the very man I was so anxious not to harm? It was an absurd notion, yet everything else seemed to have gone wrong this morning. But Staunton had been visibly ill before I fired; surely that was what had felled him, not the pistol shot.

Still holding my hands up, I walked with the policeman to the group huddled over Percival Staunton. Staunton lay flat on his back, his face a dreadful ashen hue. He was breathing very shallowly, and I thought I saw an occasional involuntary movement of his limbs. Dr. Soupape had his hand to Staunton's wrist, counting his pulse. ''What's going on here?'' said the policeman. ''Is the fellow alive or dead?''

Dr. Soupape looked up with an irritated expression, then nodded when he saw the policeman. ''I am a physician, officer. This man is in very serious condition. I cannot guarantee his life if he is not immediately hospitalized.''

The policeman leaned forward, curiosity apparent on his face. ''Where's the wound? I don't see any blood.''

''There's no blood because there's no wound,'' said the doctor. He rose to his feet, looking very weary. ''I have every reason to believe that this man has been poisoned.''

''That settles it, then,'' said the officer. He pointed to Reynold Holt and Marcus Keyes. ''You two fellows pick him up and bring him along. We'll see that he gets to a hospital directly.

''And you!'' He whirled around to face me and slapped his billy club into his hand. ''Don't think I've forgotten you! You're under arrest for dueling and firing a gun illegally. And don't try any funny business, like running away when you think I'm not looking. You may have missed your man, but I don't miss.

"And when we've got this fellow to the hospital, you're all coming down to the station with me, and we'll let the captain sort this mess out. I don't know how this fellow managed to get himself poisoned, but I know a duel when I see one. Just in case you jaspers didn't know it, you've broken about a dozen laws just by being here with weapons drawn. And your worst mistake was doing it on Terence McLaughlin's beat!"

The policeman was remarkably efficient, all things considered. While Holt and Keyes struggled with Percival Staunton, who was little more than a dead weight, the officer commandeered a wagon, and with help from the doctor, they managed to lay Staunton on the wagon bed. Dr. Soupape threw his coat over Staunton and shook his head gravely. Then all of us climbed aboard, and the driver started up his mules. As we jarred our way along the ill-paved streets, I found it hard to take my eyes off the pathetic figure lying between us, occasionally gasping for breath. Could Dr. Soupape be right? Had Percival Staunton fallen victim to poison, just as his brother-in-law Robinson had?

Then it struck me. If Staunton and Robinson were poisoned in the same way, then Leonard Galloway, the cook, ought to be let out of prison. For while the police may have found both motive and opportunity for him to murder Robinson, there was no way a man stuck in the depths of Parish Prison could have poisoned Staunton. It was the best possible argument for setting Leonard free at once!

Somehow, that made the prospect of my own going to jail seem far less oppressive. In fact, once I got over Percival Staunton's sudden collapse, a great flood of relief came over my mind. The duel was over, and I had escaped—not only alive, but unhurt! As for being arrested, I was sure the matter could be settled quickly. Perhaps a small fine for firing the weapon in a public place—a very sensible law. But that would hardly take the luster off what was beginning to look like a beautiful day. I hoped poor Staunton would live to see it.

When we reached the hospital, Dr. Soupape wanted to stay with Staunton. The policeman had other ideas. "The doctors here will do as much for him as you could," he said. "As for you, you're either an accomplice or a witness, and you're coming with me to the station until I find out which."

Dr. Soupape argued long and hard, and Reynold Holt urged the policeman to let the victim's family doctor stay with him, but the officer was adamant, and had all the telling arguments on his side. At last, he permitted the doctor to pass on his own diagnosis and suggestions to the hospital staff; then we all climbed into the police wagon that had come to the hospital for us, and took seats on hard wooden benches for the short, bumpy ride to the nearby police station. In the dim light inside the Black Maria, Dr. Soupape looked drained. He kept shaking his head and saying, "I should have spotted the symptoms. Percival might have been saved if I'd done something sooner."

"He's not dead yet," said Marcus Keyes, laying a hand on Dr. Soupape's shoulder. "Don't give him up just yet, Doctor. They may be able to pull him through."

"Don't bet on it," said Reynold Holt in a loud voice. "If it's the same stuff that killed John, he's done for. What I'd like to know is how this damn Yankee managed to give it to him."

"What?" I said, thoroughly confused. "Why on Earth would I have poisoned Mr. Staunton?"

"To avoid having to fight him," said Holt, fixing me with an icy glare. "You knew you couldn't outshoot Percy. You couldn't hide anywhere in New Orleans where he wouldn't find you, so you poisoned him. And damn me if I won't see you hang for it." Even in the dim wagon, I could see that he shook with fury.

"Leave him alone, Reynold," said Dr. Soupape, lifting a hand in warning. "You're grasping at straws. Better we should all pray for Percival's safe recovery. He'll need all the help we can give him. And blaming the innocent helps nobody.''

"You be quiet back there," came a policeman's voice from the driver's seat. "Any more disturbance and we'll find some more charges to bring against you."

"I'll be on my front porch sipping a julep before that impertinent monkey's shift is over," muttered Reynold Holt, but he said no more.

The driver finally brought his horses to a stop, and the doors of the van opened to let us out in front of an ugly brick building, evidently the police station. The officers herded us inside, where a uniformed police captain sat behind a desk. "Well, what do we have here?" he said, peering at us over a pair of spectacles. "A fine-looking group you've brought us, McLaughlin. What are the charges?"

"Suspicion of dueling, Captain. I was patrolling near City Park when I heard a pistol shot from the direction of the oaks. I went to investigate, and found these four, with another man down on the ground. The tall fellow there was holding this." He took my pistol out of his pocket and put it on the captain's desk. "And this one was on the ground near the fellow who was down."

The captain picked up my pistol, sniffed it, then opened the mechanism and removed the empty cartridge. "One shot fired, and recently. Was the other party seriously wounded?" He looked up at Officer McLaughlin.

"Well, there's the queer part," said the arresting officer, rubbing his chin. "There wasn't a scratch on him. The old fellow there claims he's a doctor, and he thought the man had been poisoned. We took the victim to Touro Infirmary. They'll keep us informed of his condition."

The captain had meanwhile inspected Staunton's pistol. "This one hasn't been fired. Are you sure it was a duel, McLaughlin?"

McLaughlin held his hands apart, as if telling about a fish he'd caught. "Two men at the Oaks, about ten paces

174 apart, both armed, and a bunch of others around to watch—
and there was a white handkerchief on the ground about
halfway between them.'' He dug in his pocket again and
pulled out Dr. Soupape's handkerchief, placing it on the
desk. ''There must have been a couple of other seconds,
but I guess they flew the coop when the fellow went down,
since this is all I caught. It couldn't have been more than
a minute or two between when I heard the shot and when
I got to the scene.''

''It sounds mighty like a duel to me,'' agreed the captain.
''Any other witnesses?'' He motioned to a clerk, who had
been working at a nearby desk and unashamedly eaves-
dropping. The clerk eagerly came over to the captain's
desk, bringing a pad of notepaper and a pencil.

''No, sir,'' said McLaughlin. ''We might be able to find
somebody else who heard the gunshot, if we need to prove
it.''

''We'll deal with that if we need to,'' said the captain.
He turned to us. ''What do you men have to say for your-
selves?''

''This is all a mistake, officer,'' said Dr. Soupape. ''I am
Dr. Alphonse Soupape, a lifelong resident of Orleans Parish
and a veteran of the War. I have a practice on Saint Charles
Avenue, in the Garden District. I and my friends are respectable citizens, not common rowdies. I need to return to
the hospital to see to the welfare of my patient, the gentleman who collapsed in the park.''

The captain turned a long-suffering look on the doctor.
''Gee, Doc, I'd never have known I was dealing with quality. Of course, somebody of your class would never be out
by the Oaks with drawn pistols, would they now? And even
if they were, the poor benighted police shouldn't interfere
with rich folks having a little fun, should they?''

He paused, took a deep breath, and then shouted. ''I
don't give a damn who you people are! You've broken at
least one law in my jurisdiction, and maybe you've broken
a whole bunch of 'em, and I'm going to do the job the city

pays me for. Do you have anything to say besides how important you are and where you live? Because otherwise, I'll lock you right up without any more hot air.''

''I will not have any statement until I see my lawyer,'' said Marcus Keyes. ''I hereby request the use of a telephone to inform him of my whereabouts.''

''You'll have that opportunity,'' said the captain. ''What about the rest of you?''

''I also wish to see my attorney,'' said Reynold Holt, turning his hostile stare toward the clerk, and Dr. Soupape voiced the same request.

''I am a stranger in town, so I don't have a local attorney,'' I said. ''If I can send a message to my employer, he will arrange for representation.''

The captain sighed, then opened a large ledgerlike book on the counter beside him. ''Very well. I'm going to book the tall fellow here on charges of dueling, discharging a firearm in public, and attempted murder. The rest of you— and that fellow in the hospital, too—are charged with dueling and accessory before the fact to attempted murder. The judge may think of a few other charges, but these will be enough to put you on ice for a while. I'll need your names and addresses, and then you'll have your chance to send for your lawyers.''

He reached for a pen, then looked at us over the top of his spectacles. ''And you'd best hope that fellow in the hospital gets well, or we'll be looking at murder charges for the lot of you.'' He turned to the clerk. ''Okay, Burghardt, book 'em!'' And he walked away and began talking with another officer in a corner of the room. I had the feeling he had dismissed us as no longer worth his attention.

After giving our names and addresses—I listed the Royal Street pension where I was staying with Mr. Clemens—we handed over our valuables for safekeeping, including our watches, wallets, jewelry, and (to my surprise) our belts. Then we were taken to a large cell in back, where we were locked in with half a dozen other prisoners. Two of them were snoring loudly, most likely sleeping off the drink that had gotten them arrested to begin with. Another kept up a continual blasphemous rant against the police, the mayor, the government, and various other institutions he claimed were unjustly persecuting him. The rest sat sullenly or paced back and forth.

The cell was perhaps fifteen to twenty feet, with hard benches bolted to the back and side walls, and a sturdy iron grating on the front. There was no effort wasted on providing amenities for the prisoners; privacy and comfort were concepts that had never crossed the minds of the designers of the place. Neither, apparently had cleanliness. In the dim light filtering in through a heavily barred window, I could see insects scurrying across the floor, and my nose told me all I needed to know of the sanitary facilities.

There was a moment's silence as we were locked in, and the other prisoners sized us up; then, the ones who had bothered to look at all turned back to their previous concerns. As we were a group, and respectably dressed, we were somewhat set apart from the usual jailhouse rabble. Once the door had shut behind us, Dr. Soupape, Reynold Holt, and Marcus Keyes began to confer about what they would do next. "Are we all going to use Dupree?" asked Keyes. "I reckon it'll be quicker than sending for three different lawyers."

"Yes, get Gordon, by all means," said Dr. Soupape. "I have to get out quickly, so I can go back to Touro and do whatever I can for poor Percy. I wish to heaven we'd managed to talk him out of the duel, but now I understand why he wouldn't listen to reason. It was the poison, of course. It attacks the mind first."

"I'm afraid the poison would have gotten him whether he'd come out today or not," said Keyes. "But I'll agree he wasn't acting like himself, not even last night when he asked me to second him. I put it down to the distress of finding his wife with somebody else. That can unsettle the strongest mind, I fear.''

"Don't blame yourself, Alphonse," said Reynold Holt. "Gordon will get us out, and then you'll do what you can for Percy. He's in good hands at Touro, but I'd be happier knowing you were looking after him, as well. And if he recovers, maybe we can figure out how this fellow gave him the poison." He glared at me.

"I did not poison Mr. Staunton!" I protested. "You saw me fire my gun into the air; if I'd wanted to kill him, would I have done that?"

"Jesus, will you shut up and let a fellow sleep?" moaned one of the drunks on the nearby bench. He sat up and looked at us, his pathetic condition evident on his face, then rolled over to face the wall.

"Mr. Cabot has a point," said the doctor, lowering his voice. "If he'd poisoned Percy to get out of the duel, why would he show up to risk being shot?"

"To divert suspicion," said Holt. "He deloped to make us all believe he bore no grudge, knowing all the time that the poison would destroy Percy's aim. You saw how much trouble he had holding the gun straight." They had closed into a small circle, leaving me a few feet away and definitely on the outside. They spoke quietly, but made no particular effort to conceal what they were saying from me or anyone else in the cell.

"A hell of a risk to take in any event," said Keyes. I thought he was going to say more, but an officer came to the cell door and called out, "All right, quiet down in there." The other prisoners all turned to look at him; even one of the drunks sat up to see what was happening. When he had our attention, he pointed at our group. "You, the duelists. Now's your chance to call your lawyers. One at a time. Who's first?"

"You make the call, Alphonse," said Reynold Holt.

178   ''Gordon should be up and about by now. Maybe he can get us out in time for luncheon.''

''He'd better be a mighty good shyster if you expect him to do that,'' said the policeman in an ominous voice. ''We just heard from Touro. That fellow you were with this morning died. You boys are in for murder charges, now.''

18

Murder charges or no, within an hour of Dr. Soupape's call, Gordon Dupree had arrived at the police station with a writ of habeas corpus, securing the release of Reynold Holt, Marcus Keyes, and Dr. Alphonse Soupape. He had obtained their release on their own recognizance.

"I'm sorry I couldn't do the same service for you, Mr. Cabot," he said, much to my surprise; I had no reason to expect him to have tried. "I did my best," he continued, "but Judge Fogarty wouldn't hear of it—not just on my word, at least. To put it baldly, you are a transient, without connections in the community, and you don't own any property. The judge sees you as a poor risk—quite understandably, I'm afraid, especially with a possible capital charge against you. He wouldn't even name a figure for bail, although he would probably change his mind if the inquest turns up a "natural causes" verdict. Failing that, Mr. Clemens might still be able to get you bail, though, having known you longer and being a man of some reputation in the community. Have you called him yet?"

"There's not a phone where we're staying; I left him a note this morning, saying where I was going, but he wouldn't think to look for me here."

Dupree waved a hand as if to dismiss the notion of difficulties. "Write a note to him. I'll make certain that he gets it." He opened his briefcase and gave me a sheet of paper and a pencil, which I gratefully accepted.

I wrote a brief note saying where I was—I had to ask Mr. Dupree for the exact address—then folded the paper and handed it to him. "I appreciate your helping me send this, although I fear I don't know exactly where Mr. Clemens is; he left town unexpectedly, and asked me to wait for him at our pension. Unfortunately, he didn't tell me where he was going."

"I see," said Dupree, scratching the back of his head. "I'm afraid that doesn't bode well for a quick release. I can't see how anyone but Mr. Clemens could get you out except on bail. I assume you don't have access to ready money."

"Nothing really, except the pocket change the police took from me. What little I've saved is in a bank back in Connecticut; I send it to my mother, and she deposits it for me. I'd hate to have to draw on it, although if Mr. Clemens doesn't return quickly I may be forced to. But if you'll just get the note to Mme. Bechet's pension on Royal Street, just above Ursulines, I'd be much obliged," I said. I shook hands with him and with Dr. Soupape, and then they left, and the jail door closed behind me.

Some of the other denizens of the cell had been released by now, as well. The drunks were taken out, as I learned, to appear before a magistrate and pay a small fine; they did not return. And a lawyer came with walking papers for two of the others, rough-looking men who'd sat together speaking quietly in what I thought was probably Italian. "What happens now?" I asked one of the policemen who came for the released prisoners.

"You'll be took before the judge this afternoon, unless somebody can get you sprung. He'll decide whether to hold you pending the inquest. If he does, they'll probably run you over to Parish Prison until they have a verdict from the coroner. If the verdict is homicide, they hold you for trial."

"Why should I be held for murder?" I said, annoyed that I had apparently been chosen as the obvious suspect.

"Even if Staunton *was* poisoned, there's no reason to think I'm the one who killed him. I didn't see him more than three times in my entire life. Why would I have anything against him?"

The officer shrugged. "Ask the judge, mister. I lock 'em up when they tell me to, and let 'em loose when they tell me to. *Why* don't have nothing to do with it." He turned and walked back to the door leading out of the cell area to the front room. He opened the door, then turned and called to me over his shoulder, "But if I was you, I'd get me a good lawyer," before going through the door and shutting it firmly behind him.

Much of the day passed in a state made up equally of boredom and apprehension. One or two of the other prisoners attempted to strike up conversations with me, apparently impressed by my status as an accused murderer. But their speech was so untutored and provincial that I could barely understand them, and when an actual sentence or two managed to penetrate the language barrier, I had nothing to say in response. I declined the offer of a hand-rolled cigarette from one of them, at which he shrugged and went off to a far corner to share it with another fellow. As for myself, I was dog-tired from my nearly sleepless night, but I had no desire to close my eyes in my current surroundings. I doubt I would have slept a wink, even if I had.

Of course, the company of the lowest segments of humanity—I am sure that most of them richly deserved incarceration—was part and parcel of the degrading experience of jail. I have no doubt that had I been allowed to keep my valuables before being locked up, at least half the inmates would have attempted to rob me of them. At least, being the largest man in the room, I had some protection from the bullying that appeared to be the only kind of interaction many of the inmates understood.

Sometime around noon a man brought in a pot of some sort of vile stew for luncheon and dished it out into tin plates. The food was possibly the worst that had ever been put in front of me, and yet (having eaten no breakfast) I was hungry enough that I managed to get some of it past my nose. By now, most of the other inmates had been taken out, either to be released or to appear before a judge for arraignment. After all, this was not a regular prison, merely an area where arrested men could be confined until formal charges could be brought against them, or for the detainment of habitual inebriates, as much for their own protection as for that of the community.

Having grown up as a lawyer's son, I suppose I had fewer illusions about the nature of American justice than most men my age. Still, I was annoyed that even the drunks were free to walk the streets while I remained behind bars. And it was especially galling to see the others who had been present at the duel released after little more than an hour in detention. I considered Holt and Keyes to be more responsible for the duel than I had been, although they had tried to persuade Staunton to accept my apology. On the other hand, Dr. Soupape had apparently attended the duel primarily in his capacity as a physician. He, at least, seemed to have done everything in his power to prevent the confrontation.

It must have been mid-afternoon when the warder finally came to the door and called out my name. I stepped forward and he opened the cell door, then ordered me to put out my hands. I did so, and he quickly snapped a pair of handcuffs onto my wrists. "What is the meaning of this? I am not some common felon!" I protested.

"Common or uncommon, it's regulations," said the officer, gesturing with his billy club. "Now come along with ye, we can't keep Judge Fogarty waiting."

The officer hustled me through the outer precinct room and into a side room that I hadn't noticed when I was brought in. This turned out to be a small courtroom, with a black-robed judge already seated at the high desk in front. There were a few spectators scattered in the seats outside the bar, newspapermen from the look of them. I was taken directly to the front, where the judge peered down at me, an unpleasant expression on his face.

A clerk read out the charges. "William Wentworth Cabot, of New London, Connecticut, local address 1099 Royal Street. Charged with discharging a pistol in public, with dueling, and with attempted murder. He is also suspected of the premeditated murder, by poisoning, of Percival Staunton, late of First Street in Lafayette Parish." He went on to read the arresting officer's report, which except for its abominable style was a clear and objective description of the scene of the duel.

"These are serious charges," said the judge in a deep, raspy voice. "Is the prisoner represented by council?"

"No, Your Honor," I said, "not at present. I am attempting to get in touch with my employer. Unfortunately, he left town on short notice and I don't know for certain when he will return."

"And who is your employer?" asked the judge.

"I am employed as secretary by Mr. Samuel Clemens of Hartford, Connecticut," I said. "He is better known by his pen name of Mark Twain." At that there was a rustle of interest from the newspaper reporters in the courtroom, who took out pencils and pads and began to jot down notes. Normally, I would have thought it beneath my dignity to call attention to my association with a celebrity, but my present circumstances did not encourage fastidiousness.

"No local residence for either one," noted the judge, evidently unimpressed. "Do you understand the charges against you?"

"I believe so," I said. "Except for the firing of the pistol, which I freely admit having done, they are patently untrue. I most emphatically deny murdering, or attempting to murder, Mr. Staunton. The other men detained at the same time will undoubtedly corroborate me." This was pure assumption on my part, but I was grasping at straws. I heard more scribbling from the reporters.

"Undoubtedly," said the judge, with an ill-concealed smirk. "But at the present moment, you are charged with several very serious offenses, including a capital crime. You have no roots in the community, and the one person who you say could vouch for your character and employment is inconveniently absent. We shall have to look into this; Mark Twain's name is not unknown to the court, and it will not go easy with you should it be learned that he has come to harm. I have no choice but to order you to be held in Parish Prison, without bail, pending formal indictment." He turned to the policeman standing beside me. "Take him away."

"Not quite so fast, Your Honor," said a familiar voice behind me—Mr. Clemens! "This fellow works for me, and I'd like to find out what he's supposed to have done before you throw him in the hoosegow. For all I know, the rascal deserves to have the book thrown at him. But if I'm going to have to do without a secretary, I'd surely appreciate being told *why*."

I turned around and looked, as did all the spectators in the courtroom. I heard whispers of "It's really him," and "No, doesn't look a thing like him."

"Are you Mr. Samuel Clemens, of Hartford, Connecticut?" asked the judge, eyeing the newcomer suspiciously.

"Most of the time," said my employer, walking up to my side. "Every once in a while, I go by the name of Mark Twain, but that's strictly for professional appearances. Oh, there are a few impostors around, claiming to be me, but by all reports they're pretty shabby imitations—not even particularly facetious, for the most part. I assure you I'm the original."

"I see," said the judge. "Well, Mr. Clemens, I am familiar with your reputation and your writings. However, my courtroom is no place for theatrics or clowning. There are serious charges preferred against this young man, including suspicion of the premeditated murder of" —he glanced at the papers on the desk before him— "Mr. Percival Staun-

ton. If you have some argument as to why the prisoner
should not be held pending formal trial, at the very least
on the charges of dueling and attempted murder, I am willing to entertain it. But I will warn you that I do not deal
lightly with those who would waste the court's time. Do
you have anything pertinent to say?'' He banged his gavel
to quiet the audience, who had begun to crowd forward.
Someone must have passed word of my employer's presence to those outside as well, since more people (including
a few of the police officers) had begun to crowd into the
little courtroom, whispering and pointing at Mr. Clemens.

"Your Honor, while I have some reputation as a creator
of fiction, I can't pretend to be a lawyer," said Mr. Clemens, whose bushy eyebrows had raised nearly an inch at
the mention of the victim's name. "Even if I were, I
haven't had the time to familiarize myself with the laws of
Louisiana. But I believe I can speak to the particulars of
the murder charge. Tell me, does the alleged murder involve poisoning?''

"That is correct," said the judge.

Mr. Clemens struck a pose I had seen him take many
times on stage, with his chin resting on one fist, and the
elbow of that arm resting on the other. His voice had
slowed down, as well I, who had seen him perform before
an audience many times by now, recognized that he was
again playing to an audience, in this case, an audience of
only one, Judge Fogarty. "That is very interesting, Your
Honor. And has the poison been identified?''

"I have no evidence of that before me," said the judge.
He turned to the police officer, who was still standing beside me. "Has an autopsy been performed?''

"No, Your Honor," said the policeman. "From what I
understand, they'll probably do it sometime this afternoon
and send us the report tomorrow or the day after.''

"I see. Well, Mr. Clemens, we evidently don't know that
detail. What relevance does the nature of the poison have
to your line of argument, sir?''

Mr. Clemens cleared his throat. "Your Honor, I'm only a visitor to New Orleans. I used to know the town fairly well, before the War, but I've made my livelihood elsewhere for a number of years now. Even so, having been in town less than a week, I am aware—as you undoubtedly are, as well—that this is the second death by poison of a member of the same family in a short time. I am referring to the death of John David Robinson, the victim's brother-in-law.''

"I am aware of the case, yes," said Judge Fogarty, frowning. The room had fallen silent except for the sound of the reporters, scribbling furiously.

"Now, doesn't it strike you as strange that two related men would be poisoned in a short period of time? It isn't that common a cause of death, is it?"

"Not especially, as far as I know," the judge agreed. "That is what made the authorities suspicious to begin with.''

"Naturally," said Mr. Clemens, brushing his fingers through his long hair. "Now, I can establish beyond reasonable doubt that I and my secretary were on a steamboat a few hundred miles upriver at the time of the first poisoning. I could produce the captain of that boat on a couple of hours' notice.''

"The court will stipulate that point for the time being," said the judge. "You may be asked to demonstrate it at some later time, should it become material to a defense. But your secretary is not accused of murdering Mr. Robinson.''

"No, and the man accused of the murder is in jail," said Mr. Clemens. "So it's not likely that *he* poisoned Staunton.''

"I am certain that the keepers of Parish Prison keep a close eye on their wards," said the judge. "What do you mean to suggest, Mr. Clemens?"

"That when two men, related by marriage, die from the same unnatural cause, and an unusual one at that, it makes sense that the same person killed 'em both. Cabot couldn't have done the first one, and the cook couldn't have done the second one. If it turns out that the poison was the same in both cases, isn't that pretty strong proof that neither Mr. Cabot nor the Robinsons' cook is guilty? That somebody else entirely killed *both* Robinson and Staunton?''

''Your logic is persuasive, Mr. Clemens, but not quite conclusive,'' said the judge. ''After all, your secretary is also suspected of fighting a duel against the deceased, and according to the arresting officer's report, admits to firing his weapon.''

''I fired into the air!'' I said, then remembered to add, ''Your Honor. I can bring witnesses.''

''That may be so,'' said the judge. ''But I am going to wait until I have the autopsy results to make a decision. It could be argued that you poisoned him, then provoked a duel so as to make sure of him. Then, when you saw the poison was working, you fired into the air to divert suspicion.''

I was about to protest further, but Mr. Clemens cut me off. ''In that case, Your Honor, I'd like to ask you to dispatch a police officer to bring a copy of the autopsy report to this court as soon as it's available. Assuming you're willing to postpone your decision until then.''

''I consider that a fair request,'' said the judge. ''The court will instruct the captain to send a man to the hospital.''

''And one other thing,'' said Mr. Clemens. ''I made the mistake of going out of town last night, and all Hell seems to have broke loose while I was gone. Can you let me talk to my secretary in private so I can bring myself up to date?''

The judge frowned at Mr. Clemens's language, but nodded his assent. ''The bailiff will take you to the visiting area. I'll give you half an hour.''

Mr. Clemens and I followed the bailiff to a small locked room with two chairs and a small table, all bolted to the

188 floor. He closed the door behind us, pointing to an electric button, and saying, "Ring if you're done early."

We sat down. Mr. Clemens glared at me for a moment, then said, "Damn me if this doesn't beat all, Wentworth." He took his corncob pipe out of his pocket and knocked it against the palm of his hand, loosing a scatter of fine ash. He began to fish for his tobacco pouch, then stopped and glared at me again. "What the devil did you *do* last night?"

I looked at Mr. Clemens and sighed. "Do you know, I was just about to ask you exactly that question."

≈ 19

Mr. Clemens laughed. "I guess you had a lot more reason to worry about my whereabouts last night than I did about yours. One thing for certain, if I'd known you were going to get yourself into a gunfight and wind up in the clink, I wouldn't have left you to your own devices. But I figured you'd want plenty of time to talk to Mrs. Staunton, and Eulalie Echo insisted we had to leave at once."

"Well, you could hardly have known that Mr. Staunton was going to burst in and challenge me to a duel," I said. "But where on Earth did Eulalie Echo take you that was so important that you couldn't wait to write me a note? I was afraid you'd been abducted—or worse."

"Damnation, I *did* write a note," said Mr. Clemens, slapping his palm on the tabletop. "Eulalie sent one of the neighborhood boys to give it to Mme. Bechet for you. Didn't you get it?"

"No. I saw her that evening, when Staunton's seconds came. If Mme. Bechet had a message for me, she said nothing about it."

Mr. Clemens snorted and tried to lean back in his chair, then made a face as he remembered it was bolted down. The visiting area was clearly not designed for the comfort of its users. The glaring light in the little room came from a single electrical bulb, protected by a heavy wire screen. I briefly wondered why the only light in this room needed to be shielded from damage, then remembered where I was. Not everyone who came into the visiting area could be expected to be calm and rational; in fact, a good proportion of them might be drunk, drugged, or otherwise beyond caring about the consequences of their actions.

"Mme. Bechet is beginning to annoy me," said Mr. Clemens. He had his tobacco pouch out now, and was filling his pipe. "Well, maybe the messenger never got there," he mused. "That seems unlikely, though. When Eulalie Echo gives a boy a message to deliver, that message gets *delivered,* even if the boy has to swim to Spain to do it. I reckon her messages get through quicker than Western Union's. Of course, the telegraph boys don't worry about Eulalie turning them into frogs and feeding them to snakes if they don't get there on time."

"Surely you don't think she can do that," I said. I hadn't thought my employer to be so credulous.

"No, but the boys believe it, and that's all that matters," he said. "Anyhow, we have more important things to talk about. Eulalie originally asked me to come see her because she'd gotten information about one of the late John Robinson's real estate ventures. It seems that Robinson was renting an apartment in the French Quarter, not far from the section of Rampart Street where we saw those girls yesterday afternoon. Now, I can think of a few reasons why a well-to-do gentleman with a fine house in the Garden District might want an apartment in that neighborhood, but all of 'em are fishy, to put it mildly."

"Oh, but Mrs. Staunton told me that Robinson had quite a few real estate investments," I said.

Mr. Clemens shook his head. "You don't rent an investment, Wentworth. There's something more to it. I have suspicions, but no evidence yet. We'll need to spend some time finding out what that apartment was being used for, once we've got you out of the lockup. That's the first item on the menu."

"You won't find me contesting that point," I said. "I'd

be happy just to get these handcuffs taken off, right now. But it couldn't have taken more than ten minutes for Eulalie to tell you about Robinson's apartment. She could have sent you a note, if that's all she had to report.''

He finished lighting his pipe and took a couple of puffs, then looked up at me. ''Well, now you've come to the strange part. It's so odd that I don't entirely believe it myself. After Eulalie told me about Robinson's little French Quarter hideout, I asked her where she got her information. Mostly, I was fishing for other ways she could contribute to our murder investigation. Eulalie has a lot of clients, if that's the right term. She's something of a priestess, as well as a fortune-teller and herb doctor and conjuror, so you might even call them *parishioners.* As Buddy Bolden said, a lot of people talk to her, for a lot of different reasons.''

I was puzzled by his description. ''A priestess? That's a strange way of describing her. I thought most of the people in this city were Roman Catholics.''

''Most of them are,'' said Mr. Clemens, ''but a lot of them like to hedge their bets; Catholics in New Orleans have been known to burn candles to saints the Pope has never heard of. According to Eulalie, a lot of them don't see any harm in adding on a whole list of voodoo saints, as well: Papa Legba and Damballa are a couple of the names she told me.''

''How quaint,'' I said. ''I suppose the uneducated classes need some superstition to sustain them.''

Mr. Clemens snorted. ''Don't be a snob, Wentworth. You can't dismiss one man's religion as ignorance and superstition and then turn around and claim that another man who believes a batch of equally absurd things has seen the true light of faith. It won't hold water. In fact, Eulalie told me that some of her clients are from the most privileged class of New Orleans society. Including, as it happens, the very lady whose husband you're accused of poisoning.''

''Maria Staunton? I find that difficult to credit!'' I tried to imagine that literary lady, a patron of the arts, sitting in

192 Eulalie Echo's barbarously decorated front room, but the image was too incongruous.

"It does go against the grain, but I can't say I'm surprised," said Mr. Clemens. "I couldn't tell you how many supposedly intelligent people turn out to believe the most outrageous nonsense: mediums and levitation and haunted houses—you name it, and there's somebody who'll swallow it, and pay good money to somebody who'll feed it to them."

"Surely one can make a valid distinction between revealed truth and the fevered imaginings of the credulous," I said. I had seen enough of Mr. Clemens to be well aware of his skepticism, but it disturbed me that he was apparently defending what no enlightened man could see as anything but the darkest superstition.

His expression was serious now. "Maybe some people can, but I've seen some mighty strange things in my time, things regular science can't make heads or tails of. Prophetic dreams, and a sort of mental telegraphy, and magical spells that work in spite of all logic saying they can't. So somebody like Eulalie fascinates me. Part of my mind is trying to figure out how she hoodwinks the suckers, and another part is half-convinced she's the real thing. And that brings me to last night's expedition. Eulalie told me of an old voodoo woman living out near Bayou Saint John, the one *she* goes to for advice. As it happened, she was going to visit her that very evening."

"So you went with her, I take it."

"Yes; Eulalie invited me, out of the blue. And she said we had to get there before dark and stay until first light, which is why I couldn't wait for you. I'll tell you some other time what I saw out there; some of it was uncanny, Wentworth, really uncanny." He took his watch out of his pocket and examined it. "But our time is running out. I need to know what Mrs. Staunton told you, and how this crazy duel got started, and anything else you may have found out about our murder case. Why don't you tell me everything, from the start, and then if we have time, we can go back to whatever we need to talk more about.''

I quickly rehearsed the events of the previous evening and this morning. Telling my story all at once, I was surprised to realize how much had occurred in less than twenty-four hours. Mr. Clemens puffed on his pipe, nodding or frowning occasionally, but making no direct comment on my narrative until I had finished. Then he said, ''Staunton may have been poisoned before he came home and found you talking with his wife. During our ride out to the bayous, I asked Eulalie a few things about the effects of jimsonweed; from what she says, it can take anywhere from six to twelve hours to kill a man. And it attacks the mind as well as the body, which would explain Staunton's behavior.''

''That's what the doctor said after Staunton was taken ill. I was thinking yesterday that we need to know more about this poison: how easy it is to obtain, and what its effects are. It looks as if you were ahead of me,'' I said. Then another thought struck me. ''Dr. Soupape evidently knows enough about it to diagnose it on sight; I wonder why he didn't suspect much earlier that Staunton was under its influence.''

''Maybe he wasn't looking for it at first,'' said Mr. Clemens. ''Or maybe he was hiding something, although I can't figure out what, considering that he's the one that finally called attention to it. Anyhow, if we can prove that Staunton was poisoned before he challenged you, then the idea that you poisoned him because you were afraid of the duel is pure hogwash. Damn it all, I wish I'd been here. I'd have told you to go into hiding and let me talk Staunton out of the duel. Why did you even accept a challenge from the likes of Staunton? The fellow was an expert duelist, nothing more nor less than an assassin. What would you have done if he'd managed to get off a shot in spite of the poison? What the hell would *I* have done?''

''I suspect you'd have hired another traveling secretary,''

I said. "If we can't convince these people I'm not a killer, you may have to do that in any case."

He snorted. "Hogwash again. I'm going to get you out of here, today if possible. But we still haven't looked into the main question about our murder case."

"That being?"

"We have to assume that whoever killed Robinson also killed Staunton. That means we have to find somebody who had reason to kill *both* of them. I'm inclined to look at the immediate family and friends. Did Mrs. Staunton say anything to you that might indicate she and her husband were having difficulties?"

"What?" I was shocked at the suggestion that Maria Staunton might have murdered her husband. But then I remembered her odd comment just before the dinner party, when I joked about her husband walking out of his portrait, and she had been disturbed at the notion of there being two of him. And now that I was thinking along those lines, her reaction upon her husband's sudden appearance the previous afternoon was one of fear as much as of surprise. Was it possible that he had been mistreating her so severely that she had at last defended herself by taking his life? I realized that, despite my first reaction, I hardly knew her well enough to judge the likelihood of her being a murderess. But I told Mr. Clemens my thoughts, and he nodded.

"Yes," he said, "it makes a certain amount of sense. That still leaves John Robinson's death unexplained, though. Did she say anything about Robinson that might suggest a reason for her killing him?"

"Her brother Reynold ended up administrating Robinson's estate," I said. "But unless there's an enormous fortune involved, that doesn't seem quite enough reason for Maria to have poisoned Robinson. And Reynold Holt appears to have some income in his own right, although Robinson was giving him a certain amount of work, partly to keep him occupied, I think. I can conceive of Maria's wishing to be free of an abusive husband, but lacking evidence that Robinson was harming Maria or her brother, I can't see any good reason for her to poison him.''

"We don't have anything that's likely to impress a judge, anyhow,'' said Mr. Clemens. He stood up and paced a step or two, as far as the little cell permitted; then, realizing how confined a space he was in, he sat back down and continued speaking. "The problem with judging somebody else's motives is that you can't ever really get inside their mind. It'd be easier to make a case if we could find some solid evidence on how the poison was given. Who had the opportunity to poison both men?''

I mused for a moment, and then another thought struck me. "I say—Eulalie seems to know a great deal about this poison. If Maria Staunton is a believer in voodoo, is it possible she could have obtained it from her?''

Mr. Clemens frowned. "It would be a convenient explanation, wouldn't it? But I think Eulalie would have told us before now if she had supplied the poison to Maria or to anyone else who might have been the killer. It would be the quickest way to exonerate Leonard.''

"What if Eulalie were afraid of implicating herself?'' I asked. "She might face prosecution as an accomplice if it could be proved that she supplied the poison.''

"No,'' said Mr. Clemens. "If Eulalie were worried about that, why would she have agreed to help us in the first place? It draws attention to her, and I doubt she'd be anxious for publicity if she had something like that to hide. Still, that's one question we haven't really looked into, where the poison came from, assuming the killer didn't just pick it in a vacant lot somewhere. The stuff is apparently a common roadside weed. Then again, it must have been disguised in some way for the victims to have taken it without being suspicious, and that assumes somebody who knows how to prepare it. I wonder if Maria Staunton patronizes some other herb doctor besides Eulalie.''

"I still have trouble with the idea that Maria is our main suspect,'' I said. I still couldn't reconcile the literary lady

I'd spoken with only yesterday with the voodoo cultist Mr.
Clemens claimed she was or with the murderess he thought
she might be. "What about Robinson's political rivals? As
you said yesterday, Tom Anderson appears to be hiding
something. It may be some political scandal that Robinson
was involved in. For that matter, how about Reynold Holt?
He certainly acted as if he held some grudge against Staunton when we were at dinner with them. That could be political, as easily as it could be something personal."

"Oh, I haven't eliminated the political angle; believe me,
Tom Anderson and Reynold Holt are still on my list. So
far, I haven't eliminated anybody except you and Leonard
Galloway."

"Well, I'm glad *you* don't think I poisoned Staunton. I
hope the judge is as willing to believe me as you are." I
looked down at the handcuffs I was still wearing, and wondered what my mother would think if she were to see them
on my wrists. Then I remembered Staunton's pistol pointed
at me and decided that I was far better off in jail than in a
casket. At least there was reason to hope I would get out
of jail.

"Well, it sounds like Dr. Soupape believes you, too,"
said Mr. Clemens. "And if we can take her at face value,
Eugenia Robinson may believe you, as well. What did you
say her words were when she came to the dueling ground?
This boy has done nothing?"

"I can't pretend I'm flattered to be called a boy, but yes,
it does sound as if she believes in my innocence. Although
she was speaking of the supposed insult to Staunton, not
the poisoning. I have no idea whether she thinks I'm guilty
on that count." I thought back to her dramatic appearance
at the park, dressed in mourning, as she tried to intercede
in the duel. She had said something to Staunton—or was
it the other way around?—that seemed at odds with her
role as peacemaker. My memory refused to yield up the bit
of information; perhaps it was simply playing tricks with
me.

"Well, Mrs. Robinson is still among the suspects," said **197**
Mr. Clemens. He had finished his pipe, and he knocked the
ashes out on the floor of the little cell. "We're guessing at
Mrs. Staunton's motive, but the same logic applies to her
sister. Hmm . . . two sisters whose rich husbands both die,
leaving them and their brother in possession of respectable
fortunes. Do you think they could be in cahoots?"

"I suppose it's possible, although you're making an assumption about the fortunes," I pointed out. "The entire
family could be on the verge of bankruptcy without our
knowing it."

Mr. Clemens scowled, then nodded. "You're right, of
course, Wentworth. What was I thinking about? I, of all
people, ought to know how precarious wealth can be. But
that gives me another idea; what if the sisters had inherited
money, and their husbands were squandering it? From what
you've said, Reynold Holt appears to have an independent
income, so there's a good chance the sisters brought money
into their marriages, as well. Dupree's the family lawyer;
he would know how stable the family fortunes are, but he
probably won't talk to an outsider. Of course, we haven't
scratched him off our suspect list yet. Or the doctor, either."

"I suppose not," I said, somewhat puzzled. "But on the
other hand, I don't see any real reason to suspect them. In
fact, they both appear to be on our side. As you said, Dr.
Soupape seems to believe my story. And Mr. Dupree tried
to get me released along with Holt and the others."

"He *said* he tried to," said Mr. Clemens. "Talk's cheap,
Wentworth. And talk from a lawyer who's being paid by
somebody else is mighty damn close to worthless."

"I suppose I ought to take umbrage, being an attorney's
son," I said. "But I see your point. Still, do you have any
particular reason to suspect Mr. Dupree?"

Mr. Clemens stood up again and took a couple of paces
back and forth. "I suspect Dupree because I don't know
where his loyalties lie. His closest ties may well be with

Reynold Holt and his sisters. We know he served with Holt in the War, and that bond can be almost as strong as blood. Robinson and Staunton may have been comparative newcomers, frittering away their wives' fortunes, and Dupree may have seen it as his duty to stop them by any means necessary. And all that goes equally for Dr. Soupape. I have the impression he's been the Holts' family doctor since they were children. For all I know, he could have been the one who supplied the poison. If so, it's not hard to figure out why he believes your story. He knows you didn't do it, because he knows who *did* do it.''

''Yes, I suppose that is a possibility,'' I said, shaking my head. I had thought the events of the last twenty-four hours would clarify our investigation of the Robinson murder, but things seemed as complicated as ever. ''There are too many possibilities. All this would be far easier if I were free to help you.''

Mr. Clemens came to my side of the table and put his arm around my shoulder. ''Let me take care of that, Wentworth,'' he said. ''I'll have you out of here in jig time. I can tell this judge is an easy-goer.''

Unexpectedly, the buzzer rang, and a second later the door popped open. The bailiff stuck his head in and said, ''OK, gents, time's up.''

Mr. Clemens looked at his watch and then glared at the bailiff. ''We were supposed to have half an hour. It's not even twenty-five minutes yet. I expect 'em to rush me in New York, but not in New Orleans, of all places.''

''Don't make no difference. Judge Fogarty wants you,'' said the bailiff, beckoning to us. ''You want to argue about the time, you can argue with the judge. He's got the only watch that matters.''

⤳ 20

There seemed to have been a massive invasion of reporters during our brief meeting. Evidently, word
that Mark Twain was somehow involved in a murder
case was sufficient to draw every idle newspaperman in the
city of New Orleans to Judge Fogarty's courtroom, like
vultures to carrion. Even before we had reached the door,
Mr. Clemens and I found ourselves running a gauntlet of
men who considered it their sacred duty to shove a notepad
in his face and fire off a volley of impertinent questions:
"Did you see the duel?" "Who shot whom, anyway?" "Is
the other man dead?" and "Will you be canceling your
lectures?" Finally, the bailiff began shoving them out of
the way, saying, "Can't keep the judge waiting. You can
get your story inside."

Inside, it was standing room only, with a double row of
newsmen against the back wall. Although the windows
were open, the room was unpleasantly warm, and some of
the reporters had removed their coats. The smell of stale
tobacco smoke and overflowing spitoons did nothing to
make it more bearable. I longed for the bright sunlight I
could see just beyond the wrought iron bars that reminded
me clearly where I was and why I was there.

Judge Fogarty did not appear at all pleased at the sudden
explosion of interest in his courtroom. He waited with a
resigned expression while Mr. Clemens and I marched up
to the front of the room, past a sullen clerk seated at a side

table. When we stood before the bench, he banged his gavel and called for order; the noise in the room diminished noticeably as the reporters and other courtroom idlers strained to hear the proceedings. "It appears you bring an audience with you, Mr. Clemens," said the judge, a wry smile on his face.

"Your Honor, I might appreciate the attention more if the gentlemen of the press had all purchased tickets," said Mr. Clemens. "I will say that I have played before smaller audiences in my time."

"I want it understood that this is not a theater but a court of law," said the judge, raising his voice and glaring around the room. "The public has a right to observe the administration of justice, but not to interfere with it. I will not hesitate to clear the courtroom upon the least sign of disorder." The murmur of voices from the back of the room fell to a nearly inaudible level, above which the scratching of pencils could now be heard. Judge Fogarty nodded, a satisfied expression on his face, and turned to face me and Mr. Clemens, who stood on my right hand.

"Mr. Cabot, I fear I have bad news for you," said the judge, peering directly at me. "The hospital cannot deliver the results of the postmortem examination of Mr. Staunton until tomorrow morning. Therefore, pending the court's perusal of such results, I must adjourn this case until tomorrow. The usual conditions for granting bail in a capital case not having been met, I am sorry to inform you that you will remain in custody until such time as the court can determine whether your release is in the best interests of the community." He banged his gavel, and I heard the buzz of voices behind me.

My heart sank. I didn't want to spend another hour in that foul cell, let alone an entire night, a night in which I would be surrounded by filth and assaulted by noise, with violent and predatory criminals as companions. I was dog-tired, having barely closed my eyes the night before the duel. If I were forced to return to the cell tonight, it would be a miracle if I got any rest at all.

But Mr. Clemens was not about to let the judge's decision go uncontested. "Your Honor," he said, "I can't see why you need that coroner's report to make a decision. Whatever the cause of Mr. Staunton's death, I would like to point out that there is no reason to believe that my secretary had anything at all to do with it. And in that case, there is no reason to confine him. He does not represent any danger to the public."

The judge frowned, putting down the small stack of papers he had begun to gather up. "Mr. Clemens, you contradict your earlier argument. If I remember correctly, you were the one who proposed that the results of the autopsy would clear your cli—your secretary."

Mr. Clemens did not even blink at this rejoinder. "And so I believe they would, Your Honor. Mr. Cabot has been in New Orleans less than a week, and has no previous connection with Staunton or his family. My secretary met the deceased for the first time two days ago, over dinner. To propose that Cabot took an instant and homicidal dislike of his host, conceived a plan to do away with him, and put it into action, in time for Mr. Staunton to die of poisoning this morning, is preposterous. It's more preposterous than anything *I've* ever written, and I say that with no pretense of humility."

At this, some of the listening reporters laughed, and others began to whisper among themselves. Judge Fogarty lifted an eyebrow and motioned toward the back of the room. A bailiff began to advance on the crowd of reporters who, realizing that ejection from the room was imminent, fell silent. The judge nodded, then turned to my employer and replied.

"Your argument is specious, Mr. Clemens," he said. "Mr. Cabot need not have conceived an instant antipathy to the deceased to have killed him. But when he was challenged to face him with drawn pistols, he might well have found himself deficient in courage, and resorted to a weapon that did its work at a distance. He then appeared at the duel so as to avoid the accusation of cowardice, but by then the poison had done its work for him.'' The judge completed his argument, then leaned forward and looked around the courtroom with a self-congratulating grimace.

The murmurs from the back of the room became audible again, and I had the unpleasant feeling that they bore a tone of approval of the judge's comment. But Mr. Clemens was not to be dissuaded from his argument. ''I can follow that line of reasoning,'' he said. ''But there's one thing I still don't understand, if you'd be so kind to explain it to me. Suppose, for the sake of argument, that Mr. Cabot was so scared of Mr. Staunton that he decided to poison him to escape a duel, rather than do what any sensible man in that predicament would do, which is to call the police, or failing that, make himself scarce until the trouble blows over. Let's even suppose that Cabot likes to carry around a couple of doses of poison in his vest pocket, so he doesn't have to go look for a local poison shop every time he decides to kill somebody.''

There was a titter from the back benches, and the judge lifted his gavel, but someone shushed the guilty party and Mr. Clemens continued. ''Even assuming all this, just when, between the challenge and the duel, is Mr. Cabot supposed to have had the opportunity to poison Mr. Staunton? Or is it customary in these parts for the man who's issued a challenge to let his opponent fix him a doctored drink?''

The judge nodded, perhaps a bit reluctantly, but clearly struck by the force of Mr. Clemens's argument. ''The court notes that there is room for doubt on the question of opportunity. But you raise another question. You say, correctly in my opinion, that a sensible man challenged to a duel would either call the police or go into hiding. Yet your secretary did neither of these. How do you reconcile this discrepancy?''

Mr. Clemens answered without a discernible pause. "Your Honor, at no point have I contended that my secretary is a sensible man." There was a ripple of laughter from the audience, and I felt my blood rising to my face, but the judge pounded his gavel and the reporters again fell silent. My employer continued, his head partly turned so that his words would be clearly audible to the entire courtroom. I realized that he was speaking as much to the reporters as to the judge; at least my story would not go unremarked by the press. I was not entirely sure that having my name in the local papers was to my advantage, but Mr. Clemens was barging ahead full steam, and I returned my full attention to what he was saying.

"If I had been here to advise my secretary, he would never have gone to meet Staunton this morning," said Mr. Clemens. "He only went because he was told—by his opponent's seconds, of all people—that Staunton would hunt him down and shoot him if he didn't appear. Mr. Cabot decided that his best chance was to show up and apologize, hoping to end the whole packet of nonsense before it got any worse. My secretary made every effort to prevent the duel. When Staunton refused his overtures, Cabot emptied his pistol into the air, exposing himself to Staunton's fire, in an appeal to the man's sense of justice and mercy. This isn't how a murderer acts, or a coward either, Your Honor. Perhaps a damn fool, but not a murderer."

The judge listened with a stony expression, but nodded his head when Mr. Clemens had finished. "Your language is not entirely respectful of the court, sir, but I will overlook it for the moment. Your logic is hard to deny," he said. "Nonetheless, I am reluctant to release Mr. Cabot without a substantial bail bond. He has no ties to the community, and therefore nothing to prevent him from absconding from the jurisdiction of this court."

"Your Honor, there is no need for bail," said Mr. Clemens, raising his hands as if in supplication. "I can personally guarantee you that my secretary is not about to skip town. And if Mark Twain's word isn't worth anything in New Orleans these days, maybe my paycheck is. You may have seen bills posted advertising my lectures this Friday and Saturday, and I don't mind telling you that I get a pretty decent fee for my appearances. I'll pledge my fees for both those lectures against Mr. Cabot's remaining in town. And if we haven't cleared him of the charge of poisoning Mr. Staunton by then, you can hold those fees until he *is* cleared, as I have every reason to believe he will be.''

The judge glared at Mr. Clemens, and Mr. Clemens returned his stare eye to eye. There was a long moment of silence, then Judge Fogarty nodded. ''Very well,'' he said, then turned to me. ''Mr. Cabot, you are released in the custody of Mr. Clemens, who undertakes that you will remain within the city of New Orleans pending the resolution of the investigation into Mr. Staunton's death. Mr. Clemens pledges his lecture fees as surety for his promise. The court will dispatch a bailiff to the lecture hall on Friday and Saturday nights with a warrant to secure the fees. I warn you, young man, if you attempt to abscond from this jurisdiction, your employer's fees will be forfeit. And I can assure you that every effort will be made to return you to New Orleans to face the consequences of your part in the death of Mr. Staunton. Do you understand?''

There was silence in the courtroom; even the slow-moving flies seemed to have stopped buzzing to hear my answer. ''I do, Your Honor,'' I said.

''He won't skip town, Your Honor,'' said Mr. Clemens. ''He may be able to outrun the New Orleans police, but if he thinks he can outrun Sam Clemens, he's a worse fool than anybody believes.''

''Very well,'' said the judge. ''Mr. Cabot, you are free to go.'' He banged his gavel one last time, and Mr. Clemens took me by the elbow and swept me out of the courtroom before the crowd of reporters could deluge us with more questions. In a little back room, the bailiff unlocked my handcuffs and returned my possessions, and I was a free man again.

After my ordeal of the last few hours, it was a distinct pleasure to emerge into the clear air. Birds were singing, and the New Orleans sunlight had never seemed brighter. After the events of the last twenty-four hours, just being alive and free to walk the streets was an immense pleasure. A distinct adjunct to that pleasure was the sight of Henry Dodds, waiting patiently at the corner with his horse and carriage. "How d'ye do, Mister Sherlock!" said Dodds. "Looks like you've been a busy man since I dropped you off last night."

Weary as I was, I had to laugh. "Too busy, Henry," I said. "But I intend to make up for it as soon as you can get me back to Royal Street. I think I'll have Mme. Bechet draw me a hot bath, then go straight to bed and sleep until tomorrow!"

"That's a first-rate plan, Wentworth," said Mr. Clemens, as I gave him a boost up into the carriage. "But I'm afraid you're going to have to wait a little while for that nap. Henry's going to take us out to Aunt Tillie's place. I've called a meeting of everybody who's helping us, so we can get to work solving this murder case, and I need you there."

At first I was tempted to protest, but then I remembered that except for Mr. Clemens's efforts, I might still be languishing in a cell. "I'll try to stay awake," I said, climbing up beside my employer on the seat. "It's the least I can do for a man who's gotten me out of jail. I never could have persuaded the judge to free me without your help." Henry Dodds clicked his tongue, and his horse looked back at him, then unhurriedly began moving forward. As with every other living being I had seen in New Orleans, the carriage horse appeared to have all the time in the world on its hands.

"What persuaded the judge was my pledging my sacred

income to keep you from skedaddling,'' said Mr. Clemens. ''But I won't insist on your strict attention, as long as you don't snore too loud. And I reckon we can get Aunt Tillie to warm you up a plate of something, if the jail food didn't agree with your palate.''

''Good Lord, could it agree with *anyone's* palate? I thought there was no such thing as a bad meal in this town, but now I've learned otherwise.'' The cab jolted over a series of small ruts in the street, then settled down to a steady rocking motion.

''Jail food ain't no good in any town,'' said Henry, turning around and looking at me with a sympathetic frown on his face. ''Not that I know by personal experience, mind you. But there's folks I know that wouldn't mind just sitting still, minding their own business, and eating regular, if the food was any good. And last I heard, all the jailbirds was agitating to get *out*, which don't say much to compliment the cooking.''

Mr. Clemens laughed. ''Well, Henry, if you'll get us out to the Garden District in good time, I'll see what I can do to get you a sample of cooking you *will* compliment. Aunt Tillie used to make a mighty good pot of gumbo when she was cooking for George Cable.''

''I'd surely love to test it out,'' said Dodds, chuckling. By this time, he had given up the facade of discretion that seemed to be a professional requirement of cabdrivers, who would pretend not to notice anything, however outrageous, that happened in the back of their vehicles. He had heard enough of our talk about freeing Leonard Galloway to be practically a coconspirator. Mr. Clemens seemed to realize this. He winked at me, then leaned forward to talk directly to the driver.

''Fine, but there's a price, Henry. You've been driving us all over New Orleans and dropping bits of advice that nobody but a native could possibly know. Well, Henry, one of the best cooks in the city is locked up in Parish Prison for a murder he didn't commit. After this morning, I'm dead certain of that. I think it's time we brought you into the conspiracy to get Leonard Galloway out of jail.''

Dodds turned and looked at Mr. Clemens. ''Well, I reckon I can lend a hand to help that fellow get back on the street again, but if you're looking for somebody to hold a ladder, I reckon I'll pass. Poor Leonard may not be their man, but that won't stop 'em from locking me up if I get caught springing him. No sir, not even for Aunt Tillie's gumbo.''

''Oh, we won't do anything worth locking people up for,'' said Mr. Clemens. ''We plan to get Leonard out just by proving that he's an innocent man. Nobody's going to go to jail.''

Dodds shook his head, his expression dubious. ''Then what was Mr. Sherlock doing in the can?'' he asked. ''Little boys on the street was saying he shot a man down cold, though I reckon they'd have kept him in if he'd done *that*.''

Mr. Clemens laughed and slapped me on the back. ''Your reputation is made, Wentworth! *Shot a man down cold!* And on the field of so-called honor. Half the women in the city will be swooning at your feet. With a six-foot-tall cold-blooded killer to protect me, there's not a man in New Orleans who'll look at me cross-eyed.''

I heaved a deep sigh. ''This is a reputation that no cultured person would wish to have attached, even falsely, to his name. I can only pray that word of this day's dreadful business never reaches my family.''

''Don't judge the day till it's over, Wentworth,'' my employer said, looking me in the eye. ''The afternoon is young. Why, we could have a couple of hurricanes, an insurrection, and a fire before the sun sets, and still be able to call it a good day by the time it's over.''

''And how would we manage that, pray tell?'' I asked.

Mr. Clemens leaned back in his seat, as if he hadn't a worry in the world. ''Well, I got a pretty good start by getting you out of jail. I plan to keep my steam up with a bowl or two of Aunt Tillie's gumbo. And if you two are

208 smart, you'll do the same. What do you say, Henry? Are you with us?''

The driver turned around, a broad grin on his face, and stuck out his hand to Mr. Clemens. ''Well, I knew from the start you fellows was up to something. Now that I know what it's all about, I guess I'm in for the game.'' He shook hands first with Mr. Clemens, then with me; then he gave a flick to his reins. The horse actually picked up its pace a tiny bit, and we were on our way to Aunt Tillie's once more.

⇒ 21

W
hen we arrived at the little house near First and Howard, Aunt Tillie's parlor was crowded. She was there, of course, greeting us with a smile and fussing over finding comfortable seats for Mr. Clemens and me. Her nephew Charley Galloway was there, along with her neighbor Buddy Bolden; they stood by the back wall of the parlor. Henry Dodds, our new coconspirator, ambled over to join them.

Mr. Cable was also on hand. He rose to greet me, shaking my hand and saying, "Well, young man, I fear you've seen a side of New Orleans most tourists are lucky enough never to encounter."

Mr. Clemens chuckled. "Oh, I suspect a fair number of 'em end up seeing the inside of the lockup, at least the ones that visit the houses along Basin Street."

"Hardly the kind of visitor that does the city credit," said Mr. Cable. "But the natives can hold their own, no doubt of that. I thought the days of dueling under the Oaks were long gone, and good riddance to them, but I see I was overoptimistic." He shook his head.

"You should know better, George," said Mr. Clemens. A frown came over his face. "That kind of humbug has more lives than a cat. These poor fellows have been fed the old lies about honor and nobility and chivalry so many times, they can't distinguish them from reality. So they don't blink an eye at the notion that a gentleman who happens to be a crack shot is somehow acting honorably by murdering some poor fellow who's offended him. When the duelist goes to jail as a common assassin, these honorable men conspire to stack the jury and let him off. Unless it's a pair of Italians or Negroes involved, in which case the whole community rises up and condemns it and lynches the one who pulled the trigger. I say it's a humbug and a shame to the whole society that supports it.'' With that, my employer took his seat on the couch and motioned to me to do likewise.

"Why, so it is, Sam,'' said Mr. Cable. "Just as much as sending a poor cook to jail for a murder he didn't commit. Let's not forget poor Leonard.''

"Lordy, no,'' said Aunt Tillie. "I cry so bad every night, wishing that poor boy could come back home. I know you gentlemen is doing your best to get him out. I just wish it didn't take so long.''

"It won't take much longer, if I can help it,'' said Mr. Clemens. "I'm waiting for one more person, and then we can start putting our heads together about getting Leonard out.''

"One more person?'' said Cable. "I thought we were all here already. Whom else are we expecting?'' He peered around the room with a puzzled expression.

"Eulalie Echo, of course,'' said Mr. Clemens.

With that, Aunt Tillie jumped from her chair. "Mercy sakes,'' she said. "What am I goin' to do with a hoodoo woman in my house?''

"Find her a seat and offer her a cool drink and something to eat, if she wants it,'' said Mr. Clemens. "I reckon she'd do the same for you, if you went to her place.''

"I surely would,'' said a new voice. I turned to look, and recognized Eulalie Echo, wearing a plain white dress and a straw hat, with a many-colored scarf around her neck. She stepped into the parlor and said, "I'm pleased to meet you, Tillie Galloway. I know you won't turn away someone who has come to your home to help Leonard. If it's not

asking too much, I would love to taste a bowl of your
famous gumbo.''

"Well, come on in and take a seat," said Aunt Tillie,
motioning toward the easy chair she had just vacated. I
suddenly realized that a wonderful smell had filled the
room, coming from the direction of the kitchen, and my
mouth began to water. Aunt Tillie must have sensed my
appetite, because she smiled at me and then turned to her
nephew. "Charley, get another chair from the kitchen for
me to set in. I got to go dish out some gumbo."

The gumbo arrived, and a respectful silence fell, broken
only by the music of spoons on the bottoms of bowls. I
was (not surprisingly) ravenous, and went through my portion even before Aunt Tillie had finished serving all the
others. She gave me an understanding look, having learned
of my incarceration earlier that same day, and quickly re-
filled my bowl. Whatever adjectives one applies to jail
food, Aunt Tillie's gumbo was at the opposite end of the
spectrum. At last, the hungry were all fed, and Mr. Clemens
turned our minds to the business of finding a way to free
Leonard Galloway.

He called on me to tell my story first, and I recounted
the events that had begun with my visit to Mrs. Staunton
yesterday afternoon and had ended early this morning with
Mr. Staunton's collapse and my jailing. When I had finished, Mr. Clemens said, "I had Wentworth go first because
his story gives the lie to the notion that Leonard had anything to do with murdering John David Robinson. The
judge can spin his theories all he wants, but I'd sooner
believe the river runs uphill than that Staunton and Robinson could die of poison within two weeks of one another,
with no connection between them. Leonard's in jail. Ipso
facto, he couldn't have done it."

Mr. Cable raised his hand. "Samuel, I believe as much
as any of us in Leonard's innocence, but I see one flaw in
your argument. Even if the postmortem proves the two men

died of the exact same poison, there could have been some poison left over from the first murder. What if someone discovered it—someone with a grudge against Staunton—who seized the opportunity to give it to Staunton? Then we'd have two different killers using the same method, and no way to exonerate Leonard, even though he was in jail at the time of the second murder—or Mr. Cabot, either, I'm afraid. You have to admit the possibility. And if I can think of that, surely the prosecutors will.''

"And it would still be nonsense," said Mr. Clemens. "But I see your point, George. We have to look at all the possibilities, even the absurd ones, just in case one of them turns out to be true. For example, we're assuming that Robinson and Staunton were both murdered; but could their deaths be accidents? Could they have taken the poison by mistake?''

"That seems far-fetched to me," said Mr. Cable. "The odds against two separate accidental poisonings in such a short time are prohibitively large. At the very least, the death of the first victim would have alerted the second to the danger.''

"But maybe the first was an accident, and the second deliberate," said Mr. Clemens, counting on his fingers. "You've already suggested someone with a grudge against Staunton who found the leftover poison; that script plays just as well if Robinson was accidentally poisoned. Or it could have been Robinson who was murdered, and Staunton who accidentally took the leftover poison a few weeks later. Mind you, it makes more sense to me to treat both the deaths as murder, but I agree we can't ignore the other possibilities, including the possibility that our killer is lying in wait for still a third victim.''

"Good Lord!" I said. "Surely two deaths are enough!''

"One was enough for me," said Mr. Clemens. "In any case, the police say it's two murders, and they're the ones calling the shots. Unless we prove that both deaths are accidental, the only real way to save Leonard—and you, too,

Wentworth—from murder charges is to prove for certain that somebody else killed Robinson and Staunton, and we'll assume that the same person killed both of them, at least until we find some good reason to believe otherwise.''

At the mention of the poison, I remembered a question that had begun tickling at the back of my mind shortly after my departure from the Staunton home. "I've been wondering about the poison itself," I said, looking at Eulalie Echo. "I realize I don't know anything at all about jimsonweed, the stuff both men were killed by. What is it like? How easy is it to obtain?"

"I could pick a bushel of it any time I wanted to," she said. "Except I wouldn't. Some herb doctors use it in love potions or other tonics, but it's very tricky to measure the dose. A little too strong, and you've killed somebody who came to you for help. I would not risk it."

"But you say some herb doctors do use it?" I continued. "Someone could just go out and buy it?"

"If you knew the right person, and if they trusted you, yes," said the voodoo woman. "But selling poison to strangers is buying trouble for yourself. I prefer not to deal in poison, even to people I know well."

Mr. Clemens had listened, resting his chin on his fist. Now he turned to Eulalie. "Here's another question. You told me yesterday that Mrs. Staunton visits you from time to time in your, ah, professional capacity. Does she go to anyone else in your line of business—for example some of the herb doctors who *do* sell this jimsonweed?"

"I don't know. She may, but what does it matter?" said Eulalie Echo, with a shrug. "You don't need to invent esoteric sources for the poison. Anyone who wants jimsonweed badly enough can pick as much as they can carry home, out by the bayous. The real difficulty is getting someone to take it without knowing. The smell and taste of the raw plant would give it away. That usually keeps even small children from eating enough to harm themselves.''

"That's why I suggested one of the herb doctors," said Mr. Clemens. "People *expect* medicine to taste bad. So the murderer could feed it to the victims without their suspecting."

Eulalie Echo shook her head. "As Mr. Cable has already said, the death of the first victim would no doubt make the second one suspicious. And the person who sold it to Mrs. Staunton would surely learn to what use she has put it, as well. Herb doctors can read the newspapers as well as anyone else. What keeps that person from betraying Mrs. Staunton to the police? Or from blackmailing her?"

"Fear of being arrested as an accessory," said Mr. Clemens. "Or perhaps Maria didn't buy it, but brewed it up herself."

Eulalie was still not convinced. "A lady cannot cook foul-smelling things in her own house without her servants noticing. Someone would surely mention it to the police after two poisoning deaths in the family, and yet no witness has come forward. Over and above this, I cannot believe that Mrs. Staunton has murder in her soul."

"Well, somebody sure does, and we've got the bodies to prove it," said Mr. Clemens. "And since one of 'em is her husband, I have to consider her a suspect." He rubbed his chin, thinking, then turned to our hostess. "Aunt Tillie, Leonard must have come home sometimes with stories about his employers' doings. Every worker talks about the bosses now and then. Did Leonard ever say anything that led you to believe that there was trouble in the family—between Robinson and his wife, or Robinson and the Stauntons, or anything of the sort?"

I would not have believed that a Negro could blush, but Aunt Tillie came as close as humanly possible. Then she threw up her hands and said, "Oh, no, Leonard never said nothing about the white folks. He knew better than to spread stories about folks that was so good to him—"

Charley Galloway laughed, and Buddy Bolden joined him. "Well, Aunt Tillie, it ain't my business to go contradicting my elders,'' said Galloway. ''So I guess maybe Leonard just didn't tell you the same stories he told me and Buddy. But I reckon that whole family was fightin' *all* the time. If it wasn't about money it was about politics, and if it wasn't about politics it was about connivin' and sneakin' around the Vieux Carré at night. If any two of 'em got along for a couple of days, it was so they could gang up on another one. And then, something else would happen, and the first two would be fightin' again. Leonard had some mighty funny stories he'd tell after he had a few drinks.''

''Well, now we're getting somewhere,'' said Mr. Clemens. ''Did Leonard say anything about Mr. Robinson's political plans?''

''We didn't need to hear about that from Leonard,'' said Bolden. He stood against the wall with his hands in his pockets. ''You could read it in the newspapers. Seems like Robinson was calling in every favor he could think of to try to get elected. And you won't find this in the papers, but he spent an awful lot of time down at Tom Anderson's, talking to folks who could deliver votes. A couple of boys I know play in Anderson's house band sometimes, and right after Robinson died, they talked about seeing him in there.''

''Strange that a reform candidate would be so cozy with that crowd,'' said Mr. Cable, leaning forward. ''Usually they do their best to stay at arm's length from Anderson and his ilk. But of course, they don't usually get elected, and Robinson was considered a strong favorite to win the next election.''

Mr. Clemens clapped his hands together. ''This is great stuff, boys. I knew Robinson couldn't be as clean and upright as the papers painted him. If Anderson isn't in this up to his ears, I'll be surprised. Do you think maybe Robinson was done in over some crooked political deal that went wrong?''

''Or a crooked land deal,'' said Mr. Cable. ''Robinson may have been acquiring land on the sly, planning ways to increase its value after his election as mayor. If the ladies will pardon my mentioning a delicate subject, I have heard talk of setting up a zone near the French Quarter where prostitution would be tolerated, if not quite legal. I would not be surprised to learn that Robinson owned property in that area and stood to benefit from an ordinance establishing such a zone. Anderson or another of his stripe—anyone who was trying to acquire the same properties—might have found it expedient to eliminate Robinson, in hopes of keeping the price down.''

''Anything could happen down in the Quarter,'' said Henry Dodds, speaking for the first time since our arrival. He straightened up and stepped forward into the center of the room. ''But if the man got killed over politics, why did they have to kill that Staunton fellow, too? I reckon he had more business in the Quarter than Robinson—I drove him down there once or twice, myself—but weren't nothing political about it, nor any land deals, either. Not at the addresses I done dropped him off in front of, no sir.''

''I reckon I know what kind of business you mean, Henry,'' Mr. Clemens said. ''Maybe we can't explain Staunton's death by some political motive, but what about the possibility that Staunton knew too much about Robinson's death and had to be eliminated? I'm certain there's a link between the two murders, something we just haven't found yet. You can't tell me it's pure coincidence that these two men both died the same way.''

Mr. Cable nodded vigorously. ''Oh, we'll find the link if we keep looking, no doubt of that. But practically speaking, we must do it quickly. Leonard must be proven innocent before he has to face a trial.''

''I don't even want to wait that long,'' said Mr. Clemens. ''Remember, I'm pledging my lecture fees as bail for Wentworth. I'd just as soon have the case solved before the bailiff can get his hands on my money. And that means within the next couple of days.''

Aunt Tillie clapped her hands, her delight evident on her

face. "Oh, bless you, Mr. Twain! I can't wait to see poor Leonard back in his own home again."

There was a flurry of excitement in the room, but Mr. Cable had a somber expression. "I am sure everyone here is heartily in favor of a quick resolution," he said, "and I by no means least. But I fear that your timetable is unrealistic, Samuel. We have too many suspects and nothing solid against any of them. We don't even know whether to concentrate on the domestic or the political motives."

"That's the next order of business," said Mr. Clemens. "Until we know enough to narrow the field, we're going to look at all the possibilities. Everybody here will have to take a part. To begin with, I'd like to follow up one hint Eulalie Echo gave me. Robinson had a rented apartment in the French Quarter, on Customhouse Street just off Bourbon. I have a pretty fair idea what that place was used for, but I'd like to be sure."

"In fact, I have news concerning that," said Eulalie. "One of my informants saw a woman entering and leaving the apartment yesterday morning. She stayed no more than half an hour."

"A woman! Just as I suspected," said Mr. Clemens, leaning eagerly forward. "Did the one who saw her recognize her?"

"No," said Eulalie. "She arrived in a closed carriage and was only visible for a few moments entering and departing. She was wearing a heavy veil and dressed in mourning."

"Ah, then I'll lay you odds it's the widow Robinson," said Mr. Clemens. "She probably went there to grab anything that could tie her husband to the apartment."

"That's a very reasonable guess, but if she removed anything, it must have been small," said Eulalie. "The person who told me about it didn't say she carried anything, going in the place or coming out of it."

"Don't be so certain it was Mrs. Robinson, either," said Mr. Cable. "The mourning could well be a disguise, meant to make everyone assume it was the widow. And her husband is already tied to the apartment; if Mrs. Echo could find out about it, so can anyone else who wants to unearth the information.''

''Don't *you* be so certain, Mr. Cable,'' said Eulalie Echo, an enigmatic smile on her lips. ''I have many sources of information, and some of them talk only to me. I am sure that Mr. Robinson was paying the rent on that apartment, but I doubt there's anything on paper to prove it. He may have had the usual vices of his class, but he hid them very effectively.''

''Well, this may be shutting the barn door after the horse has run off, but I think we need to find out more about that apartment,'' said Mr. Clemens. He turned to me. ''Wentworth, I'm going to put you on that job.''

I was surprised at this assignment. ''Excuse me? I'm not sure I understand what you want.''

''I'll take any information you can get,'' said Mr. Clemens. ''Go by the place, try to talk to the neighbors or the landlord. See if you can get a look inside. If it's on the ground floor, maybe you can peek through a window.''

''That won't be possible; the apartment is on the second floor,'' said Eulalie.

''Well, then, Wentworth, slip a couple of dollars to the landlord or janitor,'' grumbled Mr. Clemens. ''Just don't do anything that gets you thrown back in jail.''

''I promise you, I'll do my best to avoid that,'' I said.

''I know you will,'' said Mr. Clemens, smiling at me. Then he turned back to the rest of the group. ''I need somebody to scout around Tom Anderson's. Buddy and Henry, both of you say you know some of the workers there. I'd like you to ask them about Robinson—and Staunton, too. How often were they in, who did they talk to? Find out anything you can; we don't know what'll be useful.'' Mr. Clemens had stood up, and was pacing about the room in an unusually animated fashion and pointing to each person as he gave out assignments. He was even talking more rapidly than his normal drawling style, which often sounded as if each word were followed by a full stop.

"Sure, I'll talk to the boys at Anderson's," said Henry Dodds. "Like I said, those fellows don't talk much about what they see in there. But if I tell 'em it's to get Leonard out of jail maybe they'll talk."

"They'll talk to me," said Bolden. "At least, the musicians will. Between me and Henry, we'll find out what's what."

"Good. Aunt Tillie, I'd like you to get in touch with the Robinsons' butler, Arthur, again. With a second death in the family, maybe he'll change his mind about talking to us. Charley, I'd like you to pay a visit to Leonard in prison. If I were to go again, it would attract too much attention, but nobody'll think twice about a relative visiting. I have a couple of questions for you to ask him. I'll let you know what they are before we break up. Eulalie, I reckon you can help most just by keeping your ears open for information from your usual sources. You'll recognize the kind of news we want when you hear it, I'm sure."

"And what can I do?" asked Mr. Cable, smiling amusedly at Mr. Clemens's enthusiasm. "I refuse to sit idly by while everyone else solves the case, especially since I was the one who got you started on it."

Mr. Clemens stopped pacing and turned to look at Cable. "Well, George, I need somebody to go quiz the family, and I can't very well send Wentworth to do it anymore—not after the duel with Staunton. I might not even be welcome there, myself. But as one of her literary acquaintances, maybe you can go to give your condolences, for a start. I don't need to tell you what kinds of things to ask once you're in the door."

"I'm sure I'll think of something useful," said Cable. "I'll stop by this very evening. I doubt she'll be receiving visitors so soon after her husband's death, but at least I can leave a card, and then we'll see how soon I can talk to her."

"Good; then everyone's accounted for," said Mr. Clemens.

"Except for you," said Mr. Cable. "What role do you intend to play, Samuel?"

Mr. Clemens smiled broadly, looking down at the little bearded man. "Why, the one I'm most suited for, of course, George. I'll be the mastermind of the entire operation."

"Lordy, we're in trouble now," said Henry Dodds, and even Eulalie Echo joined in the hearty burst of laughter that filled Aunt Tillie's parlor.

"No," said Mr. Clemens, grinning broadly. "We've been in trouble all along, and now I'm going to get us out." He took a large white handkerchief out of his pocket and mopped his brow. "I'll admit I haven't the faintest idea how, just yet. But I have the great advantage of having been born with a diseased imagination, and over the years, I have learned to rely on it. I'm sure it'll come up with something before long."

≈ 22

After the meeting at Aunt Tillie's, Henry Dodds dropped us off at our Royal Street pension. Mr. Clemens was still annoyed about the note he had sent me the previous night, which our landlady Mme. Bechet had evidently failed to deliver. So when Mme. Bechet appeared at the door, I feared that she was about to become the target of one of his temper tantrums. But before he could open his mouth, she said, in a tone that carried enough disapprobation for multitudes, "There is a policeman here to see you, M'sieur Clemens," and suddenly his demeanor changed.

"Confound it, Wentworth, I hope that judge hasn't changed his mind about turning you loose," he whispered to me as she turned to show us the way. I nodded gloomily, having thought of exactly that possibility myself. We followed Mme. Bechet into the courtyard, where a plump fellow in a light summer suit and panama hat sat in the waning light, reading one of the afternoon newspapers. "Here is M'sieur Clemens," she said, and the man folded his paper and looked up. It took me a moment to recognize Richard LeJeune, the police detective to whom Mr. Cable had introduced us when we first started looking into the Robinson murder case.

"Good evening, gentlemen," said LeJeune. "The boys down at the precinct tell me you had an interesting day today."

"That's a hell of a way to describe it," said Mr. Clemens. "I guess it's accurate enough for present purposes, though. I'd be happy if tomorrow's newspaper stories get that close to the truth. What can we do for you, Mr. Le-Jeune?"

The detective looked at Mme. Bechet, who was attempting to linger unostentatiously within earshot. "Let's find some place private to talk," he said, rubbing his mustache with his forefinger and thumb. "I want to hear Mr. Cabot tell what went on this morning. And I've found out a couple of things you might want to know, as well."

"Sounds good to me," said Mr. Clemens. "Come on up to the room, and if it's not against your religion, I'll give you a little something to drink while we talk."

LeJeune laughed. "No religion that tells a man he shouldn't take a drink will get many converts in New Orleans, Mr. Clemens. I do believe I'll have one. I may be here on business, but it's friendly business."

We climbed the steep stairs to the room, leaving a manifestly disappointed Mme. Bechet below in the courtyard. Mr. Clemens poured generous helpings of Scotch whisky and soda for himself and the detective; I settled for plain soda water, well aware that in my present condition, liquor would put me straight to sleep. After my anxious night and morning, I was certainly looking forward to an undisturbed sleep, but not before I had heard what the detective had come to tell us.

LeJeune took a long sip of whisky, wiped his lip with the back of his hand, and sighed. "That's just what the doctor ordered," he said, bowing his head to Mr. Clemens. Then he set down the glass and took out a notebook and pencil and placed them on the table, staring directly at me. "Well, the Robinson case just got mighty confusing, didn't it? And you right in the middle of it. Why don't you tell me what went on this morning?"

I told him the entire story, beginning with my visit to Mrs. Staunton and the unexpected return of her husband, right up to Mr. Clemens's arrival at the jail. For the most part, LeJeune listened without comment, jotting down an occasional note, and once or twice interrupting me with factual questions. He seemed particularly interested in Staunton's behavior when he had challenged me to the duel. "Maybe the autopsy can tell us exactly when Staunton was poisoned, but even without seeing it, I'd bet ten dollars it was before he challenged you," he said. "From the way he was acting, it sounds as if he was already under the influence. Did any of the seconds act as if they knew what was going to happen?"

"Not that I recall," I said. It seemed a simple enough question, but at the time, I had been far too concerned with the man trying to aim a pistol at me to pay much attention to anyone else. "Dr. Soupape suspected poison almost as soon as Staunton collapsed, but I suppose that's the kind of thing a doctor would notice."

"Interesting that he didn't notice it earlier," said the detective. "A prosecutor might argue that he was holding back his diagnosis until it was too late to do the victim any good."

"Well, I thought Staunton was behaving oddly, but for all I knew it was drink or fatigue or overpowering emotion," I said. "Of course, from my point of view, the whole affair was decidedly odd. I'm afraid duels aren't in fashion in Connecticut."

"They haven't been fashionable here for a good long time, either," said LeJeune. "Percy Staunton could have saved us all a good bit of trouble if he'd just picked up a walking stick and given you a good thrashing, instead of that old rigamarole about pistols at dawn. Well, I guess you wouldn't have liked it much, but at least you can run away from a man with a stick."

"And when Staunton ended up dead, who would you have arrested?" growled Mr. Clemens. "Don't go telling me it's the cook again."

The detective put down his notebook and spread his

hands as if to deny responsibility. "If you'll remember, I'm the fellow who thought the cook might be getting a bad deal. Anyhow, this death isn't officially homicide, yet—at least not until we have an autopsy. But I wouldn't put stock in Mr. Holt's claim that your secretary killed Staunton. For one thing, I can't see when he had the opportunity to give him the poison. So while we're waiting for the autopsy results, I'm talking to all the witnesses and trying to trace Staunton's whereabouts during the day. I've already talked to the widow and to Mr. Holt, and I'll get to the doctor and Mr. Keyes tomorrow."

Mr. Clemens raised his eyebrows. "Well, I'm glad to hear the police don't suspect my secretary. It raises my opinion of Louisiana law a little bit. That pig-headed judge seemed ready to hang him, practically before Staunton was dead. I was just as glad to get Wentworth out of there before the autopsy report came in. If there'd been anything fishy about it, I suspect he'd have strung him up on the spot."

"Oh, don't pay no mind to J. J. Fogarty," said the detective. "He's all bluff. But that's beside the point. I want to tell you what we've found out about the case so far. You'll be glad to know that the widow Staunton corroborates your story about the challenge, Mr. Cabot."

"I never expected otherwise," I said, perhaps a bit defensively. "After all, it *is* true."

LeJeune gave a noncommittal grunt, then flipped through his notebook as if searching for a particular page. "I think you'll be interested in her report of the conversation she had with him after you left, if conversation is the right word. From what she said, it was mostly him accusing and her denying. Among other things, Staunton accused her family of cooking up a conspiracy to cut him out of his rightful claim to that house they live in. It was originally the Holts' family home. Staunton bought it from her father after the War, when the Holts' fortunes had gone into decline."

"That's interesting news," I said. "But if Staunton purchased it, how would Maria have any claim on it?"

"That's simple enough. After the husband's death, it goes to the wife," said LeJeune. "And that seems to be exactly what's happened here, doesn't it?"

"Do you mean he suspected she had poisoned him?" I said. "Why wouldn't he have gone straight to the doctor, if he thought that?" It was still difficult for me to see the bookish Maria Staunton—now a widow, I realized—as capable of such a heinous act.

"Even then, it might have been too late," said the detective, matter-of-factly. "But what I think it means is that the poison had started to attack Staunton's mind, and he was seeing enemies everywhere. Right now, we're looking at several lines of inquiry. The wife would have as good an opportunity as anyone to poison Staunton. But we can't make a solid case until we know when he took the poison, and where he was and who he saw all yesterday. We're trying to put those details together now."

"Yes, that would seem to be a crucial step," said Mr. Clemens. "What have you established so far?"

LeJeune raised his eyebrows and looked Mr. Clemens right in the eye. "I could get in trouble telling you this. If my captain hears I gave this kind of information to a possible suspect, he'd take my badge. Can I rely on your discretion?"

"Nothing you say will leave this room," said Mr. Clemens. The detective looked at me, and I gave my assent, as well.

LeJeune nodded, then flipped his notebook to another page. "The butler says Staunton left home after breakfast yesterday, about nine thirty, on foot, and he didn't say where he was going. He returned right after five, which is when you saw him. The butler and the widow both verify that, too."

"And in between those times?" asked Mr. Clemens. "That's a fairly large gap to fill."

"Don't I just know it? He could've gone damn near to Texas and back in that amount of time. But there's one hint I want to follow up. The widow says he told her he'd been to a saloon, and from what I've learned about his habits, I'd be willing to bet it was Tom Anderson's place he went to."

"Why, there's a coincidence," I said, without thinking. "Mr. Clemens and I were in Tom Anderson's much of the afternoon, as well. But we didn't see Staunton at all." As I said this, I saw my employer signaling me to hush, but then he just shook his head. Too late, I realized that I had all but admitted having an opportunity to give Staunton the poison, after all.

LeJeune's face lit up, and he picked up his notebook and pencil again. "Were you, now? I assume you can prove it, if need be?"

I was about to answer, but Mr. Clemens held up a hand to stop me. "I guess Anderson will corroborate it," he said. "And he can probably tell you whether Staunton was there at the same time we were. Don't go drawing conclusions just because Staunton and Cabot may have been in the same place just before Staunton was poisoned, now. It would make about as much sense to put the blame on Anderson as on Cabot."

"Or on Anderson's chef, for that matter," said the detective, with a wry grin. "Don't worry, Mr. Clemens, I don't draw conclusions without I have all the facts. But now it looks as if there are some more facts that you have and that I need to know. Do you mind telling me what led you to visit that particular place yesterday?"

"Politics," said Mr. Clemens. "Robinson was going to run for mayor, and I hear tell that Anderson's is where the ward heelers and bosses get together to make the deals and divide the spoils. If Robinson was murdered for political reasons, we figured we might find out something useful there."

LeJeune smiled, a bit condescendingly, I thought. "And did you?"

Mr. Clemens smiled back at the detective, holding the smile a little longer than I thought was entirely comfortable. "I found out that Anderson serves a first-class T-bone steak," he said at last. "But maybe you already knew that. I've heard that his saloon is one of the favorite eating places for the police department."

The detective frowned, then lifted his whisky glass and laughed. "Touché, Mr. Clemens. I can't ask you to play fair with me if I'm not ready to do the same with you. For a supposed reform candidate, Robinson was thick with some of the dirtiest political bosses in town. I've heard talk that he didn't care a damn about reform except to get himself elected. In particular, I've heard that he was looking to buy up a lot of property down on Basin Street, which is where some people want to set up a district where the whores can work without the police bothering them."

"I've heard the same," said Mr. Clemens. "Which brings two ideas to mind. Was Anderson investing in the same territory to prevent it? Or was somebody so opposed to the idea of a semilegal vice district that they decided to kill off one of the main backers?"

LeJeune nodded. "Two good questions, and don't think I haven't thought about both of them. I don't remember Robinson making any public statements on a vice district. Sidney Story did most of the talking on that idea, not that Story is very happy to have *his* name attached to it. Of course, that doesn't mean somebody who knew Robinson's real opinions couldn't have done him in. Anderson, he's as slippery as they come, but I don't think he's got the stomach for killing. Just my opinion, to be sure, but I've watched Tom since he was a young boy delivering cocaine to the whores. He'll take a rake-off as quick as anybody in the parish and turn his eyes away if there's rough stuff going on. But I don't think he's the kind to start any rough stuff on his own, or even to hire somebody else to do it for him.''

"Thank you," said Mr. Clemens. He tapped his fingers on the arm of his chair for a moment, then continued. "Now here's something for you to chew on. We've heard that Robinson was renting an apartment in that same district—on Customhouse Street just off Bourbon. Have you picked up that information? I can't see why a man who could apparently buy up half the city if he wanted to needed to rent an apartment in that district.''

"Where did you hear that?" said the detective, obviously surprised at the revelation. "I won't claim to know everything that happens in the parish, but I've been investigating Robinson's death for damn near three weeks, and this is the first I've heard of an apartment in the Quarter. I'd love to get a look inside it.''

"So would we," said Mr. Clemens. He tamped tobacco into one of his pipes, struck a match, then paused, fixing LeJeune with his eyes. "In fact, I'd asked Wentworth to see if he could find some way to peek inside. What's the chance we could all go see it together?''

"Officially, we can't," said LeJeune. "I'd have a devil of a time getting a warrant for it, seeing as how my bosses still think the cook killed Robinson. Some of them were even trying to figure out whether one of the cook's friends or relatives might have poisoned Staunton. Some people won't believe that rich folks go in for murder as much as poor folks. Anyhow, they want me to expand my investigation, but go slow, by which they mean not to dig into respectable people's soiled linen. But there may still be a way. Give me the address of Robinson's apartment, and I'll let you know tomorrow if we can get in.''

"Fair enough," said Mr. Clemens. "We'll expect to hear from you.''

"I promise you will," said the detective. He wrote down the address Mr. Clemens gave him, then tucked his notebook and pencil in his pocket. He picked up his hat from the table and stood, then hesitated. "Oh, there's one other thing I learned."

"Yes?" Mr. Clemens had stood at the same time as LeJeune, and had come around the table to the same side as the detective.

"Dr. Soupape, when that old fox Gordon Dupree sprung him out of jail—where do you think he and the lawyer went?"

"I have no idea," said Mr. Clemens. "Presumably not to the hospital, since Soupape already knew that Staunton was dead. Not straight home, either, since you wouldn't think that was worth particular mention. Where?"

"They went straight to Tom Anderson's café," said LeJeune. "They left Holt and Keyes to get home on their own, and the pair of them went to Anderson's together. An off-duty detective saw them there and recognized them because he'd helped investigate the Robinson murder scene. When he came in to work and found out about the duel and all, he remembered seeing them."

"You're right," said Mr. Clemens. "It's mighty interesting that they went there. I suppose it's too much to hope that your man might have heard their conversation or seen who they might have met with."

The detective shook his head. "No such luck. He just saw them come in together, and then they disappeared into a back room. They could have met with the devil himself, or a couple of archbishops, for all we know."

"The former seems more likely in Anderson's," said Mr. Clemens.

"Not in New Orleans," said LeJeune with a mischievous grin. "You're likely to find the devil and the archbishops at the same dinner table, if the food's good enough. And Tom Anderson serves a mighty good beefsteak." He put his hat on his head, and Mr. Clemens showed him out the door.

After LeJeune had left, I was at the limit of my strength and mental acuteness. I had slept a fitful couple of hours the night before, gone through a brush with death far too close for comfort, and seen another man fall down, not dead, but shortly to be. I had been accused of murder, incarcerated in a foul pen with common criminals, and had sat through a long meeting at Aunt Tillie's house, then the interview with LeJeune. After all that, I had very little interest in anything but rest.

"Go have dinner without me," I said to Mr. Clemens. "I won't be capable of contributing anything intelligent until I'm rested. Maybe a couple of hours will be enough. If I'm awake when you get back, we'll talk."

My employer looked me in the eye and nodded. "Sorry, Wentworth, I forgot how much you've been through today. Well, I'll have to take you to dinner at the Absinthe House some other time. Go lie down and I'll see if you're alive when I'm back."

"Given today's events, I wouldn't joke about it," I said.

Mr. Clemens grimaced. "Given today's events, what makes you think I'm joking?"

I fell asleep with no trouble, and slept soundly until I was wakened by a loud, insistent knocking on my door. My first impulse was to ignore it, but then I remembered all that had happened over the last twenty-four hours, and I forced myself to stand. "Coming," I shouted. "Give me a minute." The knocking ceased, and I turned on a light and looked at my pocket watch. It was eight-thirty, not much more than an hour since I had gone to bed. I quickly threw on a shirt and a pair of trousers and ran a comb through my hair to give it a semblance of respectability. Whoever it was at the door—the thought crossed my mind that it might be the police—would have to accept me in my half-disheveled state or be prepared to wait for me to dress more formally.

I opened the door and there stood none other than Dr. Soupape, looking as tired as I felt. "Your pardon for the intrusion, Mr. Cabot," he said, removing his hat and stepping inside without awaiting an invitation. ''I fear it has been a long day for both of us.''

Better a long one than one that ended too soon, I thought, remembering Percival Staunton crumpling onto the ground just after dawn that morning—was it really still the same day? ''It has indeed been a long day, Doctor,'' I said. ''What brings you here tonight? Will you have a seat?''

''Thank you,'' he said, taking a chair. I sat opposite him and waited for him to continue.

''I just received news from Touro Infirmary,'' he said, after a pause. ''I know several of the doctors there, and they passed along the results of the autopsy as soon as it was done. I thought you would want to know. They found traces of atropine and hyoscyamine in Percy Staunton's body.'' Then, seeing my look of incomprehension he explained: ''These are alkaloids characteristic of several poisonous plants, notably the deadly nightshade, belladonna, and (as we suspect in this case) *Datura stramonium,* commonly known as jimsonweed.''

''The same poison that killed John Robinson,'' I said, and the doctor nodded. It was in a sense a relief to learn the cause of Staunton's death. Although the similarity of method did not entirely exculpate Leonard Galloway, it strongly suggested that someone other than he had poisoned both men.

Then the doctor's expression changed, and he looked at me with suspicion clearly written on his face. ''Yes, it is exactly the poison that killed John. Do you mind telling me how you know that?''

''Why, it was in the newspapers,'' I said, suddenly on my guard. ''Mr. Clemens and I read about the case not long after we arrived in New Orleans.''

I realized that I should not have let my knowledge of the Robinson murder slip out. I could not remember whether the papers I had read actually mentioned the specific poison. If they had not, I had just given him clear warning that I knew more about the case than a casual visitor to the city would have picked up. And if by some chance he was the murderer—or if he knew who the murderer was, and was trying to prevent the police from finding out—then I had just made a serious mistake.

"Oh, yes, I suppose it was," he said, and his face again assumed the tired look it had worn when he had arrived. "Well, I've said what I came to say, and now I'll let you get some rest. You look as if you need it." He stood, and took two steps in the direction of the door.

"One thing more, Doctor," I said, my own suspicions suddenly aroused. "Why did you come tell me this tonight? As much as I appreciate being informed of the cause of Staunton's death, I would have found out about it soon enough, without your making a special trip to tell me."

"I suppose so," he said, turning to face me. "But it seemed the only decent thing to do. You were dragged into a crazy duel, completely against your will, as far as I could see, and you did your level best to avoid bloodshed, with all the cards stacked against you. I have to respect that. The poison must have affected Percy's mind. That is the only way I can see it; the stuff destroys the victim's mind before it kills him. You had as little to do with killing him as the man in the moon. So I thought you deserved to know the cause of death. If you have to mount a defense, it may turn out to be useful. That's all."

"Why should I have to mount a defense? You know I didn't kill Mr. Staunton. Why should anyone ever believe otherwise?"

Dr. Soupape shook his head. "What I know and what other people believe may not be the same. The law is not always reasonable. I hope you will not have to face a trial, but if you do, you deserve to know as soon as possible what you may be accused of. I don't know whether I will be able to give you any further help, but I cannot stand idly by and watch someone who has nothing to do with our local quarrels become the scapegoat for someone else's wrongdoing."

He put his hat on and moved toward the door again. **233**
"Good night, Mr. Cabot. I sincerely hope this is the end
of your involvement in this matter."

He closed the door behind him and left me with a load
of new questions to ponder.

23 ⌒

Despite Dr. Soupape's troubling words, I had no trouble getting back to sleep. I had not heard Mr. Clemens come in, but neither was I tempted to wait up for him. Next I knew, the sun was shining brightly outside, and the neighborhood rooster was again announcing his presence. I gave myself a much-needed wash and shave, and before I was done, I heard Mr. Clemens's door close, followed by the sound of his footsteps in the next room. I knocked on the connecting door and he said, "Come in."

He had already been out and purchased two or three local newspapers, which he waved gleefully at me. "You're famous, Wentworth!" he crowed. "If this won't bring 'em down to the lecture hall to hear what I've got to say, I don't know the public! Nothing like a little publicity to fill the seats!"

"I would gladly forgo the notoriety," I said.

The *Morning World*'s headline read, "Mark Twain's Secretary in Jail," in type of an excessively large size. Immediately below, in only slightly smaller print, it read, "Daybreak Duel Leaves Crescent City Man Dead."

"I suppose I should have expected as much, with all the reporters in court. But in the interest of accuracy, they might have pointed out that I've been released. And I certainly won't pretend that I *like* being the butt of every scandal-monger in the city."

"Oh, you'll get used to it," said Mr. Clemens, lounging

in an easy chair. "Especially if you want to be a writer. Abuse by reporters is the first sure sign of success. As long as you're cleared of the murder charge, and you will be, there's no harm at all."

"I'm glad you think I'll be cleared," I said. "But I have news, as well. Dr. Soupape came by last night to tell me that the poison that killed Staunton *was* jimsonweed, after all. He seemed to think I might still have to account for myself to the law. And whatever our detective Mr. LeJeune says, I don't believe that he has completely discounted me as a suspect."

Mr. Clemens put down the paper he had been waving and nodded sagely. "Well, of course he shouldn't. It's LeJeune's job to find the killer, and he deserves credit for not taking the easy path, which would be to get on with other business and let Leonard Galloway take his chances with the jury. LeJeune is a good policeman; we should be grateful he's on the case, instead of some time-server who doesn't give a damn who's been put in jail, as long as he gets credit for 'solving' the crime."

"I suppose you're right," I admitted. "Still, I'd like to get myself out from under the cloud of suspicion. And the sooner the better."

"We'd best get to work on it, then," said Mr. Clemens. He stood and stretched his arms, then looked me square in the eye. "Remember, I have a personal stake in this, as well. Until you're cleared, I can't collect my lecture fees. Judge Fogarty will hold onto them like a bulldog with a marrowbone. If you're all dressed, we'll go plan our next steps over breakfast. Oh, and bring along those newspapers—just in case one of those reporters has turned up something useful that we've missed."

As I might have predicted, there was nothing at all useful in the papers—certainly not in the sensational, error-ridden, and barely literate accounts of my appearance before Judge Fogarty and the dramatic appearance of Mr. Clemens to secure my release. Two papers—the *Item* and the *Morning World*—had obtained sketches of Mr. Clemens arguing in Judge Fogarty's court (apparently done after the fact, since they did not show my face at all). The *Item*'s reporter made much of the absence of a bullet wound, offering several preposterous explanations in which Judge Fogarty's speculations on why I might have murdered Staunton were repeated word for word. The *Picayune* rumbled darkly about the evils of dueling, listing several prominent local men who'd died defending their honor over the years. Its report seemed to be the most balanced and accurate, but (to my annoyance) it managed to misspell my name as "Cabbot." Mr. Clemens helpfully pointed out that I could use the mistake to convince any of my Connecticut relatives who learned of the affair that it was a different Cabbot entirely.

Mr. Clemens and I decided that Dr. Soupape's news of the identity of the poison was the last proof we needed that the same person who murdered Robinson had evidently poisoned Staunton, as well. To find the poisoner, we had to ascertain the possible links between the two killings; and in that, we were no farther along than we had been the night before.

At last, Mr. Clemens decided to send me to learn more about the apartment the late Mr. Robinson had been renting in the French Quarter. I reminded Mr. Clemens that Detective LeJeune was supposedly working on that question as well, and that we might do better to wait for his report. But my employer pointed out that while the detective might be working toward the same end as we were, he was under no obligation to share his findings with us. Anything we were able to uncover independently would be to our benefit. I had to agree with his logic, although I was not quite certain how to go about the task.

But our plans changed when we returned to our pension. I had meant only to stop off briefly before going to investigate the apartment, but we discovered we had visitors waiting in the courtyard: Charley Galloway and another

Negro, a respectably dressed older man whom I did not recognize. Charley performed the introduction: Arthur Phillips, the Robinsons' butler, had finally agreed to talk to us. The butler shook hands with a grave expression, saying, "I didn't think I had any right to talk to you, but that business yesterday changes things. Now I'm sorry I waited. I'll always wonder if I could have saved Mr. Staunton's life." He had a deep voice, with a more refined accent than many of the other Negroes we had met in New Orleans.

"There's no way any of us could have known what was going to happen," said Mr. Clemens. "I'm glad you decided to come talk, though. We can't bring Staunton back to life, but maybe we can make sure the one who killed him doesn't hurt anyone else."

In light of Arthur's appearance, Mr. Clemens decided to postpone my inspection of the apartment in favor of my staying to take notes. Charley had to go back uptown to open his barbershop, but Mr. Clemens and I led the butler upstairs and settled down for an interview: Mr. Clemens in the easy chair, Arthur and I seated at the table. I got out my notebook and prepared to record the proceedings.

"We talked to Leonard Galloway about a week ago, in Parish Prison," said Mr. Clemens, once we were all seated. "One of the first things he suggested was that we ought to talk to you, that you would be able to clear him. Why do you think he said that?"

There was no mistaking the look of surprise on the butler's face. Arthur lifted his right hand to his cheek and said, "Oh, that poor boy. Did he really say that?" He shook his head in apparent disbelief.

Mr. Clemens raised his eyebrows. "Well, I reckon he did. You heard him, didn't you, Wentworth?"

"Oh, yes," I said, as matter-of-factly as I could. Actually, I did not recall Galloway being quite so confident as Mr. Clemens had suggested, although his Aunt Tillie had certainly put great stock in the butler's ability to clear him.

But I was not about to contradict my employer when he was clearly fishing for corroboration.

"I suppose Leonard was thinking of the incident where Mr. Robinson sent him home for being drunk. Frankly, I thought that Leonard deserved what he got." The butler's expression was cold, and his tone disapproving. I was surprised; was this the man Leonard Galloway considered his friend?

"But you can confirm that Mr. Robinson apologized to Leonard, then gave him back the amount he'd docked him?" asked Mr. Clemens, leaning forward.

"Yes, he did. I thought he was too lenient with Leonard, but it was not my place to criticize him."

Mr. Clemens seemed to consider this for a moment, then asked, "Why did you think he was too lenient?"

"A man who comes to work in that condition makes us all look bad," said the butler. "He ought to have more respect for himself and for his situation." I remembered now that Eulalie Echo had called Arthur "stiff-necked." The thought came to me that perhaps he was the sort of man who is harder than his master on those in the household whom he considers his inferiors. I had known a few gentlemen who liked their butlers to play the part of a martinet to the rest of the servants, while they themselves pretended to be kind and generous; but I had never thought such an arrangement to reflect well on either the master or the butler.

Mr. Clemens raised his eyebrows again but did not pursue the matter. Instead, he said, "Leonard suggested that you might be able to give us an idea who visited Mr. Robinson the day he was poisoned. Leonard was in the kitchen, of course, so he didn't see everyone who came and went, but *you* would have. Do you remember who came to the house that day?"

The butler pursed his lips, concentrating. "Yes, the police asked me the same question. The servants were there, of course: Leonard, Callie the cleaning girl, Tom the gardener, and myself, naturally. All except Theresa, who was out of town, traveling with Mrs. Robinson.''

"Ah, yes, I'd forgotten; Mrs. Robinson was out of town," said Mr. Clemens. "Did any of the servants except Leonard have any run-ins or arguments with Mr. Robinson?"

"No, sir," said the butler, a smug look on his face. "Mr. Robinson was well-liked by everyone in the household. He rarely had to raise his voice to the servants."

Mr. Clemens tilted his head back, digesting this bit of information, then continued. "What about other visitors? Leonard mentioned that Reynold Holt came by after dinner. Did he stay long?"

"Yes; he came by around eight o'clock. I brought them coffee and brandy in Mr. Robinson's study shortly after. I don't know when Mr. Holt left, but he often let himself out when they had been working late."

"I take it they worked late fairly regularly, then."

Arthur shrugged. "Not every night, but it was not unusual, either."

"Were there any other visitors worth noting? I'm not worried about the postman or the milkman, but anyone who actually spent time with Mr. Robinson?"

"Mr. Dupree stopped by for a short time just before noon," said the butler. "He and Mr. Robinson spoke privately for a little while, and then Mr. Robinson went into town, somewhat unexpectedly, I believe, in response to news Mr. Dupree had brought; he seemed a bit disturbed after their meeting."

"You told this to the police, of course," said Mr. Clemens, and the butler nodded. Mr. Clemens leaned forward and pointed his finger at me. "So maybe LeJeune looked into it; remind me to ask him about it when we see him again, Wentworth. Arthur, you don't have any idea where Robinson went that afternoon, do you?" He turned and looked at the butler.

"No, sir; it was hardly my place to ask," said Arthur,

not meeting Mr. Clemens's gaze. *He's hiding something,* I thought. Perhaps the butler's loyalty to his dead master prevented him, even now, from revealing something that could harm Robinson's reputation.

Mr. Clemens's brow furrowed; he had noticed the prevarication as well. "Are you certain, Arthur?" he asked, his voice quiet but forceful. "This is no time to paint over the truth, no matter how bad you think it looks. An innocent man's life is at stake—a man who thought you were his friend."

Arthur still avoided his eye, but I could see that he was wavering. Mr. Clemens waited, letting the long silence do its work. Finally, the butler clasped his hands and looked up. "Lord have mercy," he said in a voice just barely above a whisper. "I never thought I'd say anything against Mr. Robinson, but—"

At exactly this moment there came a loud knock on the door. The butler's face became a mask of fear, and he looked around as if to find an escape. Mr. Clemens put a finger to his lips, then motioned to me to take our guest through the connecting door into my own room. I took the butler by the arm and began to lead him out, as Mr. Clemens went over to the door to the outside. The knock came again, louder this time. "Who's there?" said Mr. Clemens.

"Reynold Holt," said the voice outside. "Open up, I need to see you and your man."

"Give me a moment," said Mr. Clemens, motioning to the butler to hurry. "You can wait in there and listen. We won't give you away," he whispered. The butler nodded, and I showed him into my room and closed the door behind him, as Mr. Clemens resumed his seat. Then, at Mr. Clemens's signal, I went to the other door and opened it to admit the man who, when I last saw him, had been loudly accusing me of the murder of Percival Staunton.

➣24

Reynold Holt entered the room with the manner of a man unused to being kept waiting. He walked past me to Mr. Clemens, who was sitting in his chair holding a newspaper. He leaned on his cane and held out his hand. "Good morning, Mr. Clemens," he said. "I won't take much of your time, but I felt I owed you an explanation of my remarks yesterday morning."

Mr. Clemens peered at him over the top of the paper, lowering it just enough to give the impression he had been busy reading (in fact he had read the entire paper over an hour ago). Belatedly, he seemed to notice Holt's outstretched hand, and reached out to take it; but he did not stand. I was surprised at his calculated rudeness, until I realized that he was merely repaying Holt in his own coin. "Well, I'm glad you made the effort to come by," Mr. Clemens finally said. "I suppose it's the least you could do, seeing as how you owe my *secretary* an *apology.*"

If Holt noticed Mr. Clemens's cool manner and tone, he gave no sign of it. Instead, he continued to address my employer directly, almost as if I were not present. "Yesterday, in the heat of the battle, I accused your man of contriving to poison my late brother-in-law out of cowardice. Since then, I've had the time to think about it, and I realize it couldn't have happened that way. Percy wouldn't have taken a drink or anything of the sort with a man he'd just found in a compromising position with his wife. So there really wasn't a chance for the fellow to slip him the poison. Besides, Percy would probably have said something about it, if he had.''

I was annoyed at his description of the circumstances leading to the duel, not to mention his references to me as if I were Mr. Clemens's servant, but a glance from my employer warned me to keep my protests to myself. Whatever Holt thought he was doing here, Mr. Clemens and I had our own purpose: to discover anything Holt knew about the murders of Robinson and Staunton. We could not accomplish that by letting ourselves be drawn into an irrelevant argument. Mr. Clemens nodded. ''I'm glad to hear you've withdrawn that accusation, Mr. Holt,'' he said. ''I knew that Cabot couldn't have done it, of course, but you haven't had the advantage of knowing him as long as I have. More to the point, I just heard from the police that Mr. Staunton died of the same cause as your other brother-in-law, Mr. Robinson.'' (This news had come from Dr. Soupape, not the police, but I thought I saw Mr. Clemens's purpose, and said nothing.) ''Of course, Cabot couldn't possibly be responsible for Robinson's death; he wasn't even in town at the time. And since it's the same poison, it stands to reason he didn't kill Staunton, either.''

Holt nodded. I could see that Mr. Clemens's cool reception was beginning to annoy him, but he could hardly make an issue of it, given his own behavior. ''Well, we all know who killed poor John, in any case. It was that insolent cook Galloway's doing, to put poison in the food after John called him down for showing up to work stinking drunk. It's a miracle my sister was out of town that day, or the black-faced devil might have poisoned her, as well.''

A flash of anger and disgust crossed Mr. Clemens's face at Holt's uncalled-for defamation of poor Leonard Galloway, but Mr. Clemens had evidently decided to draw the fellow out, whatever Holt said. My employer stroked his mustache, as if in thought, then said, ''Well, I'd heard the cook was in jail, of course. His arrest was in the papers just after we got to town. Say, I'll bet this gives the police a real headache. Maybe the cook poisoned Robinson, but how the hell did he manage to poison Staunton?''

Holt put his hands behind his back and looked toward the ceiling, like a schoolboy reciting a lesson. "I thought about that, once I realized your man couldn't have done it. What I suspect is that the cook's friends did the second murder, to make people think he couldn't have done the first one. It makes sense, because the niggers all stick together. That's why we white men have to look out for our own interests. I know you've argued the other way, Mr. Clemens—I've read some of your books—but these modern niggers don't want to stay in their place the way they did in the old days. There are people in this city who mean to remind them of their place, and maybe this cook will be one of the first examples.''

As Holt spoke, I began to sense a change in his personality. His day-to-day temperament was, from what I had seen, somewhat truculent but not really unpleasant. Now, as his passions became engaged in his subject, he began to take on the mien of a fanatic. There was an uncomfortable electricity in the air, as much from Mr. Clemens as from him. I could see Mr. Clemens struggling to keep his temper under control. I did not envy him the task; Holt's bigoted tirade was enough to make me want to ask him to step outside.

Somehow, Mr. Clemens managed to keep his reply calm and measured. "I can't buy that, Mr. Holt," he said, raising his voice only a little. "Like it or not, old Abe Lincoln made those black men free citizens, the same as you and me. And whatever the differences between the races, I can't see how the color of someone's skin has much to do with what's inside their heart. But even if I'm wrong about that, we can't go back to those old slavery days, however much you wish we could. We damn near destroyed this country thirty years ago; nobody sane wants to see that happen again. Or do you want to see another generation of southern boys go through what you did?''

Holt stiffened, and I saw him tighten his grip on his cane. I tensed myself, ready to protect Mr. Clemens, but then Holt sighed and slumped his shoulders. ''Well, I won't try to teach a blind man to see colors,'' he said. ''Maybe you were brought up southern, Clemens, but I reckon you've forgotten what it meant. I've said what I came to say, which is that I don't hold your man responsible for the poison, whatever else he may have done. And I see no point in prolonging the discussion. Good day, sir.'' He made a stiff bow, turned on his heel, and went out, again barely acknowledging my presence as he passed me.

I heard him limping down the stairs as I closed the door, then turned to Mr. Clemens. ''Did you ever see the like of that?'' I said. ''What in the world are we supposed to make of that performance?''

Mr. Clemens was standing, staring at the door through which Holt had left. I could see that he was still struggling to suppress his temper. Finally, he shook his head, a disgusted expression on his face, and said, ''I'm sorry to say I've seen the likes of that far too many times, Wentworth. There are too many people, North and South, still trying to refight that damned war. You'd think a man his age would have settled his accounts with the past. But the older some people get, the harder their heads become. Present company excepted, of course.'' He gritted his teeth, then took a deep breath and pointed toward the door to my room. ''We're forgetting our other guest. Go get Arthur, and we'll find out what *he* has to say about Mr. Holt's performance.''

I would not have been surprised to find the butler in an angry mood, after Holt's venomous characterization of the Negro race, which he could hardly have avoided overhearing. Instead, Arthur was practically in tears as I led him back into Mr. Clemens's room. He kept shaking his head and saying, ''I should have known, I should have known.''

Mr. Clemens took one look at him and said, ''Sometimes

we all close our eyes to things we don't want to be true. That doesn't make them any less true or any less hurtful.''

Arthur gave a wry smile, then shook himself, and I saw his back grow straight again. The sadness and disillusionment were still in his eyes, but I saw a trace of anger there, as well. He said, ''I worked in Mr. Robinson's house for twenty-two years, and I thought I was set for life. I looked after his household better than I did my own. Maybe I ought to have provided better for myself.'' He sat back down at the table, a picture of dejection.

''When I went to work for Mr. Robinson, I thought that all I had to do was work hard and do my level best, and I'd get my just rewards, whatever my color. I've always taken my position very seriously, Mr. Clemens, and there wasn't anyone who found fault with me. Nobody ever called Arthur Phillips lazy, or stupid, or disrespectful, no sir! Mr. Robinson knew I could take care of his entire household, and he was always more than generous at Christmastime. And Mr. Holt always acted the same way toward me.'' Here he stopped, clearly embarrassed by his former naïveté. I felt very sorry for the fellow, but did not know how to soften the blow to his pride.

Again, I saw the anger in his eyes. ''I never thought I'd hear that crazy Klan talk from Mr. Holt. I thought he could see what an honest, hardworking man I was, a good butler, a man they all could trust with their most important business. Why, he's known me since he was a boy! And all this time they were just seeing a 'black-faced devil.' '' He put his face in his hands. ''What a fool I've been; what a fool.''

Mr. Clemens rose from his chair and put a hand on Arthur's shoulder; at this unexpected gesture of intimacy, the butler looked up with a surprised expression. ''I know how you feel, Arthur. I've seen my own plans turn to ashes, just when I thought nothing could touch me. It's never easy to learn you've been wrong about someone you trusted. All you can do is go ahead and do your best to make things right again.''

"I guess you're right, Mr. Clemens," said the butler. "And I guess I ought to start by helping Leonard Galloway, if I can. Give me a moment to think, and I'll tell you anything you want to know.''

"Maybe a drink would settle you down," said Mr. Clemens. "I could sure use one." He pointed toward the whisky and soda bottles. I took his hint and went to the sideboard to pour drinks.

"Thank you, sir, but I'll have to decline the kindly offer," said the butler, holding up his hand. "I can't hold Leonard to a rule I won't follow myself, and I do have to go back to work for Mrs. Robinson this afternoon. For all I know, Mr. Holt could be coming by for dinner this evening. It's not going to be easy to look him in the eye after hearing him spout that Klan talk. I don't know what I might do if I start drinking liquor.''

"Perhaps another time, then," said Mr. Clemens, returning to the easy chair. "Go ahead and make me one, Wentworth. Listening's as thirsty a job as talking." I nodded my assent and began fixing a drink to his usual specifications.

"I was about to tell you where Mr. Robinson had gone that last day," said the butler, "but I wasn't going to tell you why. Now it's time to tell you both. When Mr. Dupree came by, just before noon, I overheard some of their conversation. I had just brought Mr. Robinson's mail to him, and I heard Dupree tell him he had to get to Anderson's right away, and be sure to bring enough money. Now, ordinarily I might not have thought much of it, but when Mr. Robinson turned around and looked, he was white as a sheet. I didn't hear any of the rest of what they said, but Mr. Robinson went out right after that.''

"I think we just struck pay dirt," said Mr. Clemens. He was sitting up straight in his chair. I took him his drink and he nodded appreciatively, but put it on the side table without taking a sip, as he continued talking. "I'll lay you ten to one it's blackmail, Wentworth. A mistress in town, probably, and somebody who figured he could make money by threatening to expose it. Especially since Robinson was going to run as a reform candidate. A scandal would hurt him with precisely the people most likely to support him.''

"Maybe not just money, but influence," I suggested. "Someone like Anderson might have been using the threat of exposure to put pressure on Robinson and force him to adopt policies he and his cronies wanted.''

"Yes, Anderson—that's the very name that popped into my mind," said Mr. Clemens, shaking his fist. "I didn't trust that rascal from the minute I set foot in his saloon.''

"He's a rascal for sure," I agreed. "But Mr. LeJeune knows Anderson longer and better than either of us, and he doesn't think he's capable of murder.''

"Capable or not, he's smack-dab in the middle of it," said Mr. Clemens. He got up from his chair, strode over to the window, looked out at the sky, and then turned around abruptly. "Are you sure it was Anderson's he went to?''

"That's what I heard him say," said the butler, nodding. "Of course, there's not a politician in New Orleans who doesn't go there and do a little horse-trading. Some men go for other reasons, of course, but I doubt whether Mr. Robinson had any such interests. Pardon my saying so, but I think you gentlemen might be on the wrong trail with this blackmail idea.''

"Really?" said Mr. Clemens. His eyebrows went in the general direction of the ceiling. "Perhaps you'd better explain yourself. If the blackmail idea doesn't hold water, then I've misunderstood Robinson's character entirely.''

The butler lowered his head, as if to deny responsibility for having contradicted a white man. "A butler hears talk and sees things. Sometimes people even forget I'm standing there, as if I were a piece of furniture. If Mr. Robinson had been chasing women, I'd *know* it. And now that he's dead, there wouldn't be any reason to hide it, especially if it helped catch the man that killed him, though I'd hate to see Miz Eugenia get hurt by it.''

"Look here, Arthur, I don't want to put you through an inquisition, but let's get down to brass tacks. What do you know about the French Quarter apartment Robinson was renting?''

This question caught the butler by surprise. His eyes opened wide, and he swayed back, almost as if to dodge a blow. "Why, Mr. Clemens, how do you know about that?''

Mr. Clemens leaned forward, pressing the issue. "Does it matter? We know he rented it, and we know the address. We have a report that a woman was seen entering it. If Robinson wasn't supporting a mistress there, what was it for?''

Arthur's face took on the same expression as just before Reynold Holt's knock on the door. "It's not what you think, Mr. Clemens. I know he paid the rent on it, but to the best of my knowledge, he never set foot in the place except for the first visit to determine if it was suitable. But if I were in your place, I wouldn't pay it too much mind. I don't believe it has anything to do with the murders.''

Mr. Clemens was clearly not satisfied with this answer. He stroked his mustache again, thinking. "I see,'' he said after a minute or so. "You say he went there once to determine if it was suitable. Suitable for what?''

"He didn't confide that to me. To tell you the truth, I've never seen the place, myself.'' The butler had recovered his composure, and his expression was unreadable, now.

"I wouldn't want you to betray a trust,'' said Mr. Clemens. His expression was serious, and he looked Arthur straight in the eye. "But I'll ask you once again to remember that a man who thought you were his friend is in Parish Prison, and unless we can find some way to clear him, he's a good bet to hang for murder. Reynold Holt would like nothing better than to see that, Arthur. Could you live with your conscience if that happened?''

Arthur hung his head, then looked up with a determined

expression. "I could live with my conscience easily **249** enough, if Leonard is guilty," he said.

"And if he's not?"

"I don't know that he's not," said the butler. Mr. Clemens stared at him, not saying anything. The butler met his stare for a moment, then nodded. "All right, I don't know that he is, either. I've been taking Mr. Holt's word for it, and after what I heard him say today, that word doesn't carry as much weight as it used to."

"A reasonable doubt is grounds enough to free a man," said Mr. Clemens. "It sounds to me as if you don't have near enough reason to convict him. What has he done to make you want to see him hang?"

Arthur slumped down in his seat, shaking his head again. "Nothing. Lord help me, Leonard Galloway hasn't done a thing to me, and here I sit equivocating. But the law won't free him on my word alone. What can I do? What can I do?"

"You can tell us the whole truth," said Mr. Clemens, pointing his finger at the butler. "You said that Robinson went to Anderson's that day, but then you said it wasn't that unusual—all the politicos go there. You said he had to take money with him, but then you said it wasn't blackmail, and you deny he had a mistress downtown. None of that makes sense. You're dodging around something, and I think it's something I need to know. What is it, Arthur?"

Arthur was silent for a long while, but finally he looked up at Mr. Clemens and spoke. "I already told you I worked for Mr. Robinson for twenty-two years—and for Miz Eugenia's family before that. That's a long time to stay with one man, Mr. Clemens. I thought the man deserved not to have his intimate business hauled out, even after his death. A lot of folks thought he was a good man, and he *was* a good man to me, Mr. Clemens. As good a man as anybody could ask to work for. But he didn't always do right by other folks who might have had reason to expect it." He paused, perhaps thinking of his employer of so many years. "But none of us is without sin."

Mr. Clemens's expression was all sympathy. "Who didn't he do right by, Arthur?" he asked in a quiet voice.

The butler did not reply instantly, but stared at the tabletop, as if trying to find his cue written there. At last, he looked up and began to speak, almost without emotion. "He gave his wife a fine house, and a mighty fine style of living, and at first there was a lot of love between them. They were going to have a child—a son, they thought, to carry on the name. And she lost the baby. Dr. Soupape did everything he could, but she lost it. And something went out of the marriage then."

"How long ago was that?" Mr. Clemens's voice was gentle, and his face showed sympathy and concern.

"It must be near ten years, now," said Arthur. "Mr. Robinson didn't change all that much at first, but it seemed like he started to drift away from Miz Eugenia. He was always downtown on business, but when he got interested in politics, he spent even more time down there, way late at night sometimes. Well, a man's wife might not notice everything he does, but his butler will, for sure. I knew there was something wrong between them way before she did. But eventually, even she noticed."

The butler's eyes narrowed, and his voice changed; perhaps it was a bit more calculated now. "Then Miz Eugenia started to go out in the afternoons herself, when her husband was downtown. I can't say exactly where she was going, but I do know she'd get very excited sometimes, before she went out. It seemed to me she was looking forward to something more than tea and whist. But I never really knew just what it was."

"You think she was untrue to him?" Mr. Clemens's voice was carefully neutral, but in his eyes I could see that he was disturbed by the notion.

Arthur shook his head. "I'd just as soon not say any more about Miz Eugenia. Whatever troubles she and poor

Mr. Robinson might have had, she's treated me as well as any man could ask.''

''Understood,'' said Mr. Clemens. ''But do you think she could have killed her husband?''

''No!'' said the butler, clearly shocked. ''Worst I can say about him is that he didn't pay her all the attention she might have wanted, and the worst I can say about her is that she may have decided to look for attention somewhere else. As the Lord said, 'Let him who is without sin cast the first stone.' ''

Mr. Clemens frowned. ''I guess that's as far as I'm going to get along that road,'' he said. ''One more question, unless you can think of anything else I ought to know about. We've learned what kind of poison killed both Robinson and Staunton: jimsonweed. I hear tell some of the herb doctors use it in potions. Can you think of somebody who might have had a grudge against both Robinson and Staunton, somebody who could have given them an herb potion brewed from jimsonweed? Because that's my best guess how the two victims were persuaded to take the poison. Maybe they wouldn't have eaten it in a salad, but people aren't surprised if medicine has an unpleasant taste.''

''No, sir.'' The butler was emphatic. ''That stuff is the devil's work. Some of the ignorant Negroes may believe in those potions, but no respectable person would touch them.''

''That's strange,'' said Mr. Clemens, casually. ''I've heard on pretty good authority that none other than Mrs. Staunton is a firm believer in all sorts of spirits and hoo-doos.''

''I can't testify to Mrs. Staunton's beliefs,'' said Arthur, pursing his lips. ''But I'm not betraying any confidences if I tell you that Mr. and Mrs. Robinson laughed about her fads and enthusiasms. None of the family took her seriously.''

''Pity they didn't,'' said Mr. Clemens. He belatedly remembered his whisky and soda sitting next to his chair, and sidled over to pick it up and take a sip before continuing the thought. "I wouldn't be surprised if it turned out she was the one the rest of them should have taken the most seriously."

We talked to the butler a little while longer, but it was soon clear that his well of useful information had run dry. Mr. Clemens finally shook his hand and asked him to get in touch if he saw or remembered anything that might be of further use to us. Arthur ventured a little smile and promised to keep us informed. We saw him out the door, and then Mr. Clemens sat back down in his chair and took another long sip of his drink.

I stood by the door and listened to the butler's footsteps recede down the stairs. When I was satisfied that he had really gone away, I turned to Mr. Clemens and said, "What a mess! Are these Southerners playing by their own rules of logic? Mr. Holt paints a picture as crazy as anything I've ever heard. A conspiracy of Negroes, murdering their masters on the least provocation, then murdering another man to cover up the first!"

"I don't know," said Mr. Clemens, sipping his drink. "Maybe Arthur hasn't told us the whole truth. And maybe Holt isn't completely lying."

I was astonished. "You must be joking. How could any of Holt's lurid tale be true?"

"Well, of course most of it isn't even close, except in his imagination," said Mr. Clemens, anger coming into his voice. "But there are hundreds of other white men who believe the same pernicious blather, which is why they're passing these laws to crush the Negroes back into something not much better than slavery. Next thing you know, they'll be reviving the Ku Klux Klan, or the Knights of the White Camellia, which was the local version of the Klan. It's a crime and a hoax, and a shame to every southern man who doesn't stand up and expose it for the pack of lies it is."

"I would be the last to argue with that sentiment," I said. "I confess a complete inability to understand why anyone could believe Holt's diatribe. That's why I can't see what he said that you think might be true."

Mr. Clemens propped up his feet and sat back with the air of someone completely at ease. He pulled out a cigar, snipped the end off, then looked up at me and said, "Holt told us one thing that hit the bull's-eye: *Staunton wouldn't have taken a drink with someone he'd just caught in a compromising position with his wife.* I thought of that myself, yesterday in court, but the full implications of it didn't strike me until Holt reminded me of it just now. If the poison were something that could be snuck unnoticed into food or a drink without changing the taste, then the poisoner could be almost anybody: a guest in the house, a bartender, the cook in a restaurant, take your pick. But if it's jimsonweed, the victim would notice an off taste. You could argue that Robinson might have ignored the taste, because he wasn't looking out for poison. But that argument's out the window when it comes to Staunton, a man who'd seen his brother-in-law die of poison only a couple of weeks before. He'd be damned careful what he ate and drank and who he took it from."

"True enough," I said, but I wasn't entirely satisfied with his conclusions. "I don't see how that helps us single out any of the suspects, though. Almost all of them are people he would have trusted. His wife, his family, his servants, his doctor, his attorney . . . whom else is a man supposed to trust?"

Mr. Clemens snorted. "Whom else indeed? Even a man who's made enemies has a right to think he's safe among his friends and family. Those are the people a man *ought* to feel he can trust, come Hell or high water. But I'll tell you something, Wentworth. If I had to live in the same house with these Holts and Robinsons and Stauntons, I wouldn't turn my back on a single one of them."

25

After the butler's testimony, Mr. Clemens was more convinced than ever that we needed to investigate the apartment Mr. Robinson had rented. But our plans were given a new twist by the arrival of a message from Detective LeJeune. It read: *Clemens—I've got a key to that apartment. We can all go see it together after work today—tied up on other business this afternoon. Wait for me after 5:00 at the restaurant where George Cable introduced us; I've invited him, too. We'll eat and go over afterward. Until then—R. LeJeune.*

Mr. Clemens handed me the note to read, then said, "This is mighty convenient. We're better off going in with LeJeune than if I send you over to bumble around and possibly alert the whole neighborhood that somebody's interested in the place."

"What do we do if someone's home?" I asked. "Even a policeman can't very well go barging into someone's home without a warrant, can he? For that matter, even if we find something incriminating, wouldn't it be an illegal search?"

"I reckon it would," said Mr. Clemens. "That wouldn't worry me as much as somebody's thinking we were burglars and pulling a gun. But if LeJeune's got a key, he must figure it's safe. Maybe he knows it's only used occasionally. On the other hand, his getting a key may just mean that the place has already been emptied out, and we won't find anything at all. Hmmm . . .'' He rubbed his chin and thought for a moment. ''I may be getting cynical in my old age, but I wonder if LeJeune might be pulling some sort of trick on us. What if he's putting off the inspection until this evening so as to let somebody have a chance to get rid of evidence?''

''Why would he do that?'' I said. ''He's played fair with us so far, hasn't he?''

''Don't be so sure,'' said Mr. Clemens, scowling. ''He hasn't necessarily told us everything he knows. After all, he still has to consider you a suspect in the Staunton killing, especially since you blurted out that you were in Anderson's café the afternoon Staunton was poisoned.''

''Yes, I should have known better than that,'' I said. ''But I can't see that it would diminish his desire to solve the case.''

Mr. Clemens was less willing to give LeJeune the benefit of the doubt. ''What if he's under pressure not to rock the boat?'' he countered. ''LeJeune hinted as much yesterday. It takes mighty strong principles to go against orders from the man who pays your wages.''

''I suppose you have a right to be suspicious,'' I said. ''But what are we supposed to do about it?''

''The thing to do, I think, is to plant yourself someplace where you can keep an eye on the apartment without being spotted. Maybe there's a café across the street, or a barbershop, or something like that. If LeJeune or anyone else who might know you shows up at the apartment, for God's sake don't let him see you. Find one of the local boys to bring me a message—tell him he'll get a good tip if he brings it straight to me—and keep watching the place. If nothing happens, just come to the meeting place at five, and we'll play it according to LeJeune's script.''

''What if something does happen?''

Mr. Clemens's brows furrowed as he thought. Then he shrugged and laughed. ''Hell, I can't foresee everything that might happen. I'll have to trust your judgment. But

256   don't do anything that might land you back in jail! I've already pledged my earnings for the next week as bail for you. I can't bail you out again; so, when in doubt, lay low.''

"I'll be prudent, never fear," I reassured him. "And what will you do, in the meantime?''

Mr. Clemens leaned back in his chair and folded his hands behind his head. "Now's my time to sit and figure out how all the pieces fit together while I'm waiting for news. Maybe you'll find something out, maybe not—and the same goes for LeJeune and all the others. But that doesn't mean I might not be able to come up with an answer based on what I've already got. Don't know until I try. But get a move on, Wentworth! The cops could be hauling out wheelbarrows full of evidence while we sit here gabbing, and have the firetrap cleaned out before we even know it.''

I wasn't especially sanguine about this assignment, having no experience as a spy (and, I feared, no special aptitude for the profession). But it occurred to me that I was in much the same situation as LeJeune: arguing with the man who paid my wages might be an admirable character trait in the abstract, but it was hardly in my best interest. Besides, I had no good reason not to do as he said. I put on my hat and headed out the door.

I walked up to Customhouse Street, which ran behind the building of that name (the front of which faced Canal Street, near the river). This large granite edifice was formerly a Confederate munitions plant, and later served as a prison for captured rebels during the War. It now contained the central post office for New Orleans, as well as the customs department. Mr. Clemens and I had enjoyed a fine view of the city from the flat roof of this building just a few days ago. But now I turned away from it and made my way toward Bourbon Street, a less elegant district, and a far less savory one.

The apartment house was not hard to find. I arrived there

just after lunchtime. Located on the northeast side of Customhouse Street between Bourbon and Dauphine, it was a squarish, utilitarian building, which had not seen a fresh coat of paint in several years. It had the apparently compulsory balcony with a cast-iron railing, but even with this feature, its exterior showed little of the ornament and grace of those more picturesque French Quarter buildings around Royal Street. Its front door stood nearly flush to the street, and a stout colored woman was busily sweeping the banquette in front, made, in this part of town, of bricks laid in a herringbone pattern.

A saloon across the street seemed to offer the best place from which to observe the front door of the apartment with a modicum of concealment. The shady bench along the banquette outside, currently occupied by two graybeards drinking beer from tin cups, looked inviting. But Mr. Clemens's warning not to let myself be spotted stuck in my mind, and so I went inside (stepping nimbly around a large hound sleeping in the doorway), ordered a cold beer, and stationed myself to have the best view of the apartment house through the swinging doors.

Two hours later, I was beginning to wonder how much longer I could stay. I had nursed two beers and was starting a third, and had refrained from nibbling any more of the free lunch than I needed to keep the beer from going too quickly to my head. But the stale tobacco smoke was thick and rank, and the place itself was not by any means the cleanest. Not only were the cuspidors in need of emptying, the floor around them would have benefited from the use of a mop. Fortunately for me, the saloon was not crowded at this time of day; a few out-of-work loafers and the old fellows from outside, who came in for an occasional refill of their tin cups, were the only other patrons. One or two of them had tried to start up conversations, and it was only with difficulty that I had managed to get rid of them without being outright rude. As the afternoon wore on, however, more regular customers were beginning to trickle in. I might be hard-pressed to hold on to my prime spot at the center of the bar much longer, especially if I was not drinking, and if I continued to drink beer, I was not going to be any good as a lookout very much longer.

Then, just as I was beginning to think I was on a wild-goose chase, my luck changed for the better. The door to the apartment building opened, and a man with a small suitcase came down the little flight of steps and turned left, headed toward Bourbon Street. It was none other than Mr. Gordon Dupree, Mr. Robinson's family lawyer!

I had not seen him enter, but that meant very little. Quite possibly he had arrived before I took up my watch. I set down my beer unfinished, with a tip for the bartender, and hurried to the door. Dupree was still in sight, evidently in no particular hurry. Remembering Mr. Clemens's instructions, I took out pencil and paper and began to scrawl a note: *Saw Dupree leaving building.* I stopped to think what else to add, and then realized there were no likely messengers in view. I had as much chance of finding a boy to carry the note by following Dupree as by staying where I was; and it might be more useful to know his destination than to keep watching the building he had left.

I set out after him, staying on the opposite side of the street and far enough back that a casual glance might not detect me. Dupree was almost certainly not headed for Tom Anderson's café, which was two blocks or so in the other direction. At the corner, he turned right on Bourbon Street, toward Canal. I ducked into a doorway until he was out of sight, then hurried to the corner to catch up with him. He was still less than half a block ahead, moving along with no particular urgency. There were still no small boys on the street to take my note to Mr. Clemens, and by now I had committed myself to following Dupree.

At the corner of Canal there was a newsstand, with perhaps half a dozen newspaper boys lounging nearby. Several hackney coaches waited outside for passengers. Dupree went directly to the first driver in line. Clearly, I would

have to make a choice. I could attempt to get close enough
to learn his destination and risk being seen, or I could engage one of the other cabs to follow him and learn where
he went, or I could give up the chase and report to Mr.
Clemens. Dupree was already climbing aboard, so I had
best make up my mind at once. Quickly, I scrawled two
more words on the note: *Following him.* I handed it, with
a dime, to one of the paper boys, with instructions to take
it to my employer on Royal Street. He looked at the dime
and grinned, tipped his cap, and trotted off down the street.
I turned and hailed a cab. "Follow that fellow who just
left," I said. "But don't get so close that he can see we're
trailing him."

"Sure 'nuff, boss," said the driver, a lean fellow with
an olive complexion and straight black hair pulled back
over his ears. He flicked his reins, and we set off after
Dupree, whose cab had turned onto Canal Street and was
headed toward the river. At the statue of Henry Clay, which
occupied the center of this main thoroughfare, Dupree
turned right onto Saint Charles Avenue, heading toward the
Garden District. My driver followed at a little distance.

By now, this route was very familiar to me, so I kept
my eyes on the cab ahead of us and let the scenery slide
by unnoticed. "He's probably going all the way to Jackson
Avenue," I told the driver. "You can fall back a little bit,
as long as you can see where he turns off and catch up
before we lose him."

"Don't worry, boss, I won't lose him," said the driver.
"That's Jess McNally he's ridin' with, and ol' Jess couldn't
run away from me if he had a mile head start." He eased
his horse into an ambling pace, and I sat back to speculate
on what Dupree's business at the apartment might have
been. To judge from the suitcase, he was removing something from the premises—presumably clothing or other personal items. Had Robinson kept a change of clothes in the
apartment? But according to the butler, he never went there.
Could the butler be mistaken, or was he misleading us? And

why was the lawyer only now recovering his late client's possessions, if that was what he was carrying? Had the butler warned him of Mr. Clemens's interest in the place? Between the easy rocking of the carriage, and the beer I had drunk while watching the apartment, I fell into something of a daydream, trying to construct theories that pulled all the details into a coherent whole; but without notable success.

"There he goes down First Street," said my driver, and I snapped out of my reverie to realize that we had come all the way to the Garden District. My driver flicked his reins, and our horse picked up his pace.

At the corner of First, we took a left, following Dupree's carriage. We were in the most elegant part of the Garden District, now, with attractive homes and formal lawns on either side. Ahead I saw the lawyer's carriage moving directly down the street. Now I had a good idea of his probable destination. "Drive slowly, and be ready to turn around and head back downtown, but don't stop or turn unless I tell you to," I told my driver. He nodded his assent and slowed his horse to an easy walk.

About a block ahead of me, I saw the other cab slow down at the corner of Chestnut Street. As I had expected, there Dupree's cab stopped, with the lawyer stepping down, suitcase in hand, directly in front of the late Percival Staunton's home. "That's all I need to see," I told my driver. "Now, take me to Royal Street, between Saint Philip and Ursulines." He nodded and brought his horse around, and we were off to the French Quarter again.

I returned to the pension to find Mr. Clemens pacing nervously, with my note in his hand and a cigar clenched in his teeth. He spun around to face me as I came in the door, clapping his hands and saying, "Good, you're back, Wentworth! Where did that rascal go?"

"To the place where all my trouble started," I said, and

told him the whole story. He continued pacing as I talked, and let me finish without interruption.

"Damnation! I'm glad you managed to catch him in the act. Otherwise we'd never know anyone had been there, never mind who. I wonder how Dupree knew to clean the place out just before we were going to see it," he mused.

"I'm beginning to think you were right about LeJeune's putting us off until the place could be emptied of anything incriminating," I said. "I must say I'm disappointed in him."

"No more than I am," said Mr. Clemens. He stubbed out his cigar. "But we'll soon have our chance to cross-examine him. It's nearly five o'clock. What do you say we get to the restaurant early and have a drink while we wait for him and George Cable?"

As expected, we were the first to arrive at the little café, and we took a table for four near the front. We ordered drinks and sat back to await our dinner companions. "I suppose the lawyer's going to the Staunton place confirms your suspicion of Maria," I said. "I wouldn't have thought she was capable of murder. But given her interest in voodoo and her apparent difficulties with her husband, we've got all the elements in place. She had a source for the poison and all the opportunity in the world to give it to him."

"So it would appear," said Mr. Clemens. "I can't quite figure out what she had to do with the apartment, though. It was Robinson who rented it. Why would her belongings be there?"

"What makes you think it was her belongings in that suitcase?" I asked. "We don't know if he left the suitcase there or if he took it with him when he left."

Mr. Clemens tapped his finger on the tabletop. "Hmm. Good point, Wentworth. Dupree's going to the Staunton home might have nothing to do with the suitcase. But assume for a moment it did. Suppose Maria Staunton was having an affair with her sister's husband, Robinson. That apartment could have been their meeting place, and she might well have kept a few personal effects there. That would explain Staunton's suspicions and his reaction when he found you and her together. And it would explain the suitcase.''

''I suppose so,'' I said. I was still not satisfied with the explanation, but for the moment, I had nothing better to offer.

The waiter came with our drinks, and we fell silent while he was within earshot. Then Mr. Clemens took a long sip and gave a deep sigh. ''I suppose it doesn't matter who really did it, as long as we can get Leonard off, but I would be sorry to see the most intelligent and literate member of the whole family turn out to be the killer. It undermines my whole faith in the civilizing power of literature. Not that I put any great stock in civilization for its own sake, mind you.''

''I hope you're right about our being able to get Leonard off,'' I said. ''Somebody must have warned Dupree that we were going to search that apartment this evening, and as far as I can tell, it would have to be LeJeune. And if LeJeune is working to cover up the family's involvement, we may be up against a brick wall.''

''What about Arthur, the butler?'' asked Mr. Clemens. ''He could have left us and found someplace with a telephone—there's bound to be one near our pension. He could have called Dupree and told him every word we'd said within five minutes of leaving us.''

''He could have,'' I said. ''But he didn't know we were going to go see the place tonight. *We* didn't even know it until after Arthur had left. So Dupree wouldn't have known there was any urgency about cleaning it out today. Only LeJeune actually knew we were going there tonight.''

Mr. Clemens swirled the ice cubes in his glass, scowling. ''Yes, that does make it look as if it had to be LeJeune. I reckon George Cable will be disappointed to learn that his old friend has betrayed us. Remember, he told us LeJeune was among the last honest cops in New Orleans? I think we've just reduced the total by one more. And that may **263** mean that the whole damned police department has just declared its principles: *Protect the wealthy white man, even if you have to hang an innocent colored man to do it.* Hell, from the way Reynold Holt talked, they seem to think that hanging the colored man is more important than protecting the white folks. I'm starting to think it's well past time we shook the dust of this rotten city off our feet.''

''I can't disagree,'' I said. ''It's too bad; the place does undeniably have its attractive side. But here comes Mr. Cable; we'll have to break the news to him before LeJeune arrives.''

Mr. Cable was all smiles as he sat down with us, but his manner changed when Mr. Clemens outlined our recent discoveries. He was shocked to learn that LeJeune had apparently betrayed us. ''I thought I knew Richard better than that,'' he said, shaking his head. ''There must be some other explanation for it all.''

''I'd like to think so myself,'' said Mr. Clemens. ''I thought I was a good judge of character, and it looks as if I've missed the target twice. Well, maybe I'm not as surprised by LeJeune as by Maria Staunton. A policeman spends his whole working life dealing with crime and corruption, and some of it's bound to get under his skin. But that little woman—I have a hard time imagining her killing even a fly, let alone two men. But even a mouse will bite if it's backed into a corner.''

''Samuel, this is the first time I've ever heard you admit to a deficiency of imagination,'' said Mr. Cable. The little man smiled ruefully. ''Not that I had any more suspicion of her than you did. Why, I spent the best part of an hour with Mrs. Staunton this afternoon, and if she *is* the murderer, she did the best job of acting I've seen short of Sarah Bernhardt. She seems truly heartbroken over losing her Percy, as she called him. I do believe she loved her husband.''

Mr. Clemens cupped his chin, frowning. ''I'd believe

she's a murderer sooner than that she's a good enough actor to fool us, George. I've seen some pretty good liars in my time, from card sharks and jackleg preachers right up to railway tycoons and newspaper editors, and that's not even counting senators or governors. There aren't many who can fool me anymore. I wouldn't have thought the lady was in that class.''

"It *is* hard to believe," said Mr. Cable. "But I still hope you're wrong about LeJeune, at least. I've known Richard for a lot of years, and he's always been as straight with me as any policeman could ever be with a newspaperman. After all, Dupree's being at the apartment this afternoon could be a coincidence.''

"I would like to think so, too," I said. "Then at least there's a chance of some kind of justice for the killer, and for Leonard Galloway.''

"Yes, we mustn't forget Leonard," said Mr. Cable. "He's the one I'm most concerned about. Even if the murderer goes unpunished, I can't let myself give up as long as there's a chance of that innocent man being punished for it.''

Mr. Clemens ran a hand over his brow, pushing back his long hair. Anger and frustration were evident on his face, and for a moment, I was not certain which was uppermost. Then he slapped his palm on the table. "You're right, fellows. I can't let myself get discouraged while there's still a chance we can save Leonard. If I do, the bigots and their hired hands will win the day. Maybe it's an uphill race, but if I give up now, I might as well have never started it.''

Mr. Cable smiled again. As small as he was, it made him look like a little boy, despite his full beard. "That's the right spirit, Samuel. Let's give Richard a chance to show us his true colors. If he's the man I think he is, we may be able to save Leonard yet.''

"Well, we'll find out soon enough which side of the fence our detective is on," said Mr. Clemens. "Here he comes.''

I turned just in time to see Detective LeJeune enter the café. He took off his hat and mopped his brow with a white handkerchief, then looked around and spotted us. "George! Glad you could make it," he said, coming over to our table. "Mr. Clemens, Mr. Cabot. Good evening to you all. I'm looking forward to our little scouting trip tonight." He pulled the fourth chair out from the table and sat down.

"Let's hope there's still a horse in the barn when we get there," said Mr. Clemens, in a dry tone of voice. "It seems there's someone else with a key to the apartment."

The detective frowned. "Well, of course there is . . . Wait a minute. What have you found out?"

Mr. Clemens leaned back in his chair and gestured to me. "We went ahead and took a look around on our own. Why don't you tell him what you found out, Cabot?"

I quickly summarized my afternoon's expedition, ending with Dupree's delivery of the suitcase to Maria Staunton's home, and our suspicions that she might have been the one who used the apartment. The detective listened attentively, once or twice stopping me to ask about some detail of what I'd seen. When I had finished, he nodded and said, "Good work, son. I reckon you just saved me from missing the boat entirely. I knew Gordon Dupree was a slick article, but I didn't think he was the kind to impede an investigation by removing evidence. He'll be sorry he did it, if I have any say about it."

Mr. Clemens didn't change his expression. "That's easy to say, Detective," he drawled. "But Dupree must have known we were going to search that apartment tonight, for him to clean it out this afternoon. He's had weeks since Robinson's murder to go in and get whatever he was after. Who besides you knew we were going to go there tonight?"

"You, for one," said the detective, returning Mr. Clemens's stare. "You and your secretary and Mr. Cable. Let's not throw around accusations, Mr. Clemens. That's an easy game to play, but I doubt it'll get us anywhere. My job is to put the murderer behind bars, and I'd be mighty damned ungrateful if I didn't appreciate what you and Mr. Cabot have found out today. But let's get the lid nailed on this thing so we can stop suspecting each other. I can wait for supper if you gentlemen can. Do you want to go over right now and look at that place without any more delay?''

''What's the point of it?'' said Mr. Cable. ''Dupree has probably taken away everything of any potential value as evidence.''

''He may think he has,'' said Detective LeJeune. ''But unless he had a platoon of cleaning maids in there with him, odds are he's left something behind without even knowing it. And I've spent twenty years learning how to search a crime scene for just that kind of overlooked detail. Shall we go see what we can learn from it?''

Mr. Clemens stood up. ''Hell, yes. I reckon we're close enough to the end of the trail that I can wait a little longer to put food in my belly. Let's go see this apartment and find out whether we can discover something that'll free the cook and put the real murderer in jail in his place.''

26

Detective LeJeune led us up a flight of stairs into a hallway with a dark red carpet and flowered wallpaper in the taste of two decades ago. It was lit by a large window facing on the street, through which I could see the balcony on the front of the building. There were two doors on either side of the hallway, and he led us to the one on the left.

"Out of curiosity, how'd you get a key?" asked Mr. Clemens. "It looks as if I may be deeper into the detective business than I'd ever expected, and a professional secret or two might come in handy somewhere down the road."

LeJeune chuckled. "I'll tell you, but I doubt you'll get much use out of it. The landlord runs a betting parlor over on Burgundy Street. We've known about it for years, but never had any complaints, so we've left him alone. This afternoon, I reminded him that he's technically in violation of several ordinances, and he was happy to cooperate."

He turned the key in the lock; at first it seemed to resist, but then he got it seated right and pushed the door open. The four of us stepped inside. LeJeune lit the gas to reveal a tastefully furnished room with two lace-curtained floor-to-ceiling windows opening onto the balcony. There was a bright coverlet on the bed and a painting of a vase with spring flowers on the wall above the little table. The whole room gave the impression of a better style of living than

Peter J. Heck

the exterior of the building in which it was located would
have suggested.

"Looks as if Robinson took pretty good care of his mistress, if that's who lived here," said LeJeune. "The landlord told me he'd been renting it for about five years. We'll
get the specific date if it turns out to be important."

"Remember, Robinson's butler told us he never came
here," I said. "And he claimed that Robinson wasn't a
womanizer."

"We don't have to take all that at face value," said Mr.
Clemens. He went over to the window and peeked through
the curtain onto the street, then turned around to face us.
"I wouldn't be surprised if Arthur was lying to protect his
master. The decor certainly shows a woman's touch, and
the place is clean. Maybe Dupree had that platoon of cleaning maids, after all. Did the landlord know who was living
here?"

"No," said the detective. "He's an absentee, almost
never comes by the place. But he told the concierge to
answer my questions, so we should be able to find out
more, once I run the fellow down. We'll see if the neighbors have noticed anything, as well. Meanwhile, let's look
around and see what we can find. Dupree might have
cleaned it out, but we may still be able to tell who was
using it and what for."

At first glance, I thought LeJeune was being far too op-
timistic. There was a minimum of furniture: a small table,
two straight-backed chairs, a chest of drawers, and a single
bed. They were all of good quality, but I could see no
personal effects that might identify the owner. Mr. Clemens
walked over to the chest of drawers and opened the top
drawer. "Empty," he said. The other drawers also proved
to be empty.

"It looks as if we're shooting blanks," said Mr. Clemens. "I wonder how that damned lawyer knew to clean the
place out just before we were coming to look here."

"It *could* just be coincidence that he came today," said

the detective. "What I'd really like to know about is what Dupree took out of here and why he delivered it to Maria Staunton, if that's where it ended up. It smells funny to me; why would Robinson be renting an apartment for his sister-in-law's use?"

"Well, we don't know for certain that Robinson was renting the place for Maria," said Mr. Clemens. "If she'd been staying here, I'd have expected a couple of book-shelves, at the very least. Dupree could have been taking that suitcase to somebody else at her house. Her brother or her sister might have been visiting. He could even have brought it to one of the servants, I suppose."

"Yes, or he might have simply paid a visit to Mrs. Staunton, then taken the suitcase elsewhere," said Cable. "I don't blame your secretary for not staying to watch where Dupree went afterward—there'd have been too much danger of being seen. But I wish we knew for certain what was in that suitcase and who got it. It must have been something that has to be kept quiet, if they sent the lawyer to get it, instead of one of the servants."

"Good point," said Mr. LeJeune. "Nobody uses a high-priced lawyer as an errand boy unless . . . Shh! What's that?" We all fell dead silent, listening. There were light footsteps climbing the stairs toward the second floor. "Quick! Out on the balcony. I'll douse the light," said the detective. We quickly opened the French windows and tried to make ourselves inconspicuous; the light went out behind us and LeJeune stepped out to join us, pulling the window shut behind him.

"This might have nothing to do with us, but I'd just as soon not be caught here," whispered the detective. "Be still, now."

I was uncomfortably aware of being on an open balcony, directly across from the saloon where I had spent much of the afternoon. The daylight was fading, but any curious eyes glancing upward would still have little trouble picking out the four of us, no matter how inconspicuous we tried to appear. Nor was there any guarantee that, if the person climbing the stairs entered the apartment we had just left, he or she would not come directly to the front and throw open the balcony windows to discover four trespassers. And then? My imagination summoned up dire consequences: arrest, gunfire, being thrown off the balcony to the street below . . .

But I had little time to consider these possibilities, as the door to the apartment opened and someone entered. I shrank back against the balcony railing, but the newcomer strode confidently across the apartment to the windows and opened the nearest one. "Gentlemen, I know the evening breeze is fine, but it would be more private if you would step inside for a few minutes. We have things to talk about."

It was Eulalie Echo. After a moment of stunned silence, Mr. Clemens laughed and said, "Eulalie, I'm glad I don't have a weak heart, or you'd have come close to stopping it. How in the world did you know we were here?" He stepped into the apartment through the open window, and we followed him.

"You are not the only one who has been watching this apartment, Mr. Clemens," said the voodoo woman. She relit the gas, then took a seat at the table. "But you cannot expect me to give away all my secrets, especially to a policeman. Good evening, Mr. LeJeune. I know you by reputation, but I don't believe we have met."

LeJeune smiled and gave a little bow. "I hope my reputation speaks well of me."

Mr. Clemens pulled out the other chair at the little table and took his seat opposite Eulalie Echo. "Well, it looks as if we got here too late to find anything useful," he said. "If you've been watching, you must know that Dupree cleaned the place out this afternoon."

"He's done a pretty good job of it," said LeJeune. "Once we're done talking, though, I'm going over the apartment with a fine-tooth comb, and I guarantee you I'll turn up something we can eventually use. But I reckon you wouldn't be here unless you know something we don't know, Eulalie. What's your news?''

''Wait one more minute,'' said the voodoo woman. ''I decided to come meet you here because a group of white men visiting a woman in a colored section of town is bound to attract notice sooner or later; and I don't need that kind of notice, even if nobody guesses the correct reason for your visit. I have also asked Buddy Bolden to join us; he has news for us, and I believe I hear him on the stairs right now.''

Sure enough, footsteps came up the stairs, and after a moment, there was a knock on the door; at Mr. Clemens's gesture, I opened it to admit Buddy Bolden, carrying his cornet case. ''Evenin', Miz 'Lalie,'' he said. ''I came as fast as I could.''

''Good. Let us begin,'' said the voodoo woman. ''First, let me tell something I have learned. I have found out more about the woman who was seen using this apartment. The last time she was here, she came in a closed carriage, and she wore a veil. She was well-disguised, but the driver was plainly visible. My informant saw the same driver again, just this morning, out in the Garden District, and this time he was driving a man into town. That man was Gordon Dupree, the lawyer.''

''Dupree, eh?'' said LeJeune, nodding appreciatively. He took a notebook and pencil out of his pocket and scribbled something down. Then he looked around at the group. ''If it was his driver, the woman could have been one of his clients. And the two that come to mind are Maria Staunton and Eugenia Robinson.''

''Yes,'' said Mr. Clemens. ''I suppose it could be someone else, but those two would be my first guesses. But which one?''

''I don't know,'' said Eulalie, with a shrug. ''The two sisters are similar in stature, and they would be hard to distinguish at a distance, especially to someone who doesn't know them well. I can't even be certain that it wasn't another person entirely, possibly a servant.''

"Eulalie's right. We can't just assume it was one of the sisters,'' said Mr. Cable. ''It could have been a hired coach, in which case, the fact that Dupree was in it today tells us nothing at all.''

"True enough,'' said Mr. Clemens. He leaned his elbows on the table, folding his hands beneath his chin. ''Still, we can try to see if it fits a pattern. Eulalie, I'd appreciate it if you'll see if your informant can learn where the driver works.''

"Certainly,'' said the voodoo woman. ''I have already asked him to try to learn that. When I know more, I'll tell you. Now, Buddy Bolden, will you tell us your news?''

The young colored man had been leaning against the wall; now he stepped forward and said, ''I talked to a fellow who used to play piano at Anderson's café. Not quite a month ago, he was going on his break, and he saw a white man come in, asking Anderson where he could find an herb doctor. Anderson told him, and the fellow went off.''

LeJeune looked up from his notebook. ''Did your friend describe this white man? Or say where to find the herb doctor?''

Bolden spread his hands. ''He didn't send him to anybody in particular, as far as my friend knew. There must be twenty herb doctors up on South Rampart Street, any day you go there. But the customer was an old fellow, not Mr. Robinson or Mr. Staunton, 'cause I asked particular about them, and my friend knew who both of them were; said he used to see 'em in there all the time. This fellow was dressed like he had money, wearing a beard, and walking with a cane. He was looking for a love potion, and my friend said he looked like he needed it.''

"Love potion!'' said Cable. He rubbed his hands together. ''Those herb doctors often put jimsonweed in their love potions. Isn't that true, Eulalie?''

"Yes," said Eulalie Echo, nodding. "Women buy those potions when they think their man has stopped loving them. You understand, this isn't a potion to make a person fall in love; it is a strong aphrodisiac. Sometimes it makes a man regain his vigor as a lover; sometimes, if it is too strong, it poisons him. Either way, the woman often thinks she is better off than before."

Mr. Clemens frowned. "But this was a man buying the potions."

"Yes, that is unusual," said Eulalie Echo. "It is almost always women who buy them to give to their men. Men don't like to admit that they need any such assistance."

"I can't help noticing that the description of the customer fits Reynold Holt," said Mr. Cable.

"And a few hundred other men in New Orleans," said the detective, tapping his pencil on the table. "Unless we find the right herb doctor and get him to identify a white man who bought a love potion a month ago, that description won't take us very far. And that's a thousand to one against, in my opinion. I've never known an herb doctor who wanted to answer questions from a detective."

"Can you blame them?" said Buddy Bolden. He pointed at the detective. "I wouldn't be real quick to talk to you if I'd been selling poison on the street. I might make myself real hard to find, if I heard there was a cop asking questions about that stuff."

"That's not the only problem," said Mr. Clemens, rubbing his mustache with a forefinger. "Even if we could prove the buyer was looking for a love potion, even if he specified that he wanted jimsonweed in it, how could he know it was strong enough to kill a man? All we could really prove is accidental poisoning."

"That still might be enough to get Leonard Galloway out of jail," said Mr. Cable. "All we have to do is raise a reasonable doubt. If it could have been an accident, they won't hold him."

"I wouldn't bet on that," said Mr. Clemens, with a shake

of his head. "Holt was talking up a racial conspiracy; said it was time to make an example of somebody to keep the colored folks in their place. And I get the feeling some of the people in power would agree with him. I want to get Leonard out before they get a notion to take things in their own hands. And that'll take more than a reasonable doubt; we'll have to prove beyond doubt that somebody else did it."

"Which we're nowhere near," said LeJeune. His frustration was obvious. "I'm pretty sure that Leonard is innocent, myself. But Mr. Clemens is right: there's a lot of feeling against the colored folks these days. A judge isn't likely to let Leonard free without a confession from someone else or some other proof that Leonard couldn't have done it. And I don't see where that's going to come from, short of a miracle."

"Well, I can't conjure up a miracle, but we have somebody here who might be able to," said Mr. Clemens, looking at Eulalie Echo.

"Are you referring to me?" said Eulalie. For the first time I saw a surprised look on her face. "Really, Mr. Clemens, I do have certain abilities, but I cannot create miracles to order."

Mr. Clemens stood up, leaning his jaw on his right fist, a pose I'd often seen him adopt at his lectures. "All right, not a miracle, but perhaps a confession. Cable tells me that Maria Staunton is greatly distressed about her husband's death. Is that right, George?"

"It certainly is," said Mr. Cable. "She finds it most disturbing that he died still believing her to have been unfaithful. She kept saying that she wished she had been able to talk to Percy one more time."

"Well, if I could talk to him one more time, I'd be asking him who gave him the poison," said LeJeune with a scornful expression. "Not that I'd have any chance of getting it into evidence. Maybe dead men can tell tales, but you can't get judges to pay them any mind."

"And with good reason," said Eulalie. "A liar in life **275** will be a liar after death, from what I have seen."

"That should hardly surprise anybody," said Mr. Clemens. "But let's look at the evidence. The poisoner, whoever it is, appears to have used a voodoo love potion; that suggests that whoever it is might also believe in voodoo charms and magic and other kinds of superstition, no slight intended." He nodded toward Eulalie Echo, who nodded back, a tight-lipped smile on her face. Her arms were folded across her breast, and she was clearly weighing his words carefully.

Mr. Clemens continued. "Also, we have reason to believe that Robinson and Staunton were both having difficulties in their marriages, and I'd guess the poisoner used that fact to persuade both of them to try the potion. You could argue that Robinson might have taken the stuff unwittingly, but after the first poisoning, Staunton would have been on his guard against anything with an off taste. *Unless he ignored the taste because he believed that he was taking some kind of medicine.*"

"Are you accusing old Doc Soupape?" asked LeJeune. "He was the one who ordered the autopsy of Robinson to begin with. Why would he do that if he was the poisoner?"

"To deflect suspicion, maybe," said Mr. Clemens. "He's not the only suspect, though. A man will take medicine from his doctor, his wife, a servant, a nurse, even a close friend. The man who asked Anderson about herb doctors was probably Reynold Holt, the victims' brother-in-law. But Tom Anderson himself might have suggested a love potion if Robinson or Staunton confided that they were having troubles at home; from what Buddy says, they were both regular patrons. And we can't forget some of the old family friends: Dupree, or maybe even Professor Maddox."

Detective LeJeune grimaced. "Hey, Mr. Clemens, this is all backward. We ought to be narrowing down the list of suspects, and here you go making it longer again."

Mr. Clemens nodded. "Yes, because if we do what I

have in mind, we can't leave out any logical suspect.'' He stood for a moment, surveying the little group. ''LeJeune, you said that a confession would be the best way to set Leonard Galloway free. Well, I've got an idea how to get the real killer to confess. But I'll need your help, LeJeune, and Eulalie's, especially. Here's my plan. . . .''

Mr. Clemens spoke for perhaps fifteen minutes, with frequent interruptions, from both LeJeune and Eulalie Echo. But at last they both agreed to the plan. ''I guess this has as much chance of working as anything else we've got,'' said LeJeune. ''But I'll be damned if I know how I'm going to explain this to my chief.''

''Don't explain it at all,'' said Mr. Clemens. ''If it doesn't work, he doesn't even have to know we tried it. And if it does, he'll have his case solved, and I doubt he'll have any objections to how you did it.''

''I hope you're right,'' said the detective. ''Because if it doesn't work, I'm going to have Leonard Galloway's hanging on my conscience.''

''Not necessarily,'' said Mr. Cable, picking up his hat from the bed where he'd left it. ''After all, you're still doing your regular detective work—things like searching this apartment. Go ahead and carry on with your investigation while we're setting this up, and there's a good chance you might find the killer that way. If you've done that to the best of your ability, there's nobody who can find fault with you for trying something less conventional, even if it falls short.''

LeJeune shook his head wearily. ''Nobody but myself. But that's a burden I'd gladly do without.''

''There's only one thing more useless than crying over spilt milk,'' said Mr. Clemens, ''and that's crying over milk that's still in the cow. If we find the murderer, nobody's going to hang Leonard at all.''

27

The next few days were very busy. Mr. Clemens was preparing his plan to solve the murders of Robinson and Staunton, and he continued to work on his book about our trip down the Mississippi. He also kept up a lively correspondence, not only with his wife and daughters in Austria, but with literary friends across the country and overseas. And, of course, he was scheduled to deliver two lectures in New Orleans over the coming weekend. He had prepared and rehearsed for the lectures before setting out on the present tour, but still he spent some time polishing and adding finishing touches for these performances.

Unlike most of the lecturers I had seen at Yale, Mr. Clemens disliked reading from a written text. Instead, he preferred to give the appearance of an impromptu performance, although his apparently casual delivery was achieved only at the cost of extensive rehearsal. "It takes me the better part of three weeks to get ready for an impromptu lecture," he told me, and to judge from what I had seen, he did not exaggerate.

There were plenty of other things on his mind. Even on Friday night, in his dressing room, he spent an inordinate amount of time grousing about having pledged his lecture fees as surety for my remaining within Judge Fogarty's jurisdiction. A bailiff had been waiting at the theater even as we arrived, and had stationed himself in the theater manager's office to await the box office receipts. Mr. Clemens was particularly annoyed at this imposition, because it seemed clear that everyone in New Orleans except the judge himself had discarded the theory that I had any responsibility for Percival Staunton's death.

"You'd think that blamed judge would listen to his own police force," he growled, pausing to put out his cigar—he never smoked onstage. "Even that rascal Holt has figured out that you didn't have any real chance to give Staunton a dose of poison. And you were halfway up the river when Robinson got killed, but Fogarty can't grasp that point. It's about what you'd expect from a legal system that thinks the way to find the truth is to appoint a jury made up of a dozen illiterates who don't know anything and care about even less."

"Well, I can hardly take Fogarty's side in this," I said, "but I think you underestimate American justice. Is there a fairer system anywhere in the world?"

"Spoken like a lawyer's son," said Mr. Clemens, plopping himself in the dressing room chair. He took one last look in the mirror and straightened his tie. "I'm tempted to test your faith by refusing to fork over my lecture fees and seeing if Fogarty chunks you back in jail. I'd try it in a moment, but I reckon I'll need your help for the show out by the bayou tomorrow night."

"I appreciate your restraint," I said. "Perhaps I ought to skip town and leave Fogarty holding your money. Turnabout's fair play, they tell me."

Mr. Clemens chuckled. "You'd be better off taking your chances with Fogarty than fooling with me; the judge may have the law on his side, but I have no conscience whatsoever, and therefore nothing to stop me from taking revenge on you. Besides, you can't leave town yet. You'd miss the greatest dramatic production since the Royal Nonesuch."

"Very well, I shall stay. But only if you promise not to let them arrest me again."

"Don't worry," said Mr. Clemens. "I need you way too

much to let them haul you off. Even if it means I have to wait a little longer to get hold of my hard-earned lecture fees. Speaking of which, what does the house look like?''

"Filling up very nicely," I told him. I had peeked at the audience not fifteen minutes before, and already there was barely a seat unoccupied.

"Good. There's no such thing as too big an audience, at least as long as it's a paying audience." He glanced at his watch. "I guess you'd best get on out front if you don't want somebody else to grab your seat, then. The trouble is supposed to start in five minutes."

I made it out front in time to claim my seat, two-thirds of the way back in the hall, which by now was standing-room only. As usual, the boxes were filled with ladies and gentlemen dressed in the height of fashion, while the denizens of the cheap seats looked as if they might be more at home at a mule race than at a literary evening. A thick pall of tobacco smoke hung over the auditorium, and a buzz of excited conversation filled the air. From what I overheard, the first New Orleans appearance by Mark Twain in many years seemed to have gained an air of notoriety in the wake of my arrest for dueling and Mr. Clemens's appearance before the judge to plead on my behalf. I was glad that none of the newspapers that reported on that episode had been able to get an accurate drawing of me into their accounts of my day in court.

At the designated hour, Mr. Clemens made his customary entrance, ambling onstage so unobtrusively that a good portion of the audience would undoubtedly have missed it had not the few who were paying attention greeted him with applause, which swelled to a crescendo as he slowly made his way to the front of the stage.

Mr. Clemens bowed and waited for the applause to subside, then began to speak in a quiet voice, so slowly that he seemed to come to a full stop after every word. As I have said, his lectures were carefully rehearsed, and in the main identical from one performance to the next; but he liked to open each appearance with a sort of prelude tailored to the local audience, and I was curious to see what he would have to say about New Orleans, especially in view of the audience's probable familiarity with the newspaper stories.

"It's been a long time since I was in New Orleans," he began. "For the most part, things haven't changed. Neither the city, nor the people, nor the food, which is as delightful as some of the minor varieties of sin. In fact, I'd be willing to take my chances in Hades if I knew that pompano was on the menu. It stands to reason they've got plenty of your Creole peppers down there, and several sweet old ladies who'd turn up their toes and die before they told a fib have told me that whisky is the devil's invention, so I reckon they've got plenty of *that*. So all I need to learn about for sure is the pompano. Most of my old friends will be there, anyhow, so I'm assured of good company.

"I've enjoyed your Louisiana hospitality before, but for this visit, I brought along my secretary, Cabot, a young fellow from Connecticut who's seeing your city for the first time. Cabot's a Yankee. I reckon he can't help that, but that hasn't stopped him from getting into the spirit of things and acting like a true Southerner, born and bred. Not many places would have made a stranger feel as welcome, and as much like one of its own, as New Orleans has my Yankee secretary. Why, he hadn't been here a week before one of your leading citizens challenged him to a duel!

"Now, I suppose I should have warned him against that particular southern custom, but I'd been away from the South so long that it slipped my mind. It may seem an innocent sport, like shooting at newspaper editors, but in my opinion dueling's too dangerous to undertake without due advice and preparation. I've never been in favor of strenuous outdoor exercise, other than smoking cigars, you understand. And of course, the advantage of cigars is that you can smoke them indoors, as well. But dueling almost always takes place outdoors, and first thing in the morning, too. Why, a fellow could catch his death of cold unless he wraps himself up warmly. That's why I don't hold with dueling.

"Now, just in case you think I'm speaking out of ignorance and prejudice, you ought to know that I once challenged a fellow to a duel myself. This was in Nevada, back in the mining days, and I sent my challenge before I remembered I didn't know how to shoot a pistol. Then I found out the other fellow was a crack shot. So the day before the fracas was scheduled, I went out to get some practice, and he did the same—just over the hill from where I was. I fired off five or six rounds without hitting anything smaller than a church, and then one of my seconds decided to show me how it was done. Well, his first shot took the head off a little bird at about thirty yards' distance, and it just so happened that somebody from the other party saw it. They made the mistake of assuming I'd fired the shot, and I wasn't such a fool as to go and set them right. The other fellow promptly declined to fight me on any terms whatsoever. That was the triumphal end of my dueling career. I left town on the next stage, and except for slaughtering my enemies in imagination and in print, I have been a peaceful man ever since.''

When Mr. Clemens had begun, I was worried about the New Orleans crowd's response to this subject, especially in light of the duel's end, with the demise of a son of Louisiana. And I was just as glad that the auditorium was dark, so that none of the crowd could observe my blushing during his references to me, and guess my identity. But I went unrecognized, and by the time Mr. Clemens finished his preamble, the crowd was convulsed with laughter. Shortly after, he returned to his prepared script, and I settled back to observe the rest of the lecture, which, much to my relief, went like clockwork.

*   *   *

At the end of the lecture, I stood and joined the crowd in applauding my employer. Then I began to pick a path through the crowd, heading toward the entrance to the backstage area, where I knew I would find Mr. Clemens holding court to a large group of visitors outside his dressing room door. If this audience was anything like the others on the current tour, the listeners would include everyone from important local dignitaries to barely reputable characters who claimed to be intimate friends with "good ol' Sam"—and in fact, sometimes *had* been, in his riverboat and frontier days.

I had just about reached the front of the house when a soft hand fell on my elbow and a woman's voice said, "Mr. Cabot! I am glad to see you are none the worse for the unfortunate events the other day."

I turned to see who it was, somewhat apprehensive in view of my name's having been mentioned from the stage that same evening. It was none other than Mrs. Eugenia Robinson, wearing a plain dark dress, which managed to convey the impression of mourning while not seeming entirely out of place at a theater. She was accompanied by her brother, Mr. Holt, who was doing his best to pretend not to notice me, and by Mr. Dupree. "Good evening," I said, removing my hat. "I hope you enjoyed the lecture."

"Yes, I did," she said. "Maria had bought tickets when Mr. Clemens's lecture was announced, but of course she is in mourning now. I thought it would be a shame to let the tickets go to waste, and so I got Reynold and Gordon to bring me. I'm glad I did; even Reynold seemed to enjoy himself more than usual, didn't you?" She turned to her brother, smiling, and he nodded glumly and muttered something that passed for agreement, although he still did not meet my eye.

"I am glad you found it diverting," I said. "And of course I was sorry about Mr. Staunton. I hope you will believe that I never held any ill will toward him or meant him any harm." I was somewhat uncomfortable at meeting two of the dead man's family in so public a place, but other than one or two who gave me curious glances, those around us seemed not to notice, chattering happily and making their way toward the exits.

"Of course I believe you," she said. "You conducted yourself as best you could in a difficult position, and I don't believe you have any reason to feel ashamed. I think that Reynold understands that as well. Don't you, dear?" She smiled at him, and he nodded, still not looking directly at me.

"I'm glad Mr. Clemens was able to talk the judge into granting bail," said Dupree, extending his hand. "I wouldn't have thought he had the makings of a lawyer, but I suppose I shouldn't be surprised that a man of his genius can adapt his gifts to the circumstances."

"I'll pass along your compliment to him," I said, shaking hands with him.

Holt finally spoke. "While you're at it, you might tell him it's in mighty poor taste to make fun of dueling when the family of a man who's just died defending his honor is in the house." His tone of voice was gruff, and his manner stiff.

An irritated look flashed over Mrs. Robinson's face. "There's no way he could have known we were here, Reynold," she said. "And I myself wish Percy had never issued that challenge. Please drop the subject." Her brother scowled but said nothing more.

She turned to me again. "I doubt we shall see you again, Mr. Cabot, but I did want you to know that none of us holds you responsible for any of what happened on Tuesday. I believe I can speak for poor Maria, as well. She is taking her husband's passing very heavily, but we hope she will soon recover her spirits. And now, good evening, Mr. Cabot."

"Good evening, Mrs. Robinson, Mr. Dupree," I said. Then, after a moment's hesitation, "Mr. Holt." She smiled, and he gave a very perfunctory nod of the head. Mr. Dupree took her arm and they turned away, and I continued on my way to meet my employer and, if necessary, rescue him from the press of well-wishers backstage.

The hallway in front of Mr. Clemens's dressing room bore comparison to a mob scene. In addition to the usual well-wishers and would-be spongers, the gentlemen of the local press had surrounded him. Never mind that my employer was attempting to converse with various old friends and people of some importance; they persisted in sticking their notebooks in his face and quizzing him, despite his obvious reluctance to answer. As I had feared, the majority of the questions concerned my run-in with Staunton and its aftermath: "Does this secretary have any police record up North?" "When did you find out he'd been in a duel?" and "Has he told you why he killed Staunton?"

I could see that any more such questions were likely to result in an explosion of Mr. Clemens's temper, with devastating if not deadly consequences for the New Orleans press corps. I pushed through the crowd, stepping on a couple of reportorial toes in the process, and said, "Excuse me, Mr. Clemens, but we're running behind schedule. Let me help you to your dressing room."

"By all means, Wentworth," he said, looking relieved. I took his right elbow and he looked over his shoulder, saying, "You come along too, Tom." Another large body took his other elbow, and we practically carried him through the crowd of reporters into the dressing room, where I pushed the door closed behind us, not soon enough to prevent my hearing someone ask loudly, "Is that the killer?" I turned to see Mr. Clemens brushing off his formal evening suit, and for the first time noticed his other escort; none other than Tom Anderson, the Rampart Street saloon owner.

"Now that's as tight a spot as I hope I'm ever in again," said Mr. Clemens, sitting down. "Many thanks to both of you!"

"Glad to be a help," said Anderson. "I hate those damned reporters. Always prying into a fellow's business, looking for some scandal. Why, there's not a man alive, and I include the most high and mighty among 'em, who doesn't have something or another he'd just as soon keep quiet. In my business, if a fellow doesn't want to be bothered, we know how to leave him be."

Mr. Clemens nodded. "Well, one thing we know in my business is how to thank a man who's helped us out. I'm going to have a whisky, and I'd be pleased if you'd join me. Wentworth, will you pour?"

Anderson grinned. "It's not every day a man can buy Tom Anderson a drink in New Orleans, but I'd be happy to let you turn the tables on me, this time. That was a right fine speech you gave out there."

"Hell, that wasn't a speech," said Mr. Clemens. "That was a lecture. You can't get a red cent for a speech, but when you give a lecture, you get *paid.*"

Anderson responded with a hearty laugh, and I handed him and Mr. Clemens their drinks. I had poured one for myself, as well. We clinked our glasses and took a sip. "Ah, that's good after two hours' talking," said my employer. He took another sip, then turned to Anderson with a thoughtful look on his face.

"You know, Tom, I've been thinking about some of the things we were talking about in your saloon the other day," he said. "You're a man who hears and sees a lot that other people don't, because people know you won't go blabbing it all over town."

"I expect that's true," said Anderson. "I've managed to make myself useful to some important people, because they know they can trust me."

Mr. Clemens nodded and picked up one of his corncob pipes from the dressing room table. He never smoked during his lectures, and I often wondered how such an avowed tobacco fiend could manage without the weed for so long. But he rarely waited long to light up once he was offstage.

"In a sense, I envy you," he said to Anderson. "You learn a lot of things that nobody would tell to a man they think is going to put them in a book. But you must know that people can be embarrassed of the most peculiar things."

"That's for sure," said Anderson.

"Well, one thing I've always liked to put in my books is the things people believe about magic, and ghosts, and such like," said Mr. Clemens. "Cures for warts, and stories about how animals act, and love charms, and so forth and so on. But that's exactly the kind of thing people aren't willing to talk about these days. I guess they think it makes them look ignorant to believe in such things, even when they have good reason to know they really work."

Anderson took another sip of his drink, then nodded. "I know what you mean," he said. "Of course, I remember some of that stuff from that book *Tom Sawyer*: stump water, and dead cats, and witches. Folks down here still have a lot of those old superstitions."

"Doesn't surprise me," said Mr. Clemens. "I've seen some of the herb doctors up on South Rampart Street."

"Oh, yes, there must be a couple dozen of those fellows. I don't know whether their stuff is any good, but I guess it can't hurt anybody. The colored folks swear by it—more than by regular doctors—and most of them seem to live long enough."

"If Louisiana's anything like Missouri was when I was growing up, some of the white folks aren't much different," said Mr. Clemens.

"Sure, I've had white men come to me asking about that stuff. A couple of those herb doctors will sell to a white man if I give 'em the password. If a fellow thinks those voodoo herbs can fix what ails him, I'll give him the word and send him over to Rampart Street. I'd be the last to say that the white race can't learn something from the colored. Some folks say old Marie Laveau, the queen of the voodoos, had as many white women as colored at her meetings, and I bet she still would, if she were alive today," said

Anderson. "In fact, there's some will tell you she *is* alive, never mind that tomb over in Saint Louis Cemetery."

Mr. Clemens looked appropriately awed. "That would be something to talk about. How old would she be?"

"Damned if I know—better than a hundred, anyways," said Anderson. He sipped his drink. "If it's true, that would be a mighty good testimonial for those herbs, wouldn't it?"

"Good as gold," said my employer. "Hell, it's better than gold. I don't know many men who wouldn't trade a powerful lot of gold for the chance to live to a hundred. Say, do they still have those voodoo meetings like Marie Laveau's?"

A smug expression came to Anderson's face. "Well, this is telling stories out of school, but I reckon I can trust you to keep it quiet." Mr. Clemens nodded, and Anderson continued. "I got an invitation to a voodoo meeting tomorrow night, out at Bayou Saint John, and come to think of it, from what I hear, it's going to be more white folks than colored. I wouldn't usually waste my time with such stuff, especially on a Saturday night with the saloon full of customers, but there are some important people going, and they particularly asked for me to be there."

"Really," said Mr. Clemens, his eyes lighting up. "I wish you could sneak me in; I wouldn't be any trouble at all. I'd like to put something about it in my book. Of course, I wouldn't mention any names or give away any secrets."

"Well, maybe I shouldn't have said anything about it," said Anderson, looking worried. "It's strictly a private party, understand. I don't think a stranger would be welcome, but maybe I can tell you a little about it if you'll come by the saloon after it's over." He shrugged, but his expression implied that he enjoyed the feeling of having gotten an exclusive invitation that not even the famous Mark Twain had gotten.

"Well, I reckon I'll have to console myself with secondhand reports," said Mr. Clemens. Somehow he managed to keep a straight face. I wondered what Anderson would have thought had he known that his invitation to that private voodoo meeting had been arranged by the very man he was talking to.

Anderson chatted a while longer, then downed his drink and took his leave, declining a refill on the ground that he needed to return to his business. "So, it looks as if we have all our chickens ready to pluck," said Mr. Clemens, after the big saloon owner had departed.

"So it appears," I said. "But here's something you ought to know." I told him about meeting Eugenia Robinson, Reynold Holt, and Gordon Dupree after the lecture. "Interesting that she'd come to the theater with her husband so recently dead," I said in conclusion.

"Yes, she seems to take her loss much less seriously than her sister does hers," said Mr. Clemens. "Of course, they'll both be out at the bayou with us tomorrow night, so perhaps I shouldn't give Maria too much credit."

"The voodoo meeting tomorrow night is hardly the same thing as a visit to the theater," I noted. "What was your purpose in quizzing Anderson so much about it, by the way?"

"Oh, my main purpose was already accomplished: finding out whether he would admit to sending customers to those herb doctors. But when he kept talking, I decided to find out whether he actually believes in voodoo or not. Whoever our poisoner is, I think it's someone who at least partly believes in the stuff."

"And what did you decide?"

Mr. Clemens cupped his jaw in his right hand, rubbing his thumb across the chin. "Deep down in his heart, I think Anderson still believes in spirits and magic. He's not likely to admit it openly, but yes—he's as superstitious as any of Marie Laveau's followers."

"So you think he could be our murderer?"

"Sure," said Mr. Clemens. "He and about five other

people could have done it, the way I see things now. Let's
hope tomorrow night's show narrows the number of suspects down to one.'' He frowned. ''Because if it doesn't, I
don't know how the hell I'm going to get my money back
from that judge.''

28

Henry Dodds met my employer and me at the theater after the Saturday night performance, and we headed to the banks of Bayou Saint John, some little distance from where I had met Percival Staunton and his seconds for the disastrous duel. For the first time since we had met him, Henry seemed to have left behind his usual line of badinage. Tonight, he was all business. And so, under a clear sky with a bright, round moon, we rode out to our voodoo meeting. All around us, the sounds of the night echoed: birds, frogs, insects, and who knows what other creatures. I remembered that these waters were home to alligators, although I had not the slightest notion how those huge reptiles sounded. It seemed as if the night creatures had all pitched their songs in an eerie minor key; whether it was the unfamiliarity of the local fauna or my own imagination, there was a sinister air to the night music.

After what seemed a remarkably long ride, Dodds brought us to our destination. He let us off perhaps a hundred yards from the site of Eulalie Echo's ''show,'' so the noise of the horses would not alert any of the assembled suspects. Buddy Bolden met us there, and we bade Henry farewell. With Bolden leading the way, we crept as quietly as possible through the underbrush, ducking under branches and vines. I kept wondering whether the snakes and biting insects were asleep, or whether they were waiting along the path we traveled.

At last we reached a clearing in the thick semitropical forest. We took up concealed positions affording a good view of the strange scene, and waited.

My eyes having adapted to the moonlit conditions, it took a little while for them to readjust to the bright glare of the firelight. After a minute or two, looking across the clearing, I made out the faces of the assembled audience: the two widows, Maria Staunton and Eugenia Robinson, both with shawls over their shoulders, and their brother, Reynold Holt, were seated in folding chairs; Dr. Soupape and G. G. Dupree stood directly behind them; and Tom Anderson stood to one side. Mr. Cable, Professor Maddox, and Marcus Keyes stood slightly apart from the group. I could see Maddox's lips moving, but from this distance, I could not make out what he said. I knew that somewhere, out of sight, were Detective LeJeune and several other hidden participants.

It had apparently taken some persuasion to get everyone to attend tonight. Mr. Cable had told Maria Staunton that Eulalie could bring her word of her late husband from beyond the grave. Maria had sent for Eulalie, who agreed to perform the necessary rituals. According to plan, the voodoo woman had also told Maria that her spells would work best if the whole family—and some other close associates—were present, and Maria had done the rest. At first, Eugenia Robinson and Reynold Holt had spoken scornfully of "that ignorant quadroon," as they referred to Eulalie, but eventually they gave in, if only to humor their recently bereaved sister. The others, I suspected, had agreed to come as much out of curiosity as anything else; but they were here, and now it remained to see whether Mr. Clemens's plan would have the effect he hoped for.

Oblivious to the watchers, Eulalie Echo crouched by the fire, dressed all in white and stirring something in a small kettle. At last, apparently satisfied with the concoction she was brewing, Eulalie stood and nodded to her two assistants, who squatted some little distance away. One of them began to beat softly but insistently upon a large wooden drum held between his knees. The show was under way.

Buddy Bolden leaned over and whispered in my ear, "That drummer ain't bad. I ought to tell Charley to hire him for the band," but I sensed that his levity was merely a facade for a more serious mood. Whether or not he himself believed in voodoo, he understood that our purpose here was a matter of life and death—above all for Leonard Galloway, who would soon be on trial for a capital offense, if we failed to expose a more plausible suspect for the death of Robinson.

Eulalie Echo listened to the hypnotic drumming for a while, swaying gently without moving her feet. Beyond her, I could see the faces of the spectators register a range of emotions from awe to skepticism, from fervent anticipation to downright fear. Watching from backstage, as it were, I had the sense of attending a well-rehearsed performance— and yet I had not the slightest inkling how it was going to end. Indeed, I wondered whether even Eulalie knew the full script of tonight's performance beyond the opening scenes.

The drumming became louder, and Eulalie Echo began to move her feet rhythmically, stepping gracefully to one side and then another. I could see some of the spectators responding to the rhythm, as well. Next to me, Mr. Clemens was nodding his head and tapping his feet, watching Eulalie dance—if that is the correct term for what she was doing. Even I found it hard not to watch her, but I forced myself to keep my eyes on the assembled suspects. Who could tell when some movement or facial expression might betray the presence of a murderer in our midst?

I gradually realized that the drumming was accompanied by a soft vocal chant, so quiet at first that I could not recognize the language, if indeed the words were in any articulate language at all. Was Eulalie the singer, or was it the second assistant, squatting beside the drummer and rocking softly to the beat? From behind them, I could not tell whether their mouths were moving. As I tried to decide, the drumming became louder again, and the beat more insistent. Eulalie's dance became more animated, almost lascivious in its movements. It was only with difficulty that I kept my eyes on the spectators rather than on her. Something in the back of my mind told me that my respectable Connecticut relatives would never understand why I was standing near the banks of a bayou, as a dark-skinned woman danced to rhythms that might have come directly from the African shore.

The rhythms built inexorably, and then suddenly they stopped—and a frightening metallic sound, akin to maniacal laughter, erupted from the darkness, so close to me that I nearly jumped out of my skin. I looked for the source of the sound, and there stood Buddy Bolden, lowering his cornet from his mouth. In his left hand was a tin cup or something of the sort, which he had been using alternately to cover and uncover the bell of the horn. He looked at me and winked, and I understood that he had been the source of the eerie interlude.

Back in the clearing, the spectators peered into the darkness trying, as I had, to ascertain the origin of the strange sounds. I held perfectly still, hoping that the glare of the fire between us would keep anyone from picking out my position just outside the clearing. Evidently, no one saw me, although several pairs of eyes swept past my position as I stood there waiting for whatever would come next.

It was not long in coming. Eulalie struck a stance and threw back her head, crying, "The spirits are among us!" in a loud, impressive voice. I had heard her use the same manner of speech when Mr. Clemens and I had visited her in her apartment, and she had tested us with her offer of finding the killer by torturing a fowl. Bolden's cornet wailed again, another eerie laugh, but this time I was prepared for it. Even so, had I not been standing next to the player, I would readily have believed that the sound of his horn was some voice from beyond the normal pale of human experience. I could only imagine what it sounded like to those out in the clearing. Even Mr. Clemens, who surely knew what was coming, had given a little start when Buddy first blew his horn.

Eulalie Echo turned her back to the spectators and bent over her cauldron again, dipping in a spoon and sniffing the bubbling mixture. Then she poured a spoonful of the mixture onto the fire, which flared up suddenly in a bright yellow blaze. "The spirits are pleased!" she said, and several of the watching faces noticeably relaxed, although they had nothing but her word to indicate even the presence of spirits, let alone anything about their state of mind. Mr. Cable was clearly doing his best to conceal his discomfort at the pagan ritual, but most of the rest of the faces were rapt, intent on Eulalie's performance. I wondered whether we were seeing authentic voodoo rituals or something concocted for the occasion. Perhaps I would have the chance to ask Eulalie afterward.

The drumming began again, a different rhythm now: subtly more energetic than before, without being faster or louder. Suddenly, I became aware of a new figure in the clearing, moving slowly in time to the drumbeats. Whence it had come I had no idea, although I thought I had been watching carefully. The new figure was hooded in a long, dark blue garment that concealed its exact shape, and from where I was, I could not see its face, although its movements gave the impression simultaneously of frailty and of feminine grace. I recalled Mr. Clemens having spoken of Eulalie's mentor, an older woman from whom she had learned her art, and wondered if this could be that person.

Eulalie was dancing again, as well, in slow counterpoint to the new arrival. The chanting resumed. This time, I was able to make out the occasional word in French, although the accent was far from any my teachers would have considered proper Parisian. At last, they came to a stop on opposite sides of the fire. The drumming became muffled, and the hooded figure leaned over and stirred the cauldron, pouring out more of the contents into the fire, which this time blazed blue and orange. Buddy Bolden lifted his cornet to his lips, and the wild laughing sound filled the woods a third time, this time with a more sinister note. "The Widow Paris has come to join us," said Eulalie. At this, the figure threw back her hood, revealing an elderly woman's face, wearing a curiously knotted kerchief over her hair, and large hoop earrings that gleamed like gold.

The name meant nothing to me, but the effect on the spectators was electrical. Maria Staunton's eyes grew wide, while Dr. Soupape whispered something to Mr. Dupree that made him raise his eyebrows and peer intently at the new arrival. Reynold Holt sat rigidly upright, gripping his cane tightly, while Tom Anderson visibly turned pale. Gradually, everyone in the clearing seemed to focus their attention on the new arrival. Then the old woman began to speak, and I strained to hear what she was saying.

"I am not the only widow here," she said. "There are two others, two sisters made widows before their time." The voice matched her appearance of extreme age, and I detected a trace of the Creole accent in its harsh inflections; yet it had a volume and power that belied the frail appearance of its owner. Obviously feeling that power, Maria Staunton and Eugenia Robinson exchanged glances, then turned their eyes hurriedly back toward the speaker. I could see others in the audience glancing at Maria and Eugenia, as well, trying to ascertain what might be about to happen.

"Let the widowed sisters come to me," said the Widow Paris. She raised her arms straight out to her sides, shoulder-high, and with the motion, her sleeves fell back to reveal heavy gold bracelets on her arms. As all eyes were on the Widow Paris, Eulalie Echo made a furtive motion with her left hand. Was she throwing something? Suddenly the fire flared up in strange colors, and the drums became insistent once again. The woods around were dark and strangely silent; no bird or insect sent its song out into the night, as if they feared to compete with the music of the drum.

Hesitantly, Maria Holt Staunton stood; seeing her sister

holding back, she extended a hand to her, and Eugenia Holt Robinson rose to her feet, somewhat reluctantly, I thought. The two women held hands and stepped tentatively forward into the circle of light around the fire. All eyes were on them, mine included. I think that at that moment one of the spectators could have taken out a pistol and fired it without anyone else's noticing who had pulled the trigger. Certainly, the only things that penetrated my consciousness were the two sisters, holding hands and dressed in black, the old woman standing before them with raised arms, and the hypnotic rhythm of the drum.

The Widow Paris led the Holt sisters to the center of the clearing, where she had each of them stir the cauldron, then repeat the ritual of pouring a spoonful of the contents onto the fire, which blazed up vividly each time. Maria was the first to perform this ceremony, and she flinched back from the leaping flames; Eugenia poured out her spoonful of the brew more quickly, and (perhaps forewarned by her sister's experience) she did not flinch.

Then the Widow Paris said something quietly to the sisters, and they returned to their seats; as they sat, their faces were a study in contrast: Eugenia Robinson's visage bespoke a mixture of skepticism and condescension, but Maria Staunton looked on the proceedings with unmistakable awe.

I glanced at the other faces to see how they were responding to the curious ritual. Their expressions ranged from boredom (Mr. Dupree) to lively curiosity (Dr. Soupape) to apprehension (Reynold Holt and Tom Anderson). Mr. Clemens still stood silently by my side; whether or not he was impressed by the performance so far, he was clearly looking for some sign to betray the presence of the murderer we believed must be in our midst. I hoped his hunter's eye, or LeJeune's, would discern whatever they were looking for; as for myself, I had no idea what to expect, and no reason to believe I would recognize it if I saw it.

A gasp from the direction of the clearing drew my eyes

back to the circle around the fire. The Widow Paris now had an enormous snake draped over her shoulders and around her waist; I wondered how she had produced it in the few moments my eyes had been turned away. I wondered, too, how she supported its weight. The creature must have been at least fifteen feet long, and its head looked out at the seated spectators, moving back and forth as if searching for something. I looked at the audience, and saw many of the watchers shrink away from the creature in fear and distaste; but on Maria Staunton's face, there was something akin to wonder. As for Dr. Soupape, he nodded and gave a little smile, as if in appreciation of a cleverly performed conjuring trick.

The widow danced a few more steps with the snake around her shoulders, the drum beating faster. I was impressed that a woman apparently of such advanced age could still move so gracefully, especially with the heavy reptile as a burden. City-bred as I am, I had little experience with snakes, but from its size, I assumed it might be one of the great pythons I had read about. If so, it was probably not poisonous, so there was nothing to fear from its bite, at least. She came to a stop directly in front of the two sisters; whether by instinct or by training, the snake fixed its eyes on the two of them, shifting its ugly head back and forth. Eugenia Robinson shrank away from the serpent's gaze, as did Mr. Dupree. But Dr. Soupape looked on with interest, and I could see Maria Staunton's eyes gleaming, as if she had been granted a glimpse of something transcendent, and I wondered what might be going through her mind.

In his seat directly to the left of his two sisters, Reynold Holt seemed torn between fear and determination. Possibly he was steeling himself to protect them, should the creature break loose from its mistress's control and attack. As I had seen, his temperament was mercurial: at one moment he could be calm and steady, as when he seconded Percival Staunton at the duel; and at another, seething with barely

298   controlled fury, as he had been when Mr. Clemens and I had dined at the Stauntons' house. The bizarre spectacle he now found himself part of must be taking its toll on his nerves.

After a long, tense moment while the great serpent stared at the two sisters, the drum fell silent and Eulalie Echo spoke. "These two sisters have seen much pain, but all pain comes to an end. Damballa has looked upon them and seen their pain. Tonight Damballa will help them end their pain."

At these words, the Widow Paris turned and walked back toward the fire. A cloud moved in front of the moon. Those who had been closest to the snake (which from Eulalie's speech I assumed was named Damballa) visibly relaxed as it was borne away from them. Now Eulalie and one of her assistants brought forth a large wooden chest and set it between the fire and the spectators. They opened the chest, and the Widow Paris placed the snake inside and closed the lid. The drums began again, and Eulalie gave the widow a bottle of some sort of spirits, from which she took a drink, spitting some of it into the fire. Her body jerked as if with convulsions. For a moment, I was reminded of Percival Staunton's movements the morning of the duel, and worried that she might have taken poison. But then I recalled that Eulalie did not deal in poison, and my fears abated.

The drum began beating an ever wilder and more complex rhythm, as the Widow Paris came to the chest and, with a hand from Eulalie and her assistant, climbed up on it as if upon a rostrum—or perhaps a pulpit would be a better comparison. "Now the Widow Paris speaks the words of Damballa," cried Eulalie, and the drum suddenly stopped.

All eyes were on the Widow Paris, standing stock-still atop the chest. The tension was palpable, with muted night sounds now audible from the bayou, and the flickering firelight adding to the weirdness of the scene. An ominous, deep-pitched grunt echoed in the distance, from what sort of creature I know not. The silence in the little clearing **299** stretched out, almost intolerably, as everyone waited to see what would happen next.

"Damballa is angry!" It was the Widow Paris who shrieked out the words, but the voice was far different from the one she had used before. It would have been easy to mistake it for a man's voice, had it not come from the frail old woman's body, and it had a resonance as if we were hearing a trumpet from a great distance, but with the volume and power of an entire orchestra. Several of the listeners recoiled as from a physical shock, and Maria Staunton's eyes went from eager anticipation to fear.

The Widow Paris began to move again in response to the muffled drumming, slow but still complex rhythmically. After an interval, she spoke again—or perhaps I should say, the voice of Damballa spoke again, for that was surely what the watchers were expected to believe. "There is an evil one here tonight," she said, and heads nodded in the audience. "Damballa knows what is in the evil one's heart. The spirits of John and Percival have told Damballa. The evil one has taken the gifts of the earth and turned them to foulness. What is meant to inspire love has been turned to the dealing of death, and that is the greatest evil of all."

By those last words, I understood her to mean the poisonous love potion, which Mr. Clemens and I believed had been the death of John David Robinson and Percival Staunton. To most of the audience it would be meaningless, but if the poisoner was among them, perhaps it would strike home. It would be difficult for anyone without nerves of steel to hear that voice and not be afraid. Reluctantly, I took my eyes away from the old woman standing on the wooden chest and scanned the audience.

Maria Staunton was transfixed, somewhere between awe and fear. Next to her, Eugenia Robinson sat open-mouthed, her earlier skepticism clearly wavering. Reynold Holt sat stiffly, his hands gripping his cane so tightly that I could see his white knuckles even at a distance, and his eyes seemed to bulge. Dr. Soupape looked around as if searching for the evil one Damballa spoke of, while Mr. Dupree stood with his hands in his pockets, his face grim. Tom Anderson was visibly shivering; clearly the ceremony was affecting him strongly. Could he be the murderer, after all? I leaned over to whisper my suspicion to Detective LeJeune, but before I could say anything, the eerie voice rang out again.

"You cannot hide from Damballa! John and Percival have told him of your evildoing! You will lie in your bed at night, and think your evil is hidden, but Damballa will find you and torment you in your dreams! In the day you will walk the earth like a living man, but inside you will be dying every day. Damballa will do all this, and more, until you give up your evil and confess!" The drums pounded louder, and the widow's voice rose to a terrifying pitch. "Confess! Confess!"

And then, without warning, Reynold Holt gave a terrible cry and prostrated himself on the ground before the Widow Paris, calling out, "Forgive me! Oh, God! Forgive me! 'Genie told me the medicine couldn't hurt them unless they were untrue! They must have been guilty; don't you see?"

Suddenly, the scene dissolved into chaos. Eugenia Robinson drew back in horror. "Reynold! Be quiet!" she said, her eyes wide. Maria Staunton fell back in a dead faint, and Dr. Soupape rushed forward to her side. The Widow Paris stepped off the wooden chest, and Eulalie Echo came to her side. The two voodoo women stood quietly and surveyed the startling results of their weird night's work.

Eugenia Robinson looked about with a terrified expression. Mr. Dupree had come up from behind her, and was tugging at Reynold Holt's sleeve. "Get hold of yourself, man!" he shouted. But Holt kept on blubbering, not responding to the lawyer's admonitions.

Eugenia knelt down beside her brother, shouting into his ear. "Reynold, be quiet. You don't know what you're saying!"

In the background, I noticed Tom Anderson trying to

sidle away from the tumultuous scene; I wondered briefly exactly how he intended to escape back to the city. Did he plan to walk back home? Then my attention shifted to Dr. Soupape, who stood next to Maria Staunton in a commanding posture: "Give her room to breathe," he shouted. "Stand back!" Mrs. Staunton lay on the ground, her face pale and her limbs splayed lifelessly about her.

In the midst of all this, Detective LeJeune and two uniformed policemen pushed into the clearing. Mr. Clemens and I remained in the shadows, watching. Despite the confused scene in the clearing, it was but a moment's work for LeJeune to produce a pair of handcuffs and snap them on Holt's wrist. "Mr. Holt, you are under arrest. I warn you that anything you say may be used against you."

Holt's eyes were wild. He stared around the firelit clearing until his eyes lit on the lawyer. "Dupree! Tell him I didn't mean to kill anybody. 'Genie, tell them! This is all some kind of trick, isn't it? That quadroon woman made it all up. . . ."

But LeJeune was turning to Mrs. Robinson. "Ma'am, in view of what I have heard tonight, I have no choice but to take you into custody as well, as an accessory to murder. If you'll give me your word to come along quietly, the handcuffs won't be necessary."

Mrs. Robinson looked first at her brother, who stared about him with a confused look, then at LeJeune, and nodded. "I will cause no trouble," she said. "I can explain everything. I have done nothing wrong. Gordon, will you come with me?"

"Yes, but for now I advise you both to remain silent," said Mr. Dupree. I saw anger and disbelief contending on his face. Then he summoned his professional detachment and said, "I'll do the best I can for you. For God's sake don't say anything more until we've talked."

By this time, Maria Staunton had regained her senses, and she threw herself at her brother's knees. "Reynold! Tell me it isn't true! Not you, Reynold. I loved him, in spite of everything, and now he's gone.'' It tore my heart to see her in such pitiful condition. Her sister moved to stand next to her, reaching down to pat her on the shoulder in an effort to comfort her, but there was a distant look on Eugenia's face, as if she were thinking of something else entirely.

Holt bent over her, saying, ''I'm sorry, Maria, I'm sorry. I didn't mean to, forgive me. It was all a trick by that woman with the snake.''

But it was Eulalie Echo who had the last word. ''Believe it was a trick if you wish to, Mr. Holt. But there is more to the world than your eyes will ever see.'' As if to underline her words, there came still another burst of maniacal laughter from the darkened forest, the sound of Buddy Bolden's cornet writing the coda to the strangest scene my eyes had ever looked upon.

29

"We finally got some sense out of Reynold Holt," said Detective LeJeune. We were sitting in the courtyard of our Royal Street pension, sipping long, cool drinks and waiting for Henry Dodds. "He kept switching his stories, and that old fox Dupree did what he could to keep him from talking at all. At least Eugenia Robinson has managed to keep her statements consistent with one another."

Mr. Clemens sighed. "It's hard not to feel some sympathy for poor Reynold Holt. I reckon he came out of the War pretty badly damaged—not just physically, either. Damnation, Holt was just a boy at the time. He wasn't even eighteen when the War ended. It's a mighty strong mind that can watch men die by the thousands and not be affected. After a few months as a prisoner of war . . . well, if Dupree puts on an insanity defense, I'd say he has a good chance of getting his client off. Maybe there's justice in it; I don't know."

LeJeune leaned back in his seat and looked up at the sky, then looked at Mr. Clemens and shrugged. "I don't know, either, Mr. Clemens. If it means Holt will be spending the rest of his days in an asylum, I can't say I envy him. Sometimes I wonder if there's ever justice this side of the grave. If you want my opinion—and you'd be the only one who does, the way things are looking—Eugenia Robinson ought to be in the prisoner's dock right beside him. But it looks

Peter J. Heck

304 as if Dupree's going to get her off scot-free.''

"She still claims that her husband's death was an accident?'' I asked. I, for one, found it difficult to believe that a woman who knowingly procured a poisonous mixture to give to her husband could be judged innocent.

"Yes, and the prosecutor's buying her story. He says she couldn't have known it was deadly, since it was being sold on the street. But it wouldn't surprise me if Eugenia went and spiked it with a little extra jimsonweed before she sent Holt to talk her husband into taking it. No way to prove it, of course.''

"How in the world did Holt persuade Robinson to take it?'' I wondered. "I wouldn't try such a potion for all the money in the world.''

"You're a young man,'' said LeJeune. "You haven't had to face the possibility that you've missed your last chance to sire a son, or that your wife may be playing around with another man, and there's nothing you can do because you're not the man you used to be. These herb doctors say their stuff will make a man young again, if you take my meaning. Robinson was desperate, and his wife knew that. So she sent Holt to tell him there was a way to win her affections back and fulfill his husbandly duties again. He took the bait.''

Mr. Clemens nodded. "Have you figured out who the other man was? That might open a few other doors of investigation.''

The detective lit one of his cheroots, then said in a lowered voice, "My guess would be a certain lawyer. Why else was he there to clean out that apartment? The place was rented in Robinson's name, but that butler said Robinson never set foot in it after the first couple of visits— maybe to visit a mistress or a whore. I'd bet the butler's telling the truth. I don't think Robinson had much more success there than with his wife. I'd guess the wife found out about it and took a kind of revenge on him by using it to carry on her affairs. If Dupree was the other man, it wouldn't have been hard for him to cover up the rent by commingling it with Robinson's other business in the district.''

Mr. Clemens rubbed his chin, considering what the detective had said. ''Interesting,'' he finally conceded. ''A lot of it makes sense. Have you got any solid evidence to connect Eugenia to the place?''

''I found a couple of long, blonde hairs on the floor under the dresser,'' said LeJeune. ''They're the right color to be hers. I'd bet good money she was the one who used the place.''

''You won't get me to bet against you,'' said Mr. Clemens. Then he looked LeJeune in the eye. ''But if the apartment was Eugenia's, why did Dupree take that suitcase to Maria's house?''

''Eugenia was over there, consoling her sister. We found that out when we questioned her. She's a calculating one; she knew Maria would be so unhinged by Staunton's death that she'd never notice what was going on around her, so she just had Dupree bring her things by, thinking nobody would notice.''

''So eventually Eugenia got tired of her husband and sent her brother out to buy some poison,'' said Mr. Clemens, swirling his glass. ''Or maybe Eulalie Echo's suggestion is closer to the mark. Either the potion would make him love her again, or it would kill him—and she considered either one an improvement.''

''I suppose all this makes a kind of mad sense,'' I said, ''but what on Earth possessed Holt to poison Staunton?''

''Staunton was a different proposition entirely,'' said the detective. ''Robinson may have been not quite enough of a man to satisfy his wife, but Staunton didn't have any problems with his manhood; he was a tomcat. We learned that he'd been spending a good bit of time in some of the cribs and French houses up on Basin Street, in between bouts of drinking and gambling. Eugenia had convinced Holt that the potion wouldn't harm a man who truly loved his wife. That's why he didn't have any qualms about offering it to Robinson. But after Robinson's death, Staunton evidently made overtures to Eugenia. Holt found out about it, and it pushed him over the brink. He saw it as a wrong against both his sisters, and he felt he was honor-bound to revenge it.''

''I can imagine,'' said Mr. Clemens. He took a sip of his drink and contemplated the tabletop before setting down his glass. ''So here was Holt, with a leftover dose of extra-strength love potion and a philandering brother-in-law. But he couldn't have persuaded Staunton to take the stuff just on his own say-so, could he? Why would a man who's just seen his brother-in-law poisoned take a dose of something he suspected might kill him?''

''Staunton was a gambler, a duelist, a libertine. A man like that thinks of himself as better than others,'' said Mr. LeJeune, watching the smoke from his cheroot curl toward the ceiling. ''Maybe he even believed the potion would make him more powerful, more than an ordinary man. And, of course, he didn't know that Robinson had been poisoned by a love potion. I'll give you odds he bought the story about the cook poisoning his master.''

''Yes, easier to blame the disgruntled servant than to believe your sister-in-law and her brother are murderers,'' said Mr. Clemens. ''So when Holt offered him the potion, Staunton may not even have connected it with Robinson's death.''

LeJeune nodded. ''I've wondered if Eugenia was urging Staunton to take the stuff, as well. If she made taking a dose a condition for winning her—*it won't hurt you if you really love me*—maybe that would have been enough to persuade him. She may be as guilty of Staunton's death as of her husband's.''

''But the prosecutor isn't listening,'' said Mr. Clemens, with a frown.

''No, he looks at Eugenia and sees a widow who's been deprived of her loving husband, and that's all he sees,''

said LeJeune. "I'll keep poking around for some hard evidence, but I'm not sure anything short of a signed confession will change anybody's mind. And it'll be a long wait
before we get that. She's way too smart; talking about how
sad she is that poor John's dead, and how she only wanted
to make him love her again. She says the herb doctor didn't
tell her the potion was dangerous, that we ought to go arrest
him for selling it to her. At least the prosecutor wasn't
buying that. He just patted her hand and said, *The darkies
take it all the time without any harm, so it must have been
an accident.*"

Mr. Clemens snorted. "How sweet of her: blame the
colored man again. I wish they would find some way to
pin this all on her. Doesn't she have any remorse?"

"She does seem sorry that her brother's going to take
the blame for Staunton's killing," said LeJeune. "But not
sorry enough to take any responsibility on herself. I think
she's using him to stay clear of the gallows herself, and I
don't think she gives a damn about her dead husband, either. But my opinions don't count with the prosecutor, especially when she hauls out her hanky and blubbers about
poor John."

Mr. Clemens looked thoughtful. "I wonder if that prosecutor ever needed some love potion himself?"

LeJeune laughed—a nasty, scornful laugh. "Harvey An-
drews? Could be, now that you mention it. I figured it was
just that he and Gordon Dupree are old-time buddies. Them
two shared an office when they were both just starting up.
But whatever the reason, Harvey's not likely to press
charges against Mrs. Robinson."

"No, and more's the shame, because she is a murderess,
as far as I'm concerned," growled Mr. Clemens.

"Not necessarily," I said. "After all, Robinson's death
could have been an accidental overdose, and Holt still may
have poisoned Staunton without her knowledge."

Mr. Clemens waved his hand dismissively. "And even
if you're right about that, she was willing to let Leonard

Galloway hang for a crime she knew damned well he didn't commit. That would have been cold-blooded, intentional murder just as surely as if she'd pointed a gun and pulled the trigger herself. But it looks as if she's going to get away with it.''

"Don't be so sure," said LeJeune. "I've got a few cards to play before I give up that game. I still might be able to implicate her, if only as an accessory to manslaughter. But even if she never spends a night in jail, I guarantee you Eugenia will pay for what she's done. People will learn that she didn't lift a finger to save the cook, even though she knew he wasn't guilty. I and some of my friends will make sure the story gets around. Believe me, most people down here will be as disgusted as you are when they learn that she was ready to let Leonard hang. Even if the law can't touch her, she'll be an outcast in the eyes of every decent man and woman in the city.''

"And at the same time, Leonard Galloway's a free man again," I reminded them. The morning's papers had the story of his release, which had been the occasion for great rejoicing in the colored community. In fact, we were invited that very afternoon to a grand celebration of his return home, and we would be leaving for the party as soon as Henry Dodds arrived to convey us there.

"Yes," said Mr. Clemens. "I reckon it's worth something to set one innocent man free. It's too much to expect that we could stop the bigots in their tracks.''

"Well, that's true," said LeJeune. "But remember, there are plenty of us down here who don't support the bigots. This city has too many different kinds of folks living right next door to each other for us not to do our level best to get along and try to help each other where we can. I know that if I could have saved Leonard from the gallows and didn't, it would have been on my conscience forever. And I've got enough to carry around without adding that to it.''

"Don't we all?" said Mr. Clemens. "But you don't have anything to be ashamed of, LeJeune. I hope you can get the proof you need to close the books on Mrs. Robinson; let us know how it comes out, will you? Cabot will give you an address where mail will reach me, whenever you get things finally wrapped up.''

Henry Dodds took the three of us to the foot of First Street, where Charley Galloway greeted us. ''Welcome, welcome! You folks are just in time for the start of the big party. There's chicken and ribs and greens and rice—all you can eat or drink! Come on down, Leonard and Aunt Tillie's both waiting to see you! I got to hurry and go play with the band.''

We stepped along the banquette through a celebration the likes of which I had rarely seen. The entire neighborhood seemed to have turned out to welcome Leonard Galloway home. The aroma of frying fish and barbecue pervaded the air, and somewhere down the block the band was indeed tuning up. Every house was decorated, and almost everyone we saw was holding a large drinking cup. The crowd was thickest in front of Aunt Tillie's house, where there were picnic tables set up on sawhorses, with lines of servers dishing out food: red beans and rice, fried chicken, potato salad, jambalaya, and a dozen other treats that made my mouth water just to see them. At each end, there were kegs of beer and large bowls of lemonade, iced tea, and punch to wash down the plentiful food.

On the street in front there was a large wagon converted into a bandstand, with the team unhitched and the tailgate let down. Besides Buddy Bolden, there were a trombone, a clarinet, and a bass fiddle in the little band. Someone reached a hand down to Charley Galloway, and he hopped up and picked up a guitar that had been sitting on the wagon bed. Buddy Bolden looked to see that all the musicians were ready, then stomped his foot four times, and the band started to play a spirited dance tune. The young people on the street pressed close to the wagon, clapping their hands to the music. Even with the cornet to his lips,

310   I could see Buddy Bolden smiling; he caught my eye and winked as we passed by. The rhythm was hard to resist, and I found myself shuffling down the banquette in time to the music.

People waved and smiled at Mr. Clemens. He and LeJeune and I were conspicuous, but hardly uncomfortable in the friendly crowd. Aunt Tillie greeted us with open arms, and behind her came Leonard, already looking like a different man than the one I had seen behind the bars of Parish Prison. He shook hands with us all, smiling broadly despite his obvious fatigue; the sight of his face was all I needed to tell me my own ordeal had been well justified by the final outcome. We'd learned that he had a new job already, as head cook in one of the top West End resort restaurants, thanks to Mr. Cable's recommendation.

Arthur Phillips had a new job, as well. The Robinsons' former butler had moved to the Staunton residence, the old Holt family home where he had worked as a young man. He came up to Mr. Clemens and me, apologizing for his wild talk in our interview. "I thought I knew where my loyalty lay," he said. "But Miss Maria needs me more than anybody else does, now. She didn't have anything to do with Mr. Holt's wicked deeds, and I'm just glad to be back in the old home again."

On the banquette, I saw Eulalie Echo sitting in the shade, balancing a plate of food and talking animatedly with another woman; she looked more relaxed than I had ever seen her. A small boy stood by her chair, staring intently at the bandstand. George Cable was there, as well, one of the few other white faces on the street. He was clearly delighted at the celebration, and proud of his part in interesting Mr. Clemens in the case. "Samuel, this is a great day," he said, shaking Mr. Clemens's hand. "I guess there's justice in the world after all."

"I sure hope so," said Mr. Clemens warmly. Then he smiled and turned to the man for whom all our efforts had been expended. "Leonard, I hope Cable told you what he'd promised me if I helped get you out, because I'm going to call in the debt. You're going to cook me a pompano before my secretary and I leave New Orleans, or make poor Cable renege on his promise.''

Leonard laughed and gave Mr. Cable a conspiratorial nudge. ''Well, Mr. Sam, I'm glad I caught you 'fore you ate any of this other trash they're serving, 'cause Mr. Cable bought the nicest fresh pompano in town this morning. It's cooking special, right now, just for you. I may be tired, but I'm not too tired to celebrate—or to show I appreciate what you've done for me. And after sitting in that jail, it sure feels good to get back to my own kitchen again.''

Mr. Clemens beamed. ''George, you rascal, I should have known you'd put this poor fellow to work before he's had a chance to recover. But I reckon I'll forgive you, just this one time, provided the pompano's as good as you said.''

''Never fear,'' said Mr. Cable with a shy smile. ''It will be. I can guarantee you that.''

After such a promise, it would have been hard for anything to live up to my expectations; but I can say without reservation that it was the best meal I have ever tasted. Even Mr. Clemens stopped talking for once and paid strict attention to the royal fish. Finally, he wiped his lips and said, ''Now I can die happy.''

Aunt Tillie shook her finger at him, frowning. ''Now, don't you dare do that, Mr. Clemens. Why, we're just getting ready to serve dessert!''

Mr. Clemens sighed and patted his stomach, then looked at our hostess with a contented expression. ''Thank you, Aunt Tillie,'' he said. ''You just gave me all the reason I need to live another fifty years.''